D0688543

ETIQUETTE AND VITRIOL

ETIQUETTE AND VITRIOL

THE FOOD CHAIN
AND OTHER PLAYS

NICKY SILVER

THEATRE COMMUNICATIONS GROUP

Copyright © 1996 by Nicky Silver

The Food Chain copyright © 1993, 1995, 1996 by Nicky Silver
Pterodactyls copyright © 1994, 1996 by Nicky Silver
Free Will & Wanton Lust copyright © 1990, 1996 by Nicky Silver
Fat Men in Skirts copyright © 1988, 1993, 1996 by Nicky Silver

Etiquette and Vitriol: The Food Chain and Other Plays is published by Theatre Communications Group, Inc., 355 Lexington Ave., New York, NY 10017–0217.

All rights reserved. Except for brief passages quoted in newspaper, magazine, radio or television reviews, no part of this book may be reproduced in any form or by any means, electronic or mechanical, including photocopying or recording, or by an information storage and retrieval system, without permission in writing from the publisher.

Professionals and amateurs are hereby warned that this material, being fully protected under the Copyright Laws of the United States of America and all other countries of the Berne and Universal Copyright Conventions, is subject to a royalty. All rights including, but not limited to, professional, amateur, recording, motion picture, recitation, lecturing, public reading, radio and television broadcasting, and the rights of translation into foreign languages are expressly reserved. Particular emphasis is placed on the question of readings and all uses of these plays by educational institutions, permission for which must be secured from the author's representative: George Lane, William Morris Agency, Inc., 1325 Avenue of the Americas, New York, NY 10019, (212) 586-5100.

Excerpts from Bertolt Brecht's "Ten Poems from a Reader Who Lives in Cities," found on page 112, are from Bertolt Brecht Poems 1913–1956, copyright © 1976 by Methuen.

ISBN 1–56865-380-8

Cover design by Chip Kidd
Book design by Lisa Govan

THIS VOLUME OF PLAYS IS DEDICATED
TO THE GENEROUS ACTORS AND
ACTRESSES WHO, OVER THE YEARS,
HAVE BROUGHT MY PLAYS TO LIFE.

CONTENTS

INTRODUCTION

As I write this there is some debate going on as to what I should call this collection. The publishers would like me to call it *The Food Chain and Other Plays.* Their thinking is this: *The Food Chain,* being a commercial production currently in the seventh month of it's Off-Broadway run, is the most recognizable of my titles. Do they expect this volume to just fly off the shelves and give Stephen King a run for his money? I'm skeptical. I mean who buys play collections anyway? Theatre students, actors and playwrights' families, I assume. (If they really want to sell some copies, they'll take my advice, stop worrying about the title and put some naked people on the cover.) Besides, naming the collection after one play seems a slight to the others. And plays, after all, are like children. Should I inadvertently offend one it will, no doubt, grow up to hate me, use vulgar language in public and spend years in therapy.

I liked the title *Etiquette & Vitriol,* which comes from the play *Free Will & Wanton Lust.* But friends tell me it sounds snooty. As if all of a sudden I'm putting on linguistic airs. I also like the title *Stop Talking! Four Plays by Nicky Silver.* But I know that sounds negative. (It's like naming a play *This Play Stinks.*) The title conundrum has me stymied. I find I can't sleep at night. I can't concentrate on other things! I break out in spontaneous sweats! Perhaps, I should just let it go for now.

. . .

All I ever wanted was to have *"a life in the theatre."* It didn't matter how I got there—playwright, director, actor, designer (lighting technician was out because I have a neurotic fear of heights, electricity, tools, ladders and work boots). I don't remember ever wanting anything else. I *also* don't remember any early magical event, any epiphany that turned me into such a single-minded fiend. I *do* remember, as a small child, my parents took me to see *The Fantasticks*. I don't know how old I was, but apparently I was too young to sit still. I got crabby and had to be taken for a walk. It was years before I saw plays I liked. I think it was my eleventh birthday when my father let me pick a play I wanted to see. We drove to New York from Philadelphia and I picked *Equus*. I thought it was great! A play where people talked to the audience! A play NOT set in a living room! A play where actors played horses! And naked Peter Firth masturbating to orgasm as an Act I finale! It was swell! My father was less enthusiastic.

In any event, I started to read plays and found I loved them. I waited impatiently for high school to end, and when I could wait no longer I left, after eleventh grade. I'd enrolled in NYU, early admission. (That's a program where you skip twelfth grade and go straight to college, thus avoiding all of your requirements like chemistry, geometry and gym.) For a while I just went nuts in New York, dyeing my hair very unattractive colors and enjoying my freedom. (This was the seventies after all.) I went to Studio 54 a lot, despite being underage, and wore over-priced, demented clothing such as hard vinyl pants and tunics made from Twister boards. I was in some plays, saw a lot of plays, read a few plays and thought about writing plays.

I was in a special part of NYU called the Experimental Theater Wing, ETW. The idea of ETW was to expose its students to various aesthetics in hopes that they'd develop their own. There were only eight or nine people in each class and they all ate alfalfa sprouts and drank mung bean extract. I never fit in. I ate Snickers bars and took my clothes off a lot. But I must admit, I adored ETW and I got to work with people whom I considered heroes. My whole final year I was on independent study, which meant I got to sleep very, very late. At night I worked on my first play. I'm not going to tell you the title. It was very bad, both the play and the title—but, suddenly, I knew what I was going to do with the rest of my life, how I'd get "*in.*"

FAT MEN IN SKIRTS

I wrote a few plays right out of college. My second full-length was called *Bridal Hunt*. David Copelin was the director of script development at the Phoenix Theatre and he seemed to like it quite a bit—enough to option it after a reading. It was a mean-spirited, funny, vulgar play and he couldn't raise the money. Instead he produced *The Foreigner* and I got to check coats on opening night!

Shortly after that I lost someone to whom I was very close, to AIDS. This was the very beginning of the epidemic, so early in fact that it wasn't called AIDS when he was diagnosed. In any event, looking back, I realize the powerful effect this had on me. I didn't write anything for at least two years. I went to work (waiting tables), came home, watched TV and went to bed. Then one day I was walking down the street, honest to God, and someone said to me, "Did you write a play called *Bridal Hunt* a few years ago?" "Why do you ask?" I responded, wanting to know if he liked it before I fessed up. He liked it. He had a theatre company and they were looking for a play for six actors, all in their twenties, on a bare stage. He commissioned me for about three hundred dollars. And let me tell you, he got exactly three hundred dollars' worth of art. The play stunk.

They put it on at the Sanford Meisner Theatre, a tiny, tiny space on Eleventh Avenue. No one came. But the man who ran the theatre asked if I'd like to write some more. Robert Coles operated the Vortex Theater Company and he offered me a space, complete freedom, real encouragement (which was rare at the time) and no help whatsoever.

Here's how it worked: when he couldn't get someone to rent out the theatre he'd call me. I usually had four weeks to write a play, then four weeks to rehearse. I paid for the rehearsal space with money from my day job. I used my friends in the plays whether they were right for their parts or not.

I directed most of the time, not because I thought I was brilliant or anything, but at that economic bracket the options are slim. We rehearsed for four weeks, in the evenings. Then on Sunday, at midnight, the set designer went to the theatre (another show, some rental, performed at eight—but they had to be out by midnight). We built the set overnight, painted it in the morning, rehearsed once, Monday night, to set lights and opened on Tuesday. Usually we'd have eighteen or twenty people in the audience on opening night. We worked so hard! We were so young! I was so thin!

I worked that way for five or six years, putting on plays with no money for very small audiences comprised mostly of my friends. (We even did a performance of a play called *Wanking 'Tards* on the Fourth of July for an audience of one!—the stage manager's mother. I didn't attend.) I wrote a lot of plays and some of them were just awful. Others, however, weren't too bad. *Fat Men in Skirts* was the third play I put on in that space and I have to admit, I am as proud of that production as anything I've ever done. The cast, particularly Chuck Coggins and Stephanie Correa, was wonderful.

There was virtually no set, but what there was, was simple and clean. The text calls for a beach. Well, we couldn't afford sand—how sad is that? I think the budget for the set was about three hundred dollars. I wanted something natural, from the earth. And yet it had to be cold and sterile in Act III, which is set in a mental hospital. My solution was marble. Well, if we couldn't afford sand, obviously we couldn't afford marble. But we could afford a feather and some paint. I remember quite clearly sitting with my feather in the middle of the night, marbleizing the entire set! By hand! It took hours, I had terrible cramps in my hands and literally couldn't stand up straight for weeks.

But it's astonishing to look back and realize that this play, which cost about four hundred dollars to produce, got no reviews, was seen by just a handful of people and dealt with such charming topics as incest, rape and cannibalism, went on to have quite a life. It was produced two years later at the Woolly Mammoth Theatre in Washington D.C. and was a big success. Since then it's been done all over this country and in several others. The last production I worked on was at Naked Angels, directed by Joe Mantello. Marisa Tomei played Pam/Popo and was swell. She'd just won the Oscar so the audience was jammed with celebrities every night. If it sounds like I'm bragging, I don't mean to, honestly. But as I said, plays are like children and look how far this, this runty, odd, disturbing, child went.

FREE WILL & WANTON LUST

Another play that I wrote while working for the Vortex Theater Company. Again, my friends Chuck and Stephanie were wonderful, despite the fact that he was way too old for his part and she was way too young. Frankly, they were seldom right for their parts, but they're talented actors and they understood my writing. They saved many evenings from total disaster.

What's interesting is this was the first play I wrote *in response* to something. I'd read *The Vortex* by Noël Coward and was really fascinated by it. But I also felt that Mr. Coward was constrained by the morality of his time. How's that for presumptuous! I'd claim I was drunk but I don't drink. I can only claim I was young.

Free Will was also produced at the Woolly Mammoth. Again, a play that started in a showcase grew up to be a hit—and this time it won the Helen Hayes Award for best new play. *Fat Men* had been nominated, but I lost to Athol Fugard. I remember telling a reporter that I was "glad for Mr. Fugard as his career clearly needed the jump-start an award like this could provide."

A word on awards. I've been nominated for a few and won a couple. It's a strange phenomenon. I arrive feeling quite above the fray. I, personally, NEVER think I have the remotest chance of winning, so I adopt an "artists shouldn't compete" attitude. Within five minutes of the evenings commencement, I start to think . . . "What the hell, I could win. You never know." By the time my category rolls around I'm in a white-knuckled frenzy of competitive zeal, ruthless to win the damn thing! "Let me at MY statue and why is everyone clapping for Terrence McNally!" (By the way, Mr. McNally, Congratulations.)

Free Will is an odd play, even for me. I experiment with style quite wildly, careening from farce to Brecht to something else without a pause. I never intend a play to be strange. I simply use whatever tools I have to tell a story. For me, playwriting is an exciting mix of the deliberate and the unconscious. I don't know if the whole thing works. It's not for me to say. It's funny in parts and then jarring, using shifts of theatrical genre to disturb. I think Joe Orton once said you have to shock people sometimes to wake them up—or I may have imagined that to justify things. I will say, looking back, that I am very proud of the monologues that comprise the bulk of Act II. And Philip says some things that every man must have felt at some point. Or is it me? I know it's not me, so don't try to make me feel bad!

PTERODACTYLS

After a number of years at the Sanford Meisner I was tired. I was tired of working so hard. I was tired of not getting paid. I was tired of painting sets and buying props and begging for costumes. It was a grind working fifty hours a week at my day job (retail by now) then writing and rehearsing plays at night. Plus, I was frustrated that my so-called career didn't exist. Frankly, no one cared what we did on Eleventh Avenue. I decided not to do my next play with the Vortex. I'd send it out. If no one wanted to do it, fine. I'd just hold on to it and try again. Imagine my surprise when several theatres expressed interest. You see, by now the literary managers knew who I was, even if the artistic directors didn't.

I'll never forget the reading at Playwrights Horizons. First of all, I am NEVER happy with readings of my plays. Ever. They are too tricky, both emotionally and stylistically, to be served by a reading. As soon as the actors think they know what it is, it changes. Well, at Playwrights I thought the reading went particularly badly. Afterwards I met with some of the artistic staff. They told me how much they liked it AND what was wrong with it and how I might fix it. I listened, growing more petulant with every passing minute, quite sure I was right and they were wrong about everything. But I was so hungry to get a production that I went home and rewrote the whole thing—OVERNIGHT! I showed up the next morning with one hundred and forty-two new pages. Dropping them on the desk, I said, "I think the play was better before, but here's what you asked for." . . . They never got back to me.

A few months later Doug Aibel called me. How can I ever repay the debt I owe him? Doug is the artistic director of the Vineyard Theatre and such a sweet man. He liked the play and offered to do a workshop, then a production. He didn't need any readings. He didn't suggest I "fix" the play. He showed real courage and committed right there. I began hunting for a director. This was a nightmarish process, a series of meetings, usually over coffee (I don't drink coffee), where we "discussed" the play. "Discussed" is a euphemism for "the director tells me how to fix it and gives me suggestions and copious notes." For me the most important thing in collaborating with a director is that we see the same basic play in our imaginations. Suggestions like, "I think you should cut the dinosaur," indicated to me that this wasn't the case. I usually went on an inner journey during these meetings. The second ingredient in a good collaboration is more personal. I need to feel I can yell at and cry in front of my director. Although I am more apt to do the latter than the former, I like to keep my options open. This criterion for choosing a good director is largely ignored in most graduate courses.

I was in Washington D.C., directing *Free Will* when I called David Warren. Doug Aibel had faxed me his number and his bio. But I'd misplaced the second page, so I approached the phone call having no idea who he was or what he'd done. Our conversation went something like this (notice who never shuts up):

NICKY: Listen, to be frank, I'm tired of sitting through directors telling me what my play's about.—So why don't *I* tell *you* what it's about? Then you tell me if you agree.

DAVID *(Suspicious)*: Fine.

NICKY: Well, obviously, it's about denial. Denial's just dandy if it gets you through the day, but we're living at a time when, because of AIDS, it carries a terrible price. We have this epidemic because we didn't want to deal with it. Because as a culture we viewed the people who were dying as expendable. And, of course, it's a comedy, employing theatrical genre as a shield, or defense, that these characters use to survive.

DAVID: All right, sure.

NICKY: Great! Now . . . what have you directed?

DAVID: You're not familiar with my work?

NICKY: Well, no.

DAVID: Well, then, do you mind if I ask how you happened to call me?

NICKY: Doug faxed me stuff but I lost it.

DAVID: I see. Well. . . . I directed *Gus and Al*, at the Public, Bill Finn's *Romance in Hard Times, Mi Vida Loca* and *The Stick Wife* at Manhattan Theatre Club, *Pal Joey*—

NICKY *(Shrieking)*: Oh you're MUCH too big a deal to direct my little play! You'd NEVER take me seriously!

. . .

But he did. And we started a working relationship that I hope goes on until we are both very old and very crabby. David and I have worked together seven times now and it's still a complete pleasure. I learn about *everything* working with David. And I like to think he learns about something working with me.

In any event, the production turned out beautifully. What a wonderful and dedicated cast! They all believed in the project, which was surprising as no one had ever heard of me. We had neither a great deal of money (the sofa was borrowed from Manhattan Theatre Club and I'm convinced it gave Scott Cunningham lice or chiggers or something). We had no big movie star in the lead. But this, my first play to be covered by the *New York Times*, was taken quite seriously. We were treated as something important. Both critics, Ben Brantley in the daily review and David Richards in the Sunday edition, had their complaints. But they both had high praise as well. And, after ten years of putting on plays attended only by my friends, there were audiences! Night after night the theatre was full. And they laughed. And they cried. And we extended. We sold out and life was good. What a victory for the underdogs!

I was speaking at a class recently when a student asked me if *Pterodactyls* is an AIDS play. Well, it is about AIDS. But clearly it's also about family, death, marriage, parents, children, fear, love, class, economics, the end of our species and, of course, denial. Why is there this desire to place plays in narrow little categories? It seems to me that's a job for press agents. But it's not my job. And very few plays are about one thing. I was also asked if I was bitter that *Pterodactyls* didn't transfer to a commercial production. How could I be?

THE FOOD CHAIN

After *Pterodactyls*, I started work on *Raised in Captivity*. I was just beginning really, when I put it aside. I needed to take a break from the somewhat painful issues I was exploring. After all, let's face it, funny or not, there's a lot of death and dying in *Pterodactyls*. And *Raised in Captivity* explores equally painful turf (alienation, punishment, redemption). I needed to cleanse my palate, as it were. And so, having no lime sherbet on hand, I wrote *The Food Chain*.

I learned a valuable lesson working on the premiere production. I gave the play to the Woolly Mammoth, feeling they certainly deserved it, having produced me when no one else would. I felt very close to that theatre and very protected. I'd had a wonderful time working on *Free Will* the previous year and I was happy to be back. I briefly toyed with the idea of playing Otto, but chickened out and opted instead to direct.

What a miserable experience! It wasn't the cast. They were sweet and very talented. I loved the designers, particularly the set designer, James Kronzer. But for reasons that were none of my business there was a big "shakedown" among the staff at Woolly . . . a WEEK BEFORE WE OPENED! It may or may not have been good for the theatre. I wouldn't know. I only know it was terrible for me. A day before the first preview everything was falling apart. The set wasn't finished. The lights weren't hung. The props weren't even assembled! I'm sure I was very difficult as I stormed about the theatre alternately weeping and shouting. (I paint a very high-strung picture of myself. In reality I possess a calm bordering on the serene and am often mistaken for a religious figure.) On the night of the first preview, I asked the cast if they wanted to cancel. They'd NEVER worked on the set in its completed state! They said no, that they were dying for an audience. And they got one. There was a full house. I made a curtain speech wherein I warned the audience that the set may career off the stage and kill someone. Then the play began and the audience had, I think, a great time. Audiences, as a rule, love a technical disaster. They love being there the night a light falls down or a turntable breaks. It's an event. If the disaster is huge enough it takes on a mythic quality: "I was at *Sunset* the night the set collapsed, killing sixty and injuring twelve." (I actually *was* there the night Barbara Cook got caught in the set of *Carrie*! I was in London and the damn thing nearly decapitated her! But that's another story.) The lesson: It's nice if it's always fun, but ultimately something exciting can come, even out of misery.

The following season it opened in New York. This time, I wasn't directing. And this time it was fun. I had Bob Falls, who'd directed *subUrbia* (you see I learned to know a director's credits). Bob is a terrific director and, my God, what fun to be with. He never lets his sense of personal dignity prevent him from having a good time. Such a healthy attitude! We laughed and ate all day long. Again (am I lucky or what?) I had a great cast. I was a little intimidated by Phyllis Newman the first day and called her Miss Newman. She put a quick stop to that! (Her credentials and talent certainly entitle to her to some diva-esque behavior. But, quite the contrary, Phyllis is a riot.) And I had my beloved Hope Davis, who'd done such wonderful work in *Pterodactyls*. The *New York Times'* Ben Brantley said of Hope, "There is no one quite like her on the stage these days." He's mostly right—he could've left off "on the stage these days."

Cripes, I sound like a terribly sweet, cloying mess. So full of love and gratitude. If you met me in real life you'd see none of that. I'd be much more likely to spew venomous gossip about people I hate—and trust me that list is long and growing. But this looks awfully permanent. I do want to put my best foot forward. So call, or corner me at a party for the lowdown on who did me dirt, who's mean, who's talentless, who's ruthless, whom I slept with to get this published and who slept with me to get parts in plays (well no one's ever slept with me to get a part in a play, but I can plant the idea right here). Besides I feel pretty lucky and grateful. It's a rare thing to be able to earn a living doing what you love. And all I ever wanted, after all, was *"a life in the theatre."*

N. Silver
March 1996

ACKNOWLEDGMENTS

Aside from those mentioned in the introduction, I'd also like to thank the following for their help and guidance: George Lane and Mary Meagher (of William Morris, listed, please note, alphabetically), Jon Nakagawa, Barbara Zinn Krieger, Robert V. Straus, James Bart Upchurch III, Tim Sanford, Bruce Whitacre, Nancy Turner Hensley and a battery of psychiatric doctors.

THE FOOD CHAIN

The Food Chain premiered at the Woolly Mammoth Theatre Company (Howard Shalwitz, Artistic Director) July 15, 1994. The production was directed by the author. The set design was by James Kronzer; costumes were by Howard Vincent Kurtz; lighting was by Martha Mountain; sound was by Gil Thompson; the production stage manager was Anne Theisen. The cast was as follows:

AMANDA DOLOR	Kate Fleming
BEA	Cam Magee
FORD DOLOR	James Whalen
SERGE STUBIN	Christopher Lane
OTTO WOODNICK	Rob Leo Roy

The Food Chain subsequently opened August 24, 1995 at the Westside Theatre, directed by Robert Falls. It was produced by Robert V. Straus, Randall L. Wreghitt, Annette Niemtzow and Michael Jakowitz, in association with Evangeline Morphos and Nancy Richards. The associate producers were Kathleen O'Grady, Gilford/Freeley Productions, Andrew Barrett, Terrie Adams, Fanny M. Mandelberger, Richard Kornberg and Pope Entertainment Group, Inc. The set design was by Thomas Lynch; the costumes were by William Ivey Long; lighting was by Kenneth Posner; the sound by Duncan Edwards/Ben Rubin; the production stage manager was Allison Sommers. The cast was as follows:

AMANDA DOLOR	Hope Davis
BEA	Phyllis Newman
FORD DOLOR	Rudolf Martin
SERGE STUBIN	Patrick Fabian
OTTO WOODNICK	Tom McGowan

CHARACTERS

AMANDA DOLOR, Early thirties. A very attractive, high-strung intellectual. She is mercurial and has a terrific verbal capacity. It is important that she be very thin.

BEA, Mid-fifties. A Jewish matron with a heavy Long Island accent. She is abrasive and easily offended.

FORD DOLOR, Mid-thirties. A strikingly handsome man, Ford is a filmmaker and a man of ideas, not words.

SERGE STUBIN, Thirty. Serge is a sexual being, and as a runway model, he must be good-looking, although it is possible that he is less attractive than his confidence would indicate. Although intellectually out of his league with Amanda, Serge is far from stupid.

OTTO WOODNICK, Mid-thirties. Hugely overweight. Otto is flamboyant, Jewish, insecure in the extreme and full of rage. He is a verbal tornado, quite out of control.

TIME AND PLACE

SCENE 1: *Amanda*
The Dolor living room in New York City, late at night.

SCENE 2: *Otto*
Serge's studio apartment, the same night.

SCENE 3: *Fatty & Skinny Lay in Bed . . .*
The Dolor living room, the next morning.

In the interest of accuracy, I have included an alternate ending in this edition. This secondary ending was used in the play's premiere in Washington, D.C. It is my feeling that both endings work, despite one being much darker than the other, and I have decided to include them both.

SCENE 1

AMANDA

The lights come up on the Dolor living room. It is night. The room is decorated in an extremely young, "hip" manner. There is a hallway to the bedroom, a kitchen area, the main entrance and a powder room. Amanda is pacing, smoking a cigarette. She is listening to some sad, sophisticated jazz, wearing a T-shirt and leggings or casual pants. After a moment, she goes to the phone and dials.

AMANDA *(Into the phone)*: Hello, Bi— . . . Damn. Hello, Binky. This is Amanda. If you're asleep, don't get up. If you're out, don't call me back.

(She looks at the phone as if she's just spoken gibberish and hangs up. She gets a New York Yellow Pages from a bookcase and looks up a number. She turns off the music and returns to the phone. She dials. This done, she presses a button which puts the call on speaker phone. We hear the ringing, and Bea is revealed.)

5

BEA: Hello, Contact.
AMANDA: Yes, hello.

(Pause.)

BEA *(Irritated)*: This is Contact. Can I help you?
AMANDA: Yes. Well, probably not. I mean, I can't imagine how you could. I just, I wanted someone to talk to and it seemed too late to call anyone—
BEA: What's your address?
AMANDA: Pardon me?
BEA: What is your address?
AMANDA: Why do you ask?
BEA: This is a crisis hotline. I need your address.
AMANDA: I don't see how that's relevant.
BEA: I am not allowed to talk to you without an address.
AMANDA: I don't know that I want you—
BEA *(A threat)*: I'm hanging up.
AMANDA: 241 West 21st Street.
BEA: That was so painful?
AMANDA: I just don't see the purpose—
BEA: Have you swallowed anything?
AMANDA: I just wanted to talk to someone.
BEA: What floor are you on?
AMANDA: Six.
BEA: Is the window looking more and more inviting?
AMANDA: I believe you have the wrong idea.
BEA: You have any firearms?
AMANDA: Firearms?
BEA: You know, guns, whatnot.
AMANDA: Certainly not.
BEA *(Irritated)*: Are you lying to me? I will not tolerate being lied to!
AMANDA: I'm not going to do anything drastic.
BEA: Oh people say that. They always say that. People lie.
AMANDA: I assure you, I have no intention of—

6

BEA: Last week, Tuesday, I think, Tuesday or Wednesday, I can't remember—I'm on the phone forty-five minutes with this young man, *forty-five minutes*, and he's swearing up and down that he has no intention of doing anything—and after all that time, mittin-drinnen, out he sails. Right out the window. Dead.

AMANDA: Oh my.

BEA *(A fact)*: People lie.

AMANDA: What was troubling him?

BEA: Oh, I can't remember. Something. Something was wrong with him. Who can keep it straight. But I tell you, I felt *VERY* betrayed!

AMANDA: I won't jump out the window.

BEA: That's why I'm on graveyard. I had a perfectly lovely shift: six to ten. After the talk shows and before the news. Now, I'm on graveyard.

AMANDA: I'm sorry.

BEA: I felt very betrayed.

AMANDA: I understand.

BEA: Right out the window. Splattered. Dead. I heard the whole thing. It was terrible. What can I do for you, darling?

AMANDA: I just wanted to—talk to someone.

BEA: You're lonely?

AMANDA: Well, I wouldn't say that.

BEA: No. You're calling strangers in the middle of the night, but you're not lonely.

AMANDA: Alright, I'm lonely.

BEA: Well, let me tell you, *everyone's* lonely, my dear—what's your name?

AMANDA: Amanda.

BEA: Amanda, loneliness is my oxygen. I breathe loneliness. I'm Bea, and you don't know what loneliness is until you've walked a mile in my shoes. You haven't tasted loneliness, you haven't been in the same state with it. I lost my husband several years ago—I don't want to dwell. Allif a sholem. So what's the trouble?

AMANDA: My husband is . . . gone.

BEA: Gone? You mean dead gone? What do you mean? Be specific.

AMANDA: No, no. He's just gone.

BEA: Is he missing? D'you call the police? Not that they'll do anything.

AMANDA: I haven't called the police. I mean, he's fine. He called me to say he was fine. He said he needed some time to work.

BEA: When was that?

AMANDA: Two weeks ago.

BEA: How long you been married?

AMANDA: Three weeks.

BEA: And he's been missing?

AMANDA: Two weeks.

BEA: I see.

AMANDA: He's working on a film. He writes films.

BEA: Did he write *Howard's End*?

AMANDA *(Bewildered)*: No.

BEA: Too bad. I loved that picture! That is a beautiful picture. Did you see that picture?

AMANDA: No.

BEA: Ya should see it. See it on the big screen if you can. It was a lovely, lovely picture.

AMANDA *(Testy)*: Well, I didn't see it.

BEA: Oh.

AMANDA: He makes small, independent films.

BEA: Did you see *Enchanted April*?

AMANDA: No.

BEA: Me neither. I'm dying to.

AMANDA *(Lighting another cigarette)*: The point is—

BEA: Are you smoking?

AMANDA: Why?

BEA: Oh it's a terrible habit. You mustn't smoke. How old are ya darling?

AMANDA: Thirty.

BEA: You have your whole life ahead of ya, which, if you stop smoking, could be a long, wonderful adventure.

AMANDA: I'm not smoking.

BEA: I heard you.

AMANDA: I have asthma. I wheeze sometimes.

BEA: Are you lying to me!?

AMANDA: No. I'm not. I'm not. I swear.

BEA: Did you see *Room with a View*?

AMANDA *(Lying)*: Yes.

BEA: Oh was that a wonderful picture? Did you love that picture?

AMANDA: It was very good.

BEA: I loved that picture. So let me understand. You've been married three weeks and your husband's been missing for two of them?

AMANDA: Correct.

BEA: Did your husband—what's his name?

AMANDA: Ford.

BEA: That's a beautiful name! I love that name. Did Ford—I love saying it—did Ford tell you where he was going?

AMANDA: Well, it was a Monday. We'd spent the week on Martha's Vineyard. You see, it was our honeymoon and Ford has a friend who owns a house on Martha's Vineyard, which he never uses—

BEA: What's his name?

AMANDA: Who?

BEA: The friend, the friend with the house.

AMANDA: Why?

BEA: Maybe I know him.

AMANDA: Lillian.

BEA: *His* name is Lillian?

AMANDA: Yes.

BEA: Go figure.

AMANDA: In any event, we spent the week at Lillian's house. It was our honeymoon.

BEA: How was the sex?

AMANDA: It was good.

BEA: When you say "good," you mean what, exactly?

AMANDA: I mean it was good.

BEA: We'll come back to that. So you're in the city with Ford—
I love that name!

AMANDA: Yes. We're back in the city. It's Monday morning. We
had breakfast. And after breakfast, he told me that he
wanted to go for a walk. So naturally, I started to put my
shoes on. I thought he meant together.—But he said, he
wanted to go alone. He was working on an idea for a film,
mapping it out in his mind, as it were. I was a little hurt, to
be honest. But I understand that the creative process is a
very delicate dance. Ford is a genius. I'd seen all of his films
before we'd ever even met, and I always found them—searing. Just searing and penetrating in a very powerful way. So,
I didn't want to question his process. It's very important
that an artist be nurtured. . . . So he went out. And I took
a shower. This was about noon. After that, I tried to do
some writing. I'm a poet—vocationally. That's what I do. I
was working on a new poem: "Untitled 103," and I was
very absorbed in the poem. It's about wind. Wind as a
metaphor for God as a force in our lives. Or the lack there-
of. The stillness, the arbitrariness of a random world. And
the work was going very well. I was really just vomiting
images like spoiled sushi (that may be an ill-considered
metaphor, but you get my gist). I was absorbed and pro-
ductive.

I'd written—three lines, I think, when I looked at the
clock and it was ten-thirty. This happens sometimes, when
I'm writing. It's as if I fall into a hole in the time-space con-
tinuum. I am pulled—I've strayed.

So it's ten-thirty and I haven't heard from Ford. But I
didn't worry. I was unfamiliar with his process and it
seemed possible that he'd been out walking for *ten and a
half hours.*

So I tried to go to sleep. But I couldn't sleep! I tossed

and turned. I had visions in my head of Ford in a hospital, or dead in a ditch, the victim of wandering thugs. And then, of course, I started thinking . . . nothing happened to him! He hates me. He's gone. We rushed into this and now he's left me. It's over. I did something wrong. I was too aggressive! Or too passive! Or too passive-aggressive! I went into a shame spiral! And I cried, and I cursed and I prayed to God that this was a terrible dream, and that any minute I'd wake up and Ford'd be lying next to me!

And then the phone rang—thank God! I looked at the clock: six-fifteen. It was Ford! I was so relieved! "Ford! WHERE ARE YOU!?"—I tried to keep the panic out of my voice. I didn't want to seem, for a minute, the overbearing wife. He said he was fine. "I just need some time," he said. "I'm working on a film and I need some time.". . . . . And then, he hung up. He hung up. And haven't heard from him since.

(Pause) Bea? Bea? Are you still there?

BEA: You're a poet? That's what you do for a living? You're a poet?

AMANDA: Yes!

BEA: What kind of living is that? Is there money in that? How do you—

AMANDA: I have money. Money is not the issue!

BEA: I never heard of such a thing.

AMANDA: You've never heard of poetry?

BEA (Insulted): I've heard of poetry! I'm not stupid. I never heard of anyone doing it for a living.

AMANDA: Well, I did inherit some money, when I was younger.

BEA: Knew it!

AMANDA: I have published many poems! I have a poem in this week's New Yorker!

BEA: What's it called?

AMANDA: Why do you ask?

BEA: I'll pick it up. I'll take a look.

AMANDA: "Untitled 94."

BEA: I'll take a look.

AMANDA: Don't bother.

BEA: I'm very impressed. Tell me. How long did you know "Ford"—I just adore that name! How long did you know him before you got married?

AMANDA: Why do you ask?

BEA: How long?

AMANDA: What difference does that make?

BEA: Who's the professional here?

AMANDA: Are you a psychologist?

BEA: No. I am not.

AMANDA: What kind of professional are you?

BEA: I ran a needlepoint store for *several* years.

AMANDA: And that qualifies you—

BEA *(Insulted)*: We go through a very long, grueling, six-hour training process before we are allowed to man the phones!

AMANDA: I see.

BEA: Not just anyone can walk in off the street.

AMANDA: I don't think a six-hour training process qualifies you—

BEA: My life qualifies me!!

AMANDA: And how is that?

BEA: I am a survivor!

AMANDA: By that you mean, you're old?

BEA *(A threat)*: I'm hanging up!

AMANDA: I'm sorry.

BEA: My life has not been easy! Judge me not lest you be judged young lady is what I think I mean. I've been in your place! I've known the misery of abandonment—why, when my husband died, I thought my world was coming to an end! I never felt so all alone!

AMANDA: Do you have any children?

BEA: One, yes, but don't get me started. My husband's death just pulled the rug out from under me—didn't want to do a thing! I didn't want to wash or dress or go to the movies. Nothing. I just cried. I curled myself up into the fetal position and I cried. One day, honest to God, I found myself on the kitchen floor in yesterday's nightgown, curled up, like a snail, unable to move. That's the bottom. That, my dear, is the end! When you're snailed up on the kitchen floor. I just wanted to die! And I never even cared for my late husband.

AMANDA: Pardon me?

BEA: But. I pulled myself up, by my bootstraps and started over. I made a life for myself! So you want to know my qualifications? I've come back from the grave! That's my qualification!

AMANDA: I see.

BEA: So how long did you know him before?

AMANDA *(After a hesitation)*: A month.

BEA: A month?

AMANDA: Two weeks.

BEA: You marry someone you know two weeks?

AMANDA: Yes!

BEA: Does that seem foolhardy to you? It seems foolhardy to me.

AMANDA: Well, hindsight is always twenty-twenty, isn't it?

BEA: Don't be fresh. I'm just saying that that isn't very long—

AMANDA: I knew him a week!!! A week!!! All right?

BEA: How'd you meet?

AMANDA: We met at an installation.

BEA: What the hell is that? I don't know what that is.

AMANDA: An exhibit. We met at an art show by my friend, Tipper Bousché.

BEA: This is a name?

AMANDA: It is, yes. I'd been dating Cowel Selig, the performance artist. Maybe you've—

BEA: No.

AMANDA: Well, that was over.

BEA: How'd it end?

AMANDA: He killed himself.

BEA: Was that last Tuesday, or Wednesday, or something?

AMANDA: *Months* ago.

BEA: Then it wasn't my fault.

AMANDA: He died on stage: self-immolated. It was part of his performance.

BEA: My.

AMANDA: It was very well reviewed.

BEA: I prefer a musical.

AMANDA: I assume.

BEA: Did you see *Blood Brothers?*

AMANDA: No—in any event, I went with Binky to the gallery and met Ford.

BEA: And?

AMANDA: And I was very attracted to him. He is—very attractive. He has very beautiful eyes. And beautiful hair. And hands. Simply wonderful hands.

BEA: Yeah, yeah, he has hands. What happened?

AMANDA: Eventually, we came back here.

BEA: Your place?

AMANDA: Yes.

BEA: What was wrong with his place?

AMANDA: He was staying with friends. So we came back here. And, of course, we'd both been drinking a bit. I wouldn't say we were drunk, but we'd had some drinks. He said he'd like to hear some poems.

BEA: Very, very smooth.

(As Amanda speaks, Bea's light slowly dims.)

AMANDA: And so I read him some poems. I read him "Untitled 24," and "Untitled 87," and one I hadn't titled yet at all. He listened. We looked out the window, and from my apartment one can see into the building across the street. It seemed that everyone was home. There were lights in all the windows. And in each apartment, I know this sounds far-fetched, but in each apartment there was someone watching television. Every window was a painting of isolation.

Every television reflected blue, onto a solitary face. And
somehow, the power of that sight filled me with a huge sorrow—I wrote a poem about it later: "Untitled 106."—I was
overwhelmed with a mammoth despair. . . . I started to cry.
And Ford said nothing. He understood. I didn't need to
explain; he felt it as well. And he comforted me, without
words. He touched his lips to my tears and traced his hand,
so lightly, on the side of my face, touching my cheek and
jaw, then neck . . . he smelled of white wine and his own
body. I felt his lips on my ear and I shut my eyes as he
unbuttoned my blouse. He put his mouth on my nipples
and I was no longer crying. Or thinking. He shed his shirt,
so I could feel his skin as I stepped out of my skirt. Our
clothes blew, crazy down the block as he kissed my stomach. I took his head in my hands, and looked at him and his
face was very beautiful to me, so I kissed him and put my
tongue in his mouth, which tasted wonderful, and he held
me from behind, with one hand, while he slid the other
between my legs and into me, where I was wet and wanted
him to be. He was smiling, like a bad child, as we simply,
had each other, again, and again! Until it was morning.

*(A long pause. Bea's light returns revealing that she has
been deeply affected by the sexual content of Amanda's
story. Bea breathes deeply, her hand on her chest.)*

Of course later, I realized that if I could see them, my neigh-
bors could, naturally, see me and now I feel compelled to
wear dark glasses whenever I put out my garbage.

BEA: That was . . . very . . . well, there are no words.

AMANDA: It was wonderful.

BEA: So . . . you had an orgasm?

AMANDA *(Of course)*: Yes.

BEA: I never.

AMANDA: Oh?

BEA: I never much cared for it.

AMANDA: I'm so sorry.

BEA: My late husband was not an attractive person.

AMANDA: I'm sure he had fine qualities.

BEA: And that's where you'd be wrong.

AMANDA: Oh.

BEA: He had hair coming outa places you cannot imagine.

AMANDA: And yet you were devastated when he died.

BEA: Well, as for company, he was better than a book.

AMANDA: Now you have your children.

BEA: One. Child. But don't get me going. A meeskite.

AMANDA: A what?

BEA: An ugly thing. A sad thing. Pathetic.

AMANDA: That's too bad.

BEA: So. The two of you met and fucked on the first date. What happened next?

AMANDA: Well, the next day, we did, actually, talk. We got to know each other and found we had an enormous number of things in common.

BEA: Such as? List please.

AMANDA: Well, we're both intense Fassbinder fans.

BEA: Uh-huh.

AMANDA: And we both had rather unpleasant childhoods.

BEA: How so? Elucidate.

AMANDA *(Irritated)*: I don't want to go into it. I don't see how it's pertinent.

BEA *(Insulted)*: Fine.

AMANDA: So we were in bed for several days—

BEA: Does no one in your social circle have a job?

AMANDA: We have jobs!! We write!! We're artists! We make art. That's our job. People think if you don't make a shoe, or, or a desk, or something tangible that you're not worth anything. We make something for the soul, something for the spirit. Is that not tangible enough for you? Your attitude is just symbolic of everything that's wrong with people today.

BEA: I asked a question.

AMANDA: A question heavy with the Sisyphean burden of judgment.

BEA: Excuse me.

AMANDA: Where was I?

BEA: In bed.

AMANDA: And I suggested that we should spend the rest of our lives together.

BEA: And he said?

AMANDA: He . . . —smiled. He agreed. We were married by my friend Caitlin's brother. It was lovely. We wrote our own vows. I, of course, wrote a poem. Ford read from *Tess of the D'Urbervilles*— I have no idea why. And then we were off to Martha's Vineyard and now he's gone and I don't know what I'm going to do!!

BEA: What've you been doing?

AMANDA: Waiting. Waiting and waiting, as women have always done since Miss Havisham's wedding dress got covered in cobwebs.

BEA: Have you seen anyone?

AMANDA: You mean professionally? Is that what you mean?

BEA: I mean socially. A friend. Friends are very important. When my late husband keeled, I woulda dropped dead if it wasn't for my friend Thelma, a lovely human being, who picked me up with a ladle.

AMANDA: Well, I haven't. I mean I planned to. I was supposed to see—I was on my way to visit my friend, Binky, this morning. But I never made it.

BEA: What happened?

(As Amanda tells her story, Bea's light dims again. Amanda's lighting should reflect both her emotional state and the facts of the story.)

AMANDA: Well, I left my apartment. It was about noon and it was a nice day, so I thought I'd walk to her house. She lives on 75th and Columbus, which, I realize, is a very long walk, but I thought the exercise would do me good—I hadn't eaten anything yet, so I stopped at the diner on my corner, for some breakfast, and I picked up a newspaper so I'd have something to do.

I was reading my paper when the waiter came over and asked if I was . . . *alone*. Well! It was obvious that I was *alone*! I was sitting there, in a booth, by myself—did he think I thought I had an imaginary friend with me?! I was *alone*! Did he have to rub it in? Was he trying to be funny? Did he think he was, in some way, better than me? It was in his tone. He said, "Are you alone?" But what he meant to say was, "You're alone. *Aren't you!?*"—And I can't imagine that he's not alone every single day of his miserable, *pathetic* life! He has terrible skin. And it's not attractive. Not the way bad skin, or at least the remnants of bad skin, is attractive on some people. On some men!! It's never attractive on women—have you noticed that? Just one more example of the injustices we are forced to suffer! If we have bad skin, we're grotesque! Let a man have bad skin and he can be Richard Burton for God's sake! I HATE BEING A WOMAN!!

I've strayed.

The point is this waiter has terrible skin, and greasy hair and his breath stinks of something dead and his face is entirely too close to mine, and he insults me with his breath and his tone of voice and asks if I'm alone. I feel my face go flush and I want to rip his head off! I'd *like* to pull his hair out, only I'd never be able to get a decent grip—it looks as if it hasn't been washed in a decade! I want to pick up my butter knife and stab in his sunken, caved-in chest! But! I simply respond, *(Grandly)* "No, I'm married, thank you."

(Pause) I realize, now, of course, that my answer was illogical. I realize that it was inappropriate. But, at the time, it was all I could think to say.

Well, he leans back and, really, in the most supercilious manner, he leers at me and intones, "I meant, are you *eat-*

ing alone." "I KNEW WHAT YOU MEANT!" I KNEW
WHAT HE MEANT! I don't know why I said what I said,
I just said it! He made me sick. I hope he dies. I shouted, "I
KNEW WHAT YOU MEANT!" And I am not a person
who shouts, generally. I don't like shouting. It hurts to
shout and it hurts to be shouted at. My mother shouted
quite a bit and I always thought the veins in her neck looked
like the roots of a tree. But I shouted. Everyone looked at
me . . . because I was standing. I didn't mean to be standing. I didn't remember standing, but I was. I was standing.
I must've leapt up when I shouted. So I was standing and
everyone was staring at me. The place was very crowded,
much more crowded than I ever recall seeing it before. And
suddenly, it occurred to me, that these *people, my neigh-
bors,* gawking at me in endless silence, were the very same
people who had watched Ford and myself have sex that
first night when we met. I was so humiliated! I thought I
would die! Or be sick! I was certain I was going to be sick
right there at my table, standing up, being stared at! And
then everyone in the neighborhood would mutter under
their breath, every time they saw me, "Oh there goes that
woman. We've seen her have sex, and we've seen her
vomit."

I WOULD LIKE, AT SOME POINT IN MY LIFE,
TO CLING, WITH WHATEVER ENERGY I HAVE, TO
MY DIGNITY! What have we got but our dignity? Women
are worthless in this world! Every aspect of our culture
conspires to keep us subjugated under the oppressive
thumb of the beauty myth. If you're attractive, congratulations! Because you own it all! You run the world! But
God forbid you should have bad skin, or gain a pound or
lose a leg or be, in any way, a deviant from what the power-
brokers and the plutocrats and politicians and the magazines and the television and the government and the
OIL COMPANIES, WHICH OWN ALL THE OTHER
STUFF TO BEGIN WITH—God forbid you should deviate

from what the president of Shell Oil decides is attractive and YOU ARE A DISPOSABLE HUMAN BEING! YOU ARE A DEAD BIRD ON THE HIGHWAY!—Not that I'm unattractive, mind you! I am very attractive. I know I am! But I wasn't feeling very attractive this morning while I was being stared at by the same nasty, judgmental, *narrow* swine who got their rocks off watching me HAVE SEX! I just stood there in that diner, for what seemed like hours, and then, with all the composure and dignity I could muster, which was considerable, I said, "I've changed my mind!" And I left.

(A long pause) I was all the way on 43rd Street before I realized that I'd left my purse.

(Pause; her frenzy returns at once) There's another example of how we are kept under the thumb of a patriarchal culture!! PURSES! Do men have purses? No! They have pockets! Why don't we have pockets?! I'll tell you why, because they would make our hips bulge! It might make our buttocks look lumpy! And we couldn't have that!! No! So we have purses! And you can either get a dainty, little purse that you have to hold in your hand, in which case you live your whole life with only one hand available, giving the world a head start on beating you with, literally, one hand tied behind your back!! Or you can get one of those big old shoulder bags which hurt like hell and leave deep red welts on your skin and I'm certain it throws your spine out of alignment, so you end up in a panic about getting osteoporosis. And you spend all your time worrying and your money on calcium supplements, WHICH DO NO GOOD ANYWAY, BECAUSE YOU JUST KNOW YOU'LL END UP WITH A HUMP AND ALL YOUR DRESSES ARE GOING TO LOOK LONGER IN THE FRONT!! OF COURSE YOU CAN ALWAYS GET A KNAPSACK—BUT THEN, PEOPLE JUST THINK YOU'RE A LESBIAN!! I'D LIKE TO GET MY HANDS ON THE FILTHY, MISOGYNIST MOTHERFUCKER—

*I'D LIKE TO MURDER WHOMEVER THE PRICK
WAS THAT INVENTED THE HANDBAG!!*
(She composes herself a bit) I've strayed.

As I was saying, I was at Times Square when I realized
that I'd forgotten my handbag. I start to feel a little dizzy.
And nauseous. I hadn't had anything to eat. I haven't eaten
in days—I don't like to keep any food in the house because
it attracts roaches and I just end up eating it when I should-
n't. I hadn't been hungry all week. But all of a sudden I was
very hungry, famished, starved! I wasn't sure if I could
make it back to the diner on my corner without fainting.
I had to eat something! I had sixteen cents in my pocket. So
. . . I loitered at a hot dog stand. Now, I try not to eat hot
dogs because of the nitrites, but at this point they weren't
hot dogs, they were IVs! They were plasma! They were
bread and water! AND THEY COST A DOLLAR TWENTY-
FIVE!

I tried looking sweet and pathetic, like the poster for
Les Miserables: I let a tear come to my eye and looked to
heaven . . . *(She does so)* But the man selling the hot dogs
ignored me completely!

So I tried flirting with him. Subtly. I wet my lips and
held my arms in a way that I thought accentuated my bust.
(She does so) He smiled, at me, *lewdly,* and I saw that what
few teeth he had in his head were the khaki color of dead
leaves! I was dizzy and sick and swooning, but I wasn't
ready to sell myself to this fetid extortionist for a dollar
twenty-five's worth of pig snouts and feet!

I was sure there were other vendors, kinder souls
who'd take pity on me . . . and so I headed south! Back to
my corner, back to the diner, back to the hateful waiter and
my purse. At first I kept my eyes on the pavement, search-
ing all the while for a nickel, a dime—a subway token I
could barter. . . .Then I noticed . . . my hand was out, in
front of me . . . my palm was up. I wasn't begging, per se.
But if someone *wanted* to give me their spare change, who

am I not to help them purge their guilt?! FORD DID THIS
TO ME! HE REDUCED ME TO THIS! I HATE HIM!

But I did my best: groveling, begging, looking wan—
but the competition was fierce! I was surrounded, on all
sides, by people so disfigured by their misfortune I was certain I'd stumbled onto the set of a Fellini film! A woman on
my right had no shoes. I felt badly for her, until I realized
that a man on my left had no feet! He was chasing me on a
skateboard, spitting and shouting at me in a language I did-
n't recognize—but I gather I'd been working his turf—so I
ran. I ran ahead, the traffic swimming in front of me! I no
longer wanted to eat! I didn't want to see Binky! I wanted
my purse! And my key! And my bed! And a bath! I ran forward! Every block I survived was a victory! And then I
made it!

It was across the street. Home! I was standing on the
corner, surrounded by what seemed to be hundreds of children all wild and loud and out of control, and under the
care of ONE adult with a badge from the Chelsea Day
School. The sun was so hot! I was sure I standing under an
enormous magnifying glass! And soot from the cars and
buses was making me sicker and sicker! And we were all
together, standing on the corner, waiting for the light to
change. AND IT WOULDN'T! It would not! We stood for
hours! We waited weeks and the fucking light WOULD
NOT CHANGE! And then . . . it turned green—I KNOW
IT TURNED GREEN! I KNOW IT! So I staggered, or
stumbled or walked into the street and a car, FROM
NOWHERE, came zooming at me! It was headed directly
at me!! It was going to kill me!! I WAS GOING TO DIE!

It swerved! It swerved to the side! Onto the curb and
all at once the children were screaming! SCREAMING! But
I didn't look back! I RAN! I couldn't turn around! I RAN!
Past the diner!! I don't know what happened! I DON'T
WANT TO KNOW WHAT HAPPENED! I RAN!
STRAIGHT TO MY BUILDING AND HOME!

(Bea's light returns.)

BEA *(Simply)*: What do you think happened?

AMANDA: I don't know.

BEA: You think someone was hit?

AMANDA: I said, I don't know! I didn't look.

BEA: Was it on the news?

AMANDA *(With great bitterness)*: That light was green! I didn't do anything wrong! I wasn't driving the goddamn car! I didn't do anything!

BEA: Maybe nothing happened.

AMANDA: I do not want to talk about this! This is not why I called you! My husband is gone and I haven't eaten in a week and I don't have a purse and THIS IS NOT WHY I CALLED YOU! YOU ARE NOT HELPING ME!

(A long pause. General lighting has returned, but it is a good deal dimmer.)

BEA: What are you wearing?

AMANDA: What? Why do you ask?

BEa: Answer the question.

AMANDA: A T-shirt.

BEA: Change your clothes.

AMANDA: My life is in a shambles and—

BEA: Change your clothes!

AMANDA: I fail to see how that—

BEA: You have a shorty nightgown?

AMANDA: Yes.

BEA: Put it on.

AMANDA: No.

BEA: Do what I'm telling you.

AMANDA: I don't want to.

BEA: Put. It. On.

AMANDA: What are you talking about?

BEA: Everything looks one hundred percent better from inside a shorty nightgown.

AMANDA *(Ironic)*: That is very, very wise.

BEA: Listen to me. He'll be back.

AMANDA: Who cares? Who cares? I don't care anymore . . .

BEA: You fancy yourself some modern woman. But you know, things don't change. Some things are forever. The food chain is as it always was. Men rule the world. *But* penises rule men! And who rules the penises? We do, darling. People panic. People do things. But he'll be back. And when he comes back, not one word out of you! You hear me? Don't ask him where he's been. Act like nothing happened.

AMANDA: You're insane.

BEA: I will not tolerate rudeness! . . . Let me tell you, when I married my late husband, I was pregnant—not with his kid, but I was pregnant. I was very good-looking when I was younger. But the father wasn't Jewish, so I decided—or actually, my mother decided, it wouldn't go. So I married what'shisname, my dead husband. I'll never forget waking up, in Atlantic City, the day after. I'm wide awake, staring at this fat lump of hairy nothing that I married, and, let me tell you, if I coulda run, I woulda. But I was going to have a child. So, instead, I just pulled the hair on his back as hard as I could. You see my point?

(A key turns in the door.)

AMANDA: Shut up!

BEA: I will not tolerate—

AMANDA: Someone's at the door!

(Bea disappears. The door opens, revealing Ford. He and Amanda stand, just looking at each other for a moment.)

Ford. . . .WHERE'VE YOU BEEN?

BEA *(On the speaker phone)*: I told ya not to ask him that!

(Amanda hangs up the phone.)

AMANDA *(After a pause)*: I mean it doesn't really matter where you've been, does it? You've been working on a film. I understand. I know that the creative process is a very delicate flower. And you've been working. Haven't you?

(Ford sits. He is deep in thought and deeply troubled. He has something to say, but it is very difficult for him. He puts his head in his hands for a moment and agonizes.)

FORD: Well—

AMANDA: I drove you away! Didn't I? We shouldn't've gotten married. It was a bad idea. I'm sorry. It was my idea and you felt cornered, or something. Is that it? Do you want to talk about it? Is that it? . . . Are you tired? We can talk tomorrow. That's fine. You're probably tired. We can talk tomorrow after a good night's sleep.

(Ford rises, looks at her and starts to head for the bedroom.)

We do love each other though, don't we? I love you and you love me, so we love each other.

(Ford stops. He turns and looks at her.)

You're in love with someone else, aren't you! I can tell.

(Ford moves towards her, reaching out.)

I'm babbling. I realize I'm babbling. I find that I'm babbling. But you see, I've been cooped up here lately—not that I didn't go out, while you were gone. I did. But not much.

(He looks away.)

Is there someone else? Perhaps we rushed into this a bit too quickly. But then, perhaps we didn't. Time'll tell. Would you like something to eat? Are you hungry? We don't have any food—but we could order something . . . if you have a credit card. I've lost my purse.

(He sits again and struggles to find the words to say what he must. He looks around the room, scratches his head, takes a deep breath and just as he is about to speak, she cuts him off.)

YOU THINK I'M UGLY, DON'T YOU? TELL ME, WHAT PART OF ME DO YOU THINK IS UGLIEST?

(He rises to protest. She cuts him off.)

I know I'm beautiful. You're right. I'm a beautiful woman. I wasn't always. When I was a child, I was painfully fat. Did you know that?

(He shakes his head and sits.)

I never mentioned that. Did you ever wonder why there are no pictures around here, of me? Before I turned twenty? Did you think I was a vampire? Did you think I had a Nosferatu childhood?

(He shrugs.)

When I was twenty, I went on a diet. I fasted for three weeks. I lost forty-five pounds.. I dieted all summer and when I went back to school I told everyone I was my own cousin. Isn't that something?—YOU MAKE ME FEEL SO FAT!

(He puts his head in his hands.)

Everyone believed I was my own cousin. That was the summer my mother died. We had a house on the Cape. We went to the beach one day and she drowned. She went out into the ocean and swam and swam and I never saw her again. Maybe she swam to France and became a chanteuse. I changed my name to Amanda that summer.

(He looks up, surprised.)

Between my sophomore and junior years at Sarah Lawrence. Betty was a fat girl whose only friends were society's castoffs. Amanda had no more friends than Betty, but people assumed it was by choice. —Is it someone I know? The person you've found?

(He rises again, about to speak. She cuts him off.)

I can be Betty again, if you'd prefer that. My mother used to say you can be whatever you want. She meant, you can be *WHOM*ever you want. Everyone said she drowned. They said it was an accident. My father said, "Things happen." I think she killed herself. I think she wanted to die. Maybe we should talk tomorrow.

(He starts to exit.)

While you were gone, I did some work!

(He turns to her.)

I've been writing as well. I wrote a new poem. I did. It's very unusual—for me. This poem. I call it—well, I don't have a name for it yet. But it's a narrative poem, and well, it's about this man. And he's very attractive and very . . . loved. And one day, he finds himself married. And he loves his wife and she loves him, but he feels . . . confined, I think is the word I used. Maybe it was trapped. I can't remember. You see he's an artist and he's very, very sensitive. *(She is near tears)* And he wants to get away, but he knows this will

27

just . . . kill her. The wife. This will destroy her, for reasons that are absolutely not his fault. But that's the way it is. And she simply wants to kill him.

(He moves towards her.)

But instead, she just looks at him. *(She moves towards him)* And she touches his face. *(She does this, sweetly)* And she runs her fingers along his lips. *(She does this)* And she looks in his eyes . . . because she loves him. And she takes him in her hand. *(She places her hand on his crotch)* And she strokes him.

(She massages his genitalia through his trousers. His breathing deepens.)

And she kisses him.

(They kiss. It is very passionate and sexual. Lights fade out.)

SCENE 2

OTTO

The middle of the night. The lights come up on the chic studio apartment of Serge Stubin, a handsome, trim man of thirty. There is a Soloflex, a huge closet and a large bed. Serge is lounging on the bed, listening to music, wearing trendy, bike-short style underpants. After a moment, there is a knock at the door. Serge rises, turns off the CD and goes to the door.

SERGE: Who is it?
OTTO *(Offstage)*: It's me.

SERGE *(Disappointed, irritated)*: Me who?

OTTO *(Offstage)*: Me, the one true love of your life.

SERGE *(Returning to the bed)*: Go away, Otto.

OTTO *(Offstage)*: Let me in!

SERGE: It's the middle of the night.

OTTO *(Offstage)*: Serge! I'm being followed!

SERGE: Consider it flattery.

OTTO *(Offstage)*: Let me in!

SERGE: Go home!

OTTO *(Offstage)*: Today's my birthday. I'm thirty-four years old today.

SERGE: Today is not your birthday.

OTTO *(Offstage)*: Yesterday was my birthday?

SERGE: Go away. Go.

OTTO *(Offstage)*: Let me in, or I'll kill myself! I mean it. I'll do it right here on the doorstep! How'll that look? How'd you like that? Well? I mean it! I'll do it! *(Pause)* LET ME IN!!

(Serge goes wearily to the door and opens it, revealing Otto, a wildly overweight man carrying a bag of groceries.)

SERGE: What do you want?

OTTO: I got fired.

SERGE: I'm sorry.

OTTO: I want to see you.

SERGE: You can't come in. I'm expecting someone.

OTTO: I won't stay long. I promise.

(Otto forces his way in. He makes himself at home, quickly unpacking groceries, starting with doughnuts. He eats as he talks.)

OTTO: It's *unbelievably* hot in here! Is the air conditioning broken? I'm sweating already. You look well, but then you always look well. How've you been? I saw a picture of someone who looked just like you in a magazine. It was *Honcho*. I cut the penis out of the picture.

SERGE: What are you doing here?!

OTTO: I got fired—

SERGE: So you said.

OTTO: That job was everything to me! I have nothing! I *am* nothing! I'm a fat, middle-aged man with nothing to look forward to but the embrace of death.

SERGE: You're thirty-three.

OTTO: Please! With my cholesterol and my blood sugar, I'll never make sixty. This is the twilight of my life. I'm alone and jobless in my declining years.

SERGE: What happened?

OTTO: They said I wasn't funny anymore. How funny do you have to be to introduce a bunch of *no-talents*? They said I'd lost my joie de vivre! Of course, I've lost my joie de vivre— I'm fat, I'm lonely, I have a new pimple, I'm thirty-six—

SERGE: You're thirty-three!

OTTO: And I'm still getting pimples! Who could be funny under the circumstances?

SERGE: You're getting crumbs on the bed!

OTTO: Isn't that cute? Isn't that sweet? It's just like the old days. Remember how you used to scream at me when I ate in the bed? You'd scream with such rage, you turned purple. I was so happy. It can be like that again.

SERGE: It will be, if you don't—

OTTO: Do you want one?

SERGE: No.

OTTO: They're delicious!—It's hot as a pizza house in here. Are you growing pot or something?

SERGE: I like it warm.

OTTO: I'm just going to turn this up. *(He adjusts the thermostat)* Who needs them anyway?!! I survived before that crummy little nightclub and I'll survive without it! I'm not a comic. I'm an actor! I did Chekhov and Inge! It was only college, true, but I have training! I have technique!—That was the best job I ever had! Steady work, a steady paycheck, four nights a week and I could live off it! And it was so easy! What am I going to do?

SERGE: You'll get another job.

OTTO: Oh you don't care!! You never cared! You only care about you! You're self-centered, that's your problem—Are those Calvin Klein? They're cute.—You know what this means, don't you? It's back to the notions counter for me!

SERGE: You worked at Barneys in European suits.

OTTO: I just want to die!

SERGE: Well you can't die here. Not tonight.

OTTO: Do you think I made it too cold? Can I stay? Can I stay over? Can I sleep here tonight?

SERGE: Of course not.

OTTO: Please?

SERGE: I told you, someone's coming over.

OTTO: I don't believe you. I think you're lying. Who'd come over at this hour? Only an insane person, present company excluded, of course. I think you're lying. You lie with every breath. You're a liar, that's your problem.

SERGE: Go home. Get some sleep.

OTTO *(Lying)*: I can't. My house burned down.

SERGE: What are you talking about?

OTTO: It did. It burned to the ground. It's a miracle no one was killed. I think someone set it. That's what I think. I think the management company did it for the insurance. That sounds possible, doesn't it?

SERGE: No.

OTTO: You're too cynical, *that's* your problem.

(The phone rings. As Serge answers it, Otto removes a package of pretzel rods from his sack. He takes one and stacks donuts on it. He then eats this creation as if it were an ear of corn.)

SERGE *(Into the phone)*: Hello. . . . Oh, yes, I'm fine. . . . No, it's not too late. . . . Oh. . . . Oh. . . . Oh. That is too bad. *(He extends the phone to Otto)* It's for you.

OTTO *(Taking the phone)*: Oh. I left this number on my machine. *(Into the phone)* Hello?. . .Why are you calling me here?. . . Serge is fine. . . . No. No. . . . No, this does NOT mean we're back together. . . . Well, *I* visit people in the middle of the night . . . I'm sorry . . . I'm sorry . . . I'm sorry. . . . I've got to go . . . I've got to go . . . I've got to go. *(He hangs up)* It was my mother.

SERGE: You've got to go.

OTTO: She thinks I'm going to kill myself or something. She thinks I'm taking this job thing too hard. My analyst says I was overly involved in my work. My analyst says I've been looking for the wrong kind of fulfillment. My analyst makes me sick. Do you want a pretzel?

SERGE: No.

OTTO: Do you think you could ever love me again?

SERGE: No.

OTTO: Don't toy with me. Don't tease me along.

SERGE: I said no.

OTTO: Just tell me the truth. Just lay it on the line. I'm a grown-up. I can take it. Be honest. You shilly-shally, *that's* your problem.

SERGE: I'm in love with someone else.

OTTO: I remember the first time I saw you. In Barneys. You were spectacular looking, to me at any rate. Not that you're not good-looking, I don't mean that. But some people don't think you're as good-looking as me. I mean as I do. Everyone things you're better looking than I am. Even *my mother* thinks you're better looking than me. Did you know she shows your picture to people? People ask her if she has a son and she shows them your picture. You've made her very proud.

SERGE: Is there no way to stop you?

OTTO: I certainly hope not. Obviously you're good-looking.

You're a model. You have to be good-looking to be a model. But then again, you only do runway. You're not good-looking enough for print, are you? Is it chilly in here now? You could love me again, if I were thin.

SERGE: I doubt that.

OTTO: Oh, you may not think so, but I know it. I'm sure of it. I'm on a diet. I've lost eighty-five pounds. Can you tell? Do I look thinner?

SERGE: No.

OTTO: Well, actually, I gained four pounds. But I don't think four pounds really shows up. I know in the past, when I've lost four pounds, it didn't show. When was that? As I was saying, before I was so *rudely* interrupted, I'm on a new diet. I have a Slim-Fast shake with every meal. Have you tried Slim-Fast?

SERGE: Of course not.

OTTO: You're afraid to try new things, *that's* your problem. I like you're hair. Are you combing it differently, or at all? Slim-Fast is delicious! It goes fabulously with pretzels! *(He pulls a can of Slim-Fast out of his bag)* I'm not thirsty yet. Maybe later.—You'd love me again, if I was thinner. I told my analyst that I was going to come and see you, and you know what she did? She laughed! She burst into gales of laughter! She told me she was crying. She cries all the time. I don't think she's happy. I think she's got serious problems. Would you love me again if I weighed a hundred pounds? Would you love me if I weighed fifty pounds? Would you love me if I looked like one of those living corpses in the photographs from the liberation of Auschwitz?

SERGE: I can't say I'd love you. I might prefer you.

OTTO: So tell me, what've you been doing with yourself lately? I'm fascinated.

SERGE: I did the Gaultier show and Anna Sui menswear.

OTTO: Runway modeling must be soooo stimulating. Such a challenge.

SERGE: It's fine. It's easy.

OTTO: Tell me, do you ever worry that you'll fall off the ramp? D'you ever worry that you'll swagger, blindly, off the runway and into the lap of the editor from *GQ*?

SERGE: No!

OTTO: D'you ever worry that you'll put the clothes on upside down? D'you ever traipse down the catwalk with your arms in the leg holes and the pants wrapped around your back, like a bolero jacket?

SERGE: I like what I do! The money is good. The people are nice.

OTTO: I bet they are. Why shouldn't they be?—It is definitely freezing in here now. *(He adjusts the thermostat)* What have they got to be bitter about? All those stunning young boys with perfect chests and perfect hair. They all have squares on their stomachs and perfect little geometric rear ends. I'm a total failure! I'm washed up at thirty-eight!

SERGE: You're thirty-three!!

OTTO: Must you be correct all the time? What is this neurotic compulsion you have to be correct? You have a fetish, *that's* your problem.

SERGE: I don't want to hurt your feelings—

OTTO *(Pulling a pack of Yodels from his bag)* Do you like Yodels? Probably not. I've always loved Yodels. When I was a kid I used to unroll them and eat them like a piece of pizza. It made them seem like more. My analyst says my parents never paid enough attention to me, so I have a neurotic fear of there never being enough of anything. I don't know what she's talking about most of the time. *(He shoves a whole Yodel into his mouth)*

SERGE: How often are you seeing her?

(Otto chews, savoring his food for a moment. Then, cheerfully:)

OTTO: Twice a day. Remember how happy we were?

SERGE: I don't remember that we were particularly happy.

OTTO: You reinvent history, *that's* your problem. We were in an advanced state of bliss! My living here with you was the happiest two years of my life.

SERGE: Two years?!

OTTO: Did I say two years? I meant four years. It just flew by in half the time.

SERGE: You never lived here!

OTTO: Time flies when you're in love.

SERGE: We dated for a couple of weeks!

OTTO: You must've had it awful bad.

SERGE: GET OUT!!

OTTO *(Sprawling on the bed)*: I loved this bed! I adored it! It was ecstasy like death! You know that Jacques Brel song? "My death waits in a double bed—" The contortions, the experiments, the complete savage abandon!! If this bed could talk, the stories it could tell!—Is this the same bed? It smells different. Did you get a new bed?

SERGE: I'm asking you nicely. I've tried to be direct. I've tried to be blunt. Now, I'm asking you as a friend—

OTTO: We are friends, aren't we?

SERGE: I suppose.

OTTO: Then tell me, as a friend, what's wrong with me?

SERGE: You're insane.

OTTO: I'm forty years old and I have no one in my life!!

SERGE: You are THIRTY-THREE!!

OTTO: You have a terrible temper. You know that? I'm forty-one and you're twenty-eight, but with your temper and too much exercise, we'll be the same age in six months.

(The phone rings. Serge answers it.)

SERGE: Hello?. . . . Yes. . . . yes . . . yes . . . yes. *(He extends the phone to Otto)* It's for you.

OTTO *(Singing)*: I'm Mr. Popular! *(He takes the phone)* Hello? . . . Obviously, I'm still here. . . . No, we're NOT back together yet! . . . No, no, I'm not making a fool of myself. . . . Yes, I saw her today. . . . She laughed. . . . Fifty dollars. . . . I have to go. . . . I'm hanging up! *(He hangs up)* It was my mother.

SERGE: Please leave.

OTTO: She's lonely. She threw out her back. She's in traction.

SERGE: We all have our problems.

OTTO *(Sarcastic)*: Oh you are so sympathetic. You're a saint! When you look up sympathy in the dictionary, it says, "see Serge Stubin." You're too good, that's your problem.

SERGE: I'm sorry.

OTTO: Oh, no. What do you care? The poor woman is stuck in a hospital bed somewhere, out in the night, her limbs hanging like a Calder mobile. Her son's out of work, wandering the streets, a forty-four year old nebbish with no future, and not much of past to speak of.

SERGE: How did it happen?

OTTO: Who cares! Who cares how it happened. I HATE HER! SHE RUINED MY LIFE. THAT BITCH CONDEMNED ME TO AN ETERNITY OF SELF-LOATHING. Did you know I have a neurotic fear of being upside down? My analyst says I need to experience my rage. She doodles while I talk to her. She pretends to take notes, but I caught her one day. She was drawing the Lincoln Memorial on a cocktail napkin! It was very good, but I told her it stunk—I'm not giving her any satisfaction—

(He pulls a box of Snowcaps from his bag) I LOVE SNOWCAPS!! Most people only eat them at the movies, but you know they're good anytime.

SERGE: Don't eat any more.

OTTO *(Eating Snowcaps)*: I'M STARVING! Did I mention that I lie in bed at night and pretend you're there next to me? I do. Did I mention that I hung your picture in my bathroom? I taped it on the medicine chest, over the mirror. Now when I wake up and I look at myself—I'm you!! I thought it would make me like myself more. It didn't. It made me like you more—and I cut myself shaving continually.

SERGE: You have got to move on with your life.

OTTO: I put two candles in the bathroom. One on either side of your picture. It's like a shrine. Well it's not like a shrine, it IS a shrine! I sacrifice small animals to you. I use the sink. It's not as messy as you might imagine. I do mice, and squirrels. Last week I did a baby goat.

SERGE: Oh my God.

OTTO: I'm lying. Or kidding. I don't know which—about the goat.

SERGE: Still.

OTTO: And the mice. I killed a mosquito once. But it had nothing to do with you. Do you remember how terrified you were of bugs?

SERGE: You're afraid of bugs.

OTTO: You project, that's your problem. You always had a neurotic fear of insects. I love them! I adore bugs. I keep roaches as pets.

SERGE *(Pointing to a spot on the floor)*: Good. Then you can have that one, there.

OTTO *(In terror)*: WHERE!? WHERE!? KILL IT! KILL IT NOW!!

SERGE: I'm lying. Or kidding. I don't know which.

OTTO: I knew that. You are a complete sadist. You get pleasure from my abject misery. Maybe that's why I love you so much. You could love me again if I were blond. I could be blond. All those boys you work with are blond, aren't they? Except for the brunets and the redheads. I could be blond! I could bleach my hair. I'd look repulsive. I'd look hideous. You'd like that. You'd like it if I were freakishly ugly.—Is it unbelievably hot in here again? *(He goes to the thermostat)*

SERGE: You're going to break that!

OTTO: OH WHAT DO YOU CARE? YOU CAN ALWAYS BUY ANOTHER. You can buy anything you want. You have all the money in the world and I am not speaking hyperbolically. I think you do. I think you've used it all up. That's why I can't ever seem to get any: YOU HAVE IT ALL!!!

   (Otto throws open Serge's closet, which is lined with

mirrors. Upon seeing himself, he shrieks in horror and slams the doors shut)

I love your apartment! It's so *put together*. Do you remember my apartment? It's pathetic. Everything is old, and broken and chipped, from the Salvation Army. I'm *forty-five years old* and I still have bookcases made from cinder blocks like a college dormitory.

SERGE: You *have* money.

OTTO: BLOOD MONEY! Money my father left me. I hated him. He was a loathsome human being. Did I ever tell you that I went to his funeral dressed as Bloody Mary?—The character from *South Pacific,* not the cocktail.—I wore a giant mumu, a lei around my neck and a frozen daiquiri paper umbrella in my hair. I just did it to embarrass him. But then no one came anyway. His was the most ill-attended funeral I've ever seen. And I've seen quite a few. Lately I go to funerals just for the pick-me-up.

SERGE: Why don't you take some of that money and go on a trip?

OTTO: I swore to myself I'd never spend one cent of the filthy lucre that miserable old fart left me! He hated me! He drank more than any two people I've ever known. The last time I saw my father, you know what he said to me? Do you? He was in the hospital. He was on an iron lung. He was dying. Frito?

SERGE: No.

OTTO: He had a completely obsessive personality—pathetic. So he was in the hospital, clinging to life by his nicotine-yellow fingernails. And he's going on and on at me about my weight and being "light-in-the-loafers," which was the darling euphemism he used for "fairy." And his breathing was very labored—he had emphysema, or something. I can't remember. I never paid much attention. So he's on this iron lung, and his last words to me, the very last words he ever spoke: he reached out, red in the face, panic in his heart—he reached out and shrieked, "Otto! Otto! Please, no! Don't touch that plug!!"

SERGE: Oh my God!!

OTTO: But it was too late.

SERGE: You unplugged his iron lung?!

OTTO: His television! What's wrong with you?

SERGE: I thought—

OTTO: You thought I killed my father? You're insane, that's your problem. I unplugged his television. I went to visit him, I took time out of my busy schedule, which was completely empty as it happened, but he didn't know that! I went out of my way to visit that old gasbag and he has the nerve to lie there watching TV! He was the rudest person I ever knew. It was a football game, or something. I don't know. The one with the orange ball and hoops with nets. It was giving me a headache, so I unplugged it. And then he was angry—wouldn't say a word. He just lay there, like a corpse. It wasn't until later that I learned he had died.

(The phone rings.)

SERGE *(Weary)*: Go ahead.

OTTO *(Into the phone)*: Hello? . . . Oh hello. . . . No, we're not back together yet!! . . . Yes, I realize that I'm a fat, ugly, lonely failure with nothing and no one in my life and that no one will shed a single tear when I die. . . . I'll talk to you later. *(He hangs up)* It was my mother.

SERGE: I assumed.

OTTO: Let's pretend we just met. Okay? Let's pretend you picked me up in one of those bars you go to. I hate those places. Let's pretend. You be . . . you! And I'll be me. Okay? It'll be fun.

SERGE: I don't want to.

OTTO: You never want to have any fun, THAT'S your problem.

SERGE: Look! I'VE EXPLAINED TO YOU—

OTTO: I remember the first moment I saw you. How long ago was that? I can't remember now. Was it six months? Eight months?

SERGE: It was FOUR years ago!

OTTO: Was it? Was it really? Time stands still when I'm without you. Four years? How much did I weigh then?

SERGE: Considerably less than you do now!

OTTO: You're full of hate, baby! Hate just oozes out of you. Hate is gushing out of your skin. You wear hate the way the salesgirls in Bloomingdale's wear makeup. In heavy layers.

SERGE: YOU'RE DRIVING ME CRAZY!

OTTO: Did I mention that I tattooed your name on my buttocks? I did! It was extremely painful. It hurt like hell, but I did it! You know I have a neurotic fear of needles, but I tattooed your name on my rear-end, in letters THREE feet tall!

SERGE: Listen—

OTTO: NOW I SIT ON YOU ALL THE TIME!

SERGE: I HAVE TOLD YOU—

OTTO: I know, I know. You're expecting someone!! Well, where is this mystery date? I don't see him. Let him come. I'll kill him! Then you, then myself—or any order you want. But you see, I don't think there is anyone coming over. I think you're lonely and bitter. I think every day since we split up has been as torturous for you as it has for me!

SERGE: I'VE BEEN VERY HAPPY!

OTTO: OH HIDE YOUR MISERY WITH LAUGHTER! YOU CAN'T FOOL ME. YOU'RE GRIEF STRICKEN TO THE POINT OF HYSTERIA, ONLY YOU HIDE IT WITH UNCOMMON PANACHE. I KNOW HOW BROKEN YOU'VE BEEN, BECAUSE I'VE BEEN THE SAME! THE DAYS ARE LONG, BUT THE NIGHTS ARE LONGER! ADMIT YOU WANT ME BACK! DON'T LET STUPID PRIDE STAND IN YOUR WAY. WHAT'S THAT? SO SOONER THAN LATER YOU'LL BE A ONCE-BEAUTI-FUL, FADED, MALE-INGENUE TYPE, WIZENED AND WITHERED ALONE WITH YOUR PRIDE. WELL, LET ME TELL YOU, PRIDE IS A COLD COMPANION ON A BITTER WINTER'S NIGHT! I KNOW PRIDE! I KNOW WHAT PRIDE IS! I have none myself, of course, BUT I'VE

SEEN IT IN OTHERS. FORGET YOUR PRIDE, LOVE
ME!!

SERGE: For the last time, YOU HAVE GOT TO GET ON WITH
YOUR LIFE! Look at what you're doing to yourself!
You're killing yourself!

OTTO: That'd make you happy, wouldn't it?

SERGE: NO! No, Otto, it wouldn't. You can think what you
want. But I do not hate you. I don't. God knows why, but
I don't.

OTTO: Is it hot in here? I'm having a sugar drop. *(He sits on the
floor and dumps out the remaining contents of his grocery
bag)*

SERGE: I look at you and I remember what you used to be.

OTTO: Before you destroyed me?

SERGE: Before you ate yourself into this state!

OTTO: Have I put on weight? Is that what you're saying? I try
not to get on the scale.

SERGE: You were attractive.

OTTO: I get vertigo from watching the dial spin, and spin, and
spin.

SERGE: You were SANE! You were funny—

OTTO: God, I'm hot.

SERGE: I do not accept responsibility for you! I AM NOT TO
BLAME!

*(Otto eats Oreos rabidly, unscrewing them, scraping out
the middle and throwing the cookie over his shoulder.)*

OTTO: I can't imagine it's a question of blame.

SERGE: It's been four years! Four long years! We dated briefly.
There was no passion. No great love! We dated briefly! We
never lived together! We never planned a future! WE!
DATED! BRIEFLY!

OTTO *(Offering)*: Oreo?

SERGE: NO!!

OTTO *(Coy)*: They're double stuff. *(He drinks a Yoohoo)*

SERGE: WHAT IS WRONG WITH YOU!!? I thought this was over! I've held my breath! I've prayed! I've done good deeds! BUT NOTHING WORKED! YOU'RE BACK! I don't want to hurt you, but I need my peace! YOU HAVE GOT TO GET OVER ME! I'm no great catch to begin with, as you constantly remind me, while groveling, sniveling and begging me to take you back! TAKE YOU BACK!!? WE DATED BRIEFLY!!

OTTO: Finished? *(He drinks a second Yoohoo)*

SERGE: NO I AM NOT FINISHED!!! I don't know what to do—tell me what to do. I know you have needs. I know you have problems, you have obvious problems! But this is not fair! I HAVE NEEDS AND PROBLEMS TOO! THIS ISN'T FAIR! DO YOU HEAR ME? THIS JUST IS NOT FAIR!!

(A long pause.)

OTTO *(Very small)*: I don't see what you're so worked up about. I just dropped by. I brought some doughnuts. That's all.

(The phone rings.)

SERGE: ANSWER IT!

OTTO: Excuse me. *(Into the phone)* Hello? . . . Oh, hello. . . . No, we are NOT back together yet!! . . . Yes, I understand that I'm a heap of human debris, that I'm not getting any younger and that everything I touch turns to shit! . . . Well, if that's what you want, I can't stop you from killing yourself. . . . No, I *don't* care that you've taken forty-five sleeping pills!! . . . If you want to die, it's your prerogative! . . . No, I'm not calling 911 for you!! . . . I DON'T CARE! . . . THEN JUST DIE! DIE! DIE AND LEAVE ME ALONE! I CAN'T GO ON LIKE THIS! *(He slams the phone down)* It was my analyst.

SERGE: What?

OTTO: I'm sorry if I intruded. You keep telling me to get on with my life. For years now, you've been telling me that. "Get on with your life." . . . But you are my life.

SERGE: Don't be pathetic.

OTTO: If it's pathetic, it's pathetic. If it's sick or sad or whatever it is—it is the way it is. I love you. And you will love me again. Someday . . . or you won't. But I don't intend to give up trying. I see no advantage in surrender.

SERGE *(After a moment)*: You keep telling me, I'll love you again. But I *never* loved you.

OTTO: What?

SERGE: But I am in love. Now. For the first time. Do you understand me? He's on his way over here right now. He went to get his things and he's coming here, to live. So you simply have to go.

(Sadly, Otto rises. The phone rings. Otto looks at Serge, who gestures that Otto should answer it.)

OTTO *(Into the phone)*: Hello? . . . It's for you.

SERGE *(Taking the phone)*: Hello? . . . Oh. . . . I see . . . well, but . . . but . . . *(He hangs up the phone)* He's not coming.

OTTO *(Simply)*: Oh. *(Pause, then with great cheer)* So? Can I stay?

(Blackout.)

SCENE 3

FATTY & SKINNY LAY IN BED . . .

The lights come up on the Dolor living room. It is morning, perhaps we hear the sounds of birds. The doorbell rings. After a moment, the person on the other side begins pounding on the door, rather violently. Finally, Amanda enters, wearing a shorty nightgown.

AMANDA: Coming!

(She goes to the door and opens it, revealing Serge.)

Can I help you?
SERGE: Is this Ford Dolor's apartment?
AMANDA: Why do you ask?
SERGE: It is, isn't it?
AMANDA: It's nine in the morning.
SERGE: May I come in?
AMANDA: No!

(Serge pushes past her. She follows.)

SERGE: Where is he?
AMANDA: Ford's asleep. What is this about?
SERGE: I'd like to speak to Ford, please.
AMANDA: Well, I'm not going to wake him. Who are you?!
SERGE: My name is Serge. Who are you?
AMANDA: I'm Amanda. I'm Ford's wife. Now, please leave.
SERGE: Not until I speak to Ford.
AMANDA: I've asked you to leave. I'd appreciate it if you'd just—
SERGE: I'm in love with your husband.
AMANDA *(Stunned)*: What?
SERGE: I think. If he's in love with me, that is. If not then I'm not. I'm not putting myself in *that* position.
AMANDA: You're . . . ?
SERGE: I'm sorry. I didn't mean to blurt it out like that. I have no intention of hurting you. I have no interest in you. I didn't even make a mental note of your name.
AMANDA: It's Amanda.
SERGE: Would you do me a favor and get Ford? Tell him I'm here.
AMANDA: You're a man.
SERGE: Yes, I know that. I'm aware of that.
AMANDA: You're saying Ford is—

SERGE: My lover. Ford is my lover.

AMANDA *(Stricken)*: I see.

SERGE: He never mentioned he was married.

AMANDA: He didn't?

SERGE: How long have you been together?

AMANDA: Oh a long time. Several years.

SERGE: Well, he doesn't talk much.

AMANDA: Yes, I know.

SERGE: He's pretty quiet.

AMANDA: He never mentioned you, either.

SERGE: I really didn't come here to upset you. I came to see Ford. I want to find out where we stand. I have plans to make, things to do. I have an appointment at the tanning salon at ten and I intend to know what's going—

AMANDA: How long have you known my husband, Mr.—?

SERGE: Serge, please.

AMANDA: How long, *Serge*?

SERGE: We met two weeks ago.

AMANDA: I see. And at what sordid, little social club was this?

SERGE: Bloomingdale's.

AMANDA: Typical.

SERGE: I'm a model. Maybe you recognize me?

AMANDA: I'm afraid not.

SERGE: Well, I don't do much print work.

AMANDA: That is too bad.

SERGE: I was at Bloomingdale's for the fall promotions of the new Calvin Klein underwear. Ford was shopping. He remarked on the cut of my briefs and one thing led to another. We went back to my place, and I found that I could open up to him. I could really talk to him in a way I can't talk to a lot of people. You know most people look at me and they just see someone who's unusually attractive. Then they find out that I'm a model, and they assume that I'm an idiot! You know, I think that's a form of prejudice! Wouldn't you say so?

AMANDA: I don't know. I don't know *and* I don't care.

SERGE: Well, we went back to my place. We were talking and listening to some old Donna Summer tapes. And then, we didn't even discuss it—before we knew what was happening we were fucking and sucking and going like rabid dogs in the summer sun, right there in the window!

AMANDA: Oh my God.

SERGE: I know. It's pretty undignified, huh?

AMANDA: Oh my God.

SERGE: But when you connect, you connect.

AMANDA: I feel sick.

SERGE: Oh, we were safe. Not to worry. I consider myself extremely responsible.

AMANDA *(Weakly)*: Good.

SERGE: And that was it. We spent the next fourteen days together.

AMANDA: Did you?

SERGE: In bed, on the floor, in the tub, on the roof—

AMANDA: The roof?

SERGE: We only stopped for salt tablets! I was seeing someone else, this guy, Roger—and he had heart surgery last week, but I'll be honest with you. Ford made me forget all about Roger. I mean, I forgot to send flowers or call the hospital or anything. I wonder if he lived. Can I use your phone?

AMANDA: No.

SERGE: Oh well. It doesn't matter. I never really cared for Roger. He was wild about me but he talked nonstop! I couldn't get a word in edgewise. With Ford, it was different. We have something very, very unique—

AMANDA: You can't qualify unique. It either is, or it isn't.

SERGE: What?

AMANDA: Skip it.

SERGE: That's why I don't understand! This might come as a surprise, but Ford was planning on moving in with me. He left my place last night at about twelve and said he'd be back in a couple of hours with his stuff.

AMANDA: He was going to—

SERGE: Then he calls at two in the morning, and no explana-

tion! No excuse! No nothing! Just "I'm not coming." Well
I'm not used to this! I'm not used to being treated like a
piece of gum stuck under a chair! I want to see him. Now!

(Amanda blocks the hallway.)

AMANDA: Too bad.

SERGE: I'll wait.

AMANDA: Just go!

SERGE: Tell me, did he say anything? Did he talk about me? Did
you discuss it? Was it me? Was I suffocating? Is that it? I
thought he liked being suffocated! He liked the paddle! He
liked the whip! He liked the cat-o'-nine-tails! He even liked
the candle wax!

AMANDA: STOP IT! STOP IT! STOP IT!

SERGE: He told me we had something special! He told me that
he loved me!!

AMANDA *(Bitter)*: When was that?

SERGE: Over and over!

AMANDA: Oh?

SERGE: If not in so many words—

AMANDA: Well, Mr.—Serge, he told me he loved me over and
over, last night, *IN* so many words!

SERGE *(Mock casual)*: Really?

AMANDA: YES! Because Ford and I are MARRIED and we DO
love each other! So whatever sick, twisted hold you've had
on my husband is broken! He clearly regrets having met
you and has decided to stay HERE, with ME, his WIFE!

SERGE: You think so?

AMANDA: Did he return to you last night? No. He was in bed
with me last night! And that's exactly where he intends to
stay!

SERGE: I'd like him to tell me that.

AMANDA: It's over! Why don't you simply leave? Go. Go and get
yourself a tan. If you leave now, there'll be no ugly scenes
of recrimination.

SERGE *(Feigning shock)*: Maybe I—do you have a glass of water?
AMANDA: No.
SERGE: Please. I'm not used to this. I'm strikingly attractive and this comes as quite a blow.
AMANDA: Drink it. Then leave.

(Exasperated, Amanda fetches Serge a drink. He takes the moment to head toward the bedroom. Just as he gets there, Otto appears at the door, which had been left ajar, carrying a bag of groceries and pointing a gun at his temple.)

OTTO: THE WORLD IS A RANCID CESSPOOL AND I CAN TAKE IT NO LONGER!!
SERGE *(Turning)*: Otto!?
OTTO: LET MY DEATH BE ON YOUR HEAD, SERGE STUBIN! LET YOUR DREAMS BE FILLED WITH VISIONS OF MY BLOODY SKULL!
SERGE: What are you doing here!?
OTTO *(Entering)*: I followed you.

(Amanda enters and hands Serge a glass of water.)

SERGE: Oh dear God.
OTTO: When you threw me out last night, I slept in the garbage can outside your building. I ate orange rinds and an old shoe for breakfast—all right, all right I went home and had bacon and a dozen eggs—but I was up at seven a.m. and perched outside your house! I followed you! I'd've been here sooner, but that pig at the gun store refused to cash my check! A clear case of anti-Semitism! I haven't been to sleep, but then I never sleep. I haven't slept in years!
     (He falls to his knees) Do you think you could love me again if I got a good night's sleep? Do you?—Don't answer! I know what you're going to say. You're going to say "No." That's all you ever say: No, no, no, no, no. You are positively monosyllabic! You should buy a word-a-day calen-

dar to build your vocabulary—I tossed and turned all night long and I have decided that life is simply not worth living WHILE YOU LOVE SOMEONE ELSE!—It's unbelievably hot in here! Is anyone else hot? It's like a sauna. I'm waiting for the boy to come around with the cold-water hose for my wrists and temples, for God's sake!

AMANDA: Do you know this person?

SERGE: No. No, I don't. We've never met. Call the police.

OTTO: I am Otto Woodnick!

AMANDA: You're not!?

SERGE: He is.

OTTO: I am!

AMANDA: Otto! It's me! Betty Pemberton! I was in your homeroom class in New Rochelle High!

OTTO: Betty?!

AMANDA: Amanda now. Amanda Dolor!

OTTO: You were so fat!

AMANDA: You were so thin!

OTTO and AMANDA: What happened to you!!?

(Otto and Amanda embrace. Serge watches this. As they are embraced, Ford staggers groggily into the room. He sees the scene, has no apparent reaction, turns and exits, unnoticed.)

OTTO: You look fantastic!

AMANDA: I've lost some weight. That's all.

OTTO: I heard about your mother.

AMANDA: Oh yes.

OTTO: I'm so sorry.

AMANDA: Oh don't be, please. My mother was a horrible person really. For years now I've tried to convince myself that her death was somehow tragic to me, that she was a fine person. But she wasn't and it wasn't. She made me feel completely inadequate. She was very beautiful, you know. And tall and thin. She looked like Audrey Hepburn. I hated her. Her death was my liberation.

SERGE: You hated Audrey Hepburn?!

AMANDA: God no. I hated my mother. After she died I flourished for the first time. I lost all my weight and took control of my future.

SERGE: The two of you should start a club! He drones on all the time about his mother.

OTTO: She's a nightmare!

SERGE: What's wrong with you people?

AMANDA: Do you like your mother?

SERGE: Of course!

OTTO and AMANDA: Why?

SERGE: She's my mother. I love her. She's charming and witty and she believes in me. She instilled in me the confidence that lets me do anything I put my mind to.

OTTO and AMANDA: Oh.

SERGE: My father, on the other hand, is a turd.

OTTO: Listen to that! He's so pithy. It would take me paragraphs to say what he says with a word! That's the man I love! I hope you don't mind if I have a nibble while we catch up, Betty. I'm starving! I haven't eaten in minutes!

(He pulls a bag of bagels from his bag and eats as he talks) Help yourself to a bagel if you want, BUT DON'T TOUCH THE CINNAMON-RAISIN, they're my favorite—I will never forget the first time I saw him! Talk about your some-enchanted-evenings! Do you remember how popular I was in school? I was the best-liked Jewish person in our class. I had more friends than I knew what to do with. Well, I had friends. NO ONE LIKED ME! No one's ever liked me! Do I smell funny? You'd tell me if I smelled funny, wouldn't you, Betty? No, no, don't answer that. I bathe and if I smell funny there's nothing more I can do about it, so I'd just as soon not know it.—Where was I? Oh yes, we met at Barneys—

AMANDA: Department stores are meat markets!

OTTO: It's so true. Housewares are the worst! Anyway, he took me away with him, for a weekend in Bimini—

SERGE: I never did any such thing!

OTTO: Ooooo, he's got a terrible temper!

SERGE: I've never even been to Bimini!

OTTO: I think he's capable of anything.

AMANDA: *I'VE* been to Bimini.

OTTO: I keep warning him, I keep telling him with that temper and a diet void of sugar, he'll put himself in a grave before he hits twenty!

SERGE: I'M THIRTY NOW!!

OTTO: I rest my case.

SERGE: Get out of my life!

OTTO: Could you love me again if I got out of your life? Could you?

SERGE: If you got out of my life? Forever? Yes. Yes, I could.

OTTO: But then I wouldn't—I'm confused now.

SERGE: God!

(Amanda takes a bagel from Otto's bag and eats ravenously—it's a cinnamon-raisin.)

OTTO: We were going to redecorate his house. We went to Conran's and picked out all new furniture—you look amazing by the way. I can't get over it. You'll have to share your diet tips later.—We went to ABC Carpets and found the most precious Persian rugs! We picked china and flatware. I told my mother, who's in traction, by the by, now that you ask. My analyst says I have a neurotic fixation on my mother. But I ask you, at what point does a fixation become neurotic? You be the judge. DO I SEE RAISINS?!

(Amanda drops the bagel, panicked.)

The point is, we made plans. I went so far as to pick up one of those What-Shall-We-Name-the-Baby books. I voted for Shemuel. He wanted Violet. We bickered. I think it was a religious thing. What do you think?

SERGE: STOP TALKING!!

OTTO: He tortures me! He's a pig! I weep to dehydration!

AMANDA *(Confronting Serge)*: How *can* you be so cruel!?

(Otto crawls to his grocery bag, on the floor, and eats.)

SERGE: What?

AMANDA: Look at what you're doing to him!

OTTO: Yeah, look.

SERGE: You don't understand the situation.

AMANDA: How you can function under the elephantine burden of guilt you must carry is a conundrum to me!

SERGE: A *what?*

OTTO: I love the way you talk.

AMANDA: A riddle. It means riddle!

SERGE: Why don't you just say riddle!?

AMANDA: Look at the state to which you've reduced this man!

SERGE: I've reduced him to nothing!

AMANDA: Exactly my point!

OTTO: What do you mean by that?

SERGE: How is this any of your business?

AMANDA: Loyalty is everything. When I was fat Betty Pemberton, Otto Woodnick came to my aid when no one else cared if I lived or died.

OTTO: I did?

AMANDA: I was teased mercilessly by pretty girls with tiny waists and prematurely perky breasts. I spent many a long afternoon weeping in fat, solitary misery behind the bleachers. There was one group of particularly venomous anorexics. They pelted me with rocks. They stole my English Lit. midterm. Otto Woodnick came to my rescue.

OTTO: I did?

AMANDA: He stayed up all night and helped me redo it! I only got a C+, but I would've had nothing to turn in, if it hadn't been for Otto's gallant chivalry.

OTTO: Don't mention it. Rugalach?

AMANDA: He was sweet and kind and good.

SERGE: Well, he's none of those things now!

(Otto starts choking.)

AMANDA: And who's fault is that? I know what kind of feral beast you are! You think you can blithely destroy human beings without remuneration. This fat, loud, gasping, wheezing lump of despair—

(Without missing a beat, Amanda kicks Otto, who is choking, on his back. Something flies out of Otto's mouth and back into the bag. He resumes eating, contented. There has been no pause in Amanda's speech.)

—bears no resemblance to the Otto Woodnick I knew! You think I'll let you toy with Ford the way you've toyed with poor, pathetic, now-repulsive Otto?! Well, I'm here to tell you, NO! YOU MAY NOT! You've got to be stopped!

OTTO: Who's Ford?

AMANDA: My husband.

SERGE: My God!

OTTO *(Rising)*: MY RIVAL!

SERGE: I'm not toying with anyone! I'm in love with Ford—

OTTO: Where is he?

AMANDA *(Pointing toward the bedroom)*: In there.

SERGE: I think—if he's in love with me—

OTTO: PREPARE TO DIE, YOU FILTHY SCUM!

(Otto stalks off, his gun raised. Serge and Amanda realize what has just happened and stand frozen in terror. A moment passes.)

OTTO *(Offstage)*: WHERE ARE YOU COWARD! IT'S NO USE HIDING!

AMANDA: He's probably in the shower! *(She immediately regrets this reflexive response)*

OTTO *(Offstage)*: Well! I'll just wait!!

(Serge and Amanda relax.)

AMANDA: I have asked you to leave. I've told you to leave. If I must, I'll call the police.

SERGE: I'll leave when Ford tells me to.

AMANDA: What does it take to—

SERGE: You've said a lot of terrible things to me. Things you have no right to say. You don't know anything about me.

AMANDA: I know more than I care to, thank you.

SERGE: You look at me and see someone in control. Someone who's got it all together. You don't know what it's been like.

AMANDA *(Sarcastic)*: Enlighten me.

SERGE: As long as I can remember, since I was a kid, people have constantly thrown themselves at me. Otto's just one extreme case—

AMANDA: My heart bleeds for you.

SERGE: It's a curse! Wherever I go, it's just the same! Men, women, children for God's sake! I've spent night after night with hundreds of strangers. Thousands! Millions!

AMANDA: Is the touching part coming?

SERGE: Yes—I don't toy with people. I sit and listen to them profess their love for me till I could vomit!—But I never respond. I never say a thing. If absolutely pressed, I tell them, I confess, that I feel nothing. Because that's what I feel. Nothing. I've never felt a thing. I've wanted to. I've tried to. But there's just . . . nothing. *(He is working himself into a distraught state)* And yet, I attract people night and day. I never know what to do with them: the faceless throng of babbling strangers. Until Ford. It's not fair! It's just not fair. Is it my fault that their lives are so obviously empty? Is it my fault that people are simply sucked into me like a vacuum?

AMANDA *(Genuinely sympathetic)*: No.

SERGE: I have needs. I have problems. Does anyone ever really care about me? No. I seem to attract only the most destructive, broken, needy, sad, sad, sad human beings. What's wrong with me?

AMANDA *(At a loss for words)*: I'm sure there's nothing wrong with you.

SERGE: Is it my fault I'm unusually attractive?

AMANDA: Of course not.

SERGE: Is it my fault I have beautiful hair?

AMANDA: How could it be?

SERGE: Is it my fault I have nearly perfect skin, straight, white teeth and a smooth, tan stomach as hard as Formica?

(Their eyes meet.)

AMANDA: I don't, I, well, I wouldn't, I—

SERGE: Am I to blame for my well-muscled thighs?

AMANDA: Nuh-uh.

SERGE: Did I ask for my lips? Did I ask for eyes this blue? Am I to be held responsible for my butt—did you happen to notice my butt?

AMANDA: Yes, I did.

SERGE: My life has been a horrible, endless nightmare of empty, hot, pulsating, sweaty, throbbing, wild-dog anonymous sex!

AMANDA: FUCK ME!!

(She lunges at him. They kiss. It is quite passionate. Ford enters in a bathrobe. His hair is wet.)

FORD *(Quietly, without emotion)*: Who, um, who's that fat person sobbing in our bathroom?

(Amanda and Serge break their embrace.)

AMANDA: Ford!

SERGE: What happened to you last night, Ford?!

AMANDA: I know what this looks like.

SERGE: I waited and waited! Did you, or did you not say you'd be right back?

AMANDA: You mustn't jump to conclusions.

SERGE: Then you call and say you're not coming. I'm not used to this! I need to know where we stand.

AMANDA: I realize it looks as if we were embraced—and, in fact, we were. True. But not for the reasons you might think. I knew you'd come out of the shower eventually and I seduced Serge, hoping you'd walk in and find us together, in corpus delicti, or whatever it's called. I wanted to prove to you that although this "person" may claim to have feelings of some depth for you, he *obviously* does not.

SERGE: What a crock! Ford, I seduced her! I pretended to be sensitive. You know I'm not sensitive. I pretended to be all upset so she'd fall for me and you'd walk in and discover that whatever hold she's got on you is based on deception!

AMANDA: Oh shut up.

SERGE: You shut up!

AMANDA: You shut up!

SERGE: Make me.

AMANDA: Ford, I don't know if I mentioned this, maybe I did, but did you know that when my mother died, I inherited a great deal of *money*? Her father invented the Ziploc bag, and I did. I inherited an enormous amount of money.

SERGE: Ford, did you realize that as a top runway model I spend six months out of every year in Europe on all expense paid trips to Paris, Milan, Madrid and London for the spring and fall collections. Of course everyone gets to bring their spouses.

(Otto enters, unnoticed, holding a huge wad of toilet paper, into which he has been sobbing.)

AMANDA: Ford, I love you.

SERGE: Ford, me too, I think.

OTTO *(Shooting the gun into the air)*: I demand to be taken seriously!!

(There is a knock at the door as some plaster falls on Otto's head.)

AMANDA: Excuse me. *(She tosses the bag of bagels at Otto)* Here, Otto. Eat.

(She goes to the door.)

Who is it?

BEA *(Offstage)*: Is that Amanda?

AMANDA *(Opening the door)*: Can I help you?

BEA: YOU HUNG UP ON ME!

AMANDA: Pardon me?

BEA: I'm Bea. From the hotline. I will not tolerate being hung up on!

OTTO: Mother?

BEA *(Entering)*: Otto?!

OTTO: What are you doing here?

BEA: This one hung up on me! Forty-five minutes we talk and she hangs up! For all I know, she's splattered on the sidewalk this morning—you got a glass of water? I got a taste in my mouth like burned, wet feathers.

(Ford fetches Bea a glass of water.)

SERGE: I thought you said your mother was in traction?

OTTO: I was lying. Or kidding. I don't know which.

BEA: Typical.

AMANDA: Thank you for coming, but as you can see, I'm fine.

BEA: You're Serge, aren't you?

SERGE: Yes.

BEA: You look just like your picture, only with clothes. I love that picture. You know I carry it in my purse.

SERGE: I've been told.

BEA: Does this mean the two of you are back together?

SERGE: No, Mrs. Woodnick. It does not!

(Ford hands Bea a glass of water.)

BEA: Thank you, darling.

(Amanda takes the glass of water away from Bea.)

AMANDA: If you don't mind, Mrs. Woodnick—

OTTO: Mother, you remember Betty Pemberton?

BEA: Of course! The big fat girl. Oh who could forget her. Repulsive.

AMANDA: *I* am Betty Pemberton.

BEA: I thought you were Amanda?

AMANDA: I'm both.

BEA: You look fantastic!

OTTO: Doesn't she?

AMANDA: Thank you.

BEA: I heard about your mother—

AMANDA: Don't mention it—

BEA: Maybe you could help Otto? Look at him. Yuck. That's right! That's right, Otto! Eat! Keep eating those bagels! Keep shovin' 'em down your fat ugly throat! That's the boy! Maybe if you're lucky, you'll explode and bits of you'll fall all over Broadway—

(Otto points the gun at Bea.)

Ya look good, Otto. You've lost weight, haven't you? It shows up in your face.

AMANDA: It was very nice of you to stop by, Mrs. Woodnick. I appreciate your concern, but we're actually—

BEA: What are you doing here anyway, Otto? Shouldn't you be out looking for work? My son was fired recently.

SERGE: He mentioned it.

OTTO: I followed Serge.

BEA: Why Otto? Why do you have ta make such a pest of yourself? What good can come of that? None. Why'd you follow Serge here?

OTTO: So I could kill Ford.

BEA: Who's Ford?

(Ford raises his hand.)

I see. Why?

OTTO: Because Serge is in love with Ford!

BEA *(Angry)*: So what good comes of that?! EAT! GO AHEAD EAT! You make no sense when you talk, so eat.

AMANDA: I apologize for hanging up—

BEA: You know, Ford, you have the most beautiful name I ever had in my mouth. And, Amanda, or Betty, or whatever the hell you're calling yourself today, I can see why you were so upset. I'd be upset too, if I thought this one was leaving me for him—

AMANDA: He's not leaving me for anyone!

SERGE *(Grabbing Ford's arm)*: He's coming with me!

AMANDA *(Grabbing Ford's other arm)*: I HATE YOU!!

SERGE: Tell her, Ford. Let's go.

OTTO: Stay with *her,* Ford. She loves you. He stinks.

BEA: Mind your own business.

OTTO: If you fall apart, Serge, I'll pick up the pieces! You could love me again, if I picked up the pieces!

SERGE *(Releasing Ford, who falls)*: Never!

OTTO: You could love me again on the rebound!

AMANDA *(To Ford)*: Tell him you never want to see him again!

SERGE *(To Ford)*: I have a taxi waiting. We could be in bed in twenty minutes. I'll have you hog-tied, horse-whipped and begging for more—

AMANDA *(Out of control)*: IF YOU DO NOT SHUT UP I WILL NOT BE RESPONSIBLE FOR MY ACTIONS!! I'M

LIABLE TO KILL SOMEONE! I CAN DO IT, TOO! THIS IS MY HOME! WHAT ARE YOU PEOPLE DOING HERE AT THIS HOUR!? YOU HAVE COME TO DRIVE ME MAD! PERVERTS AND FAT PEOPLE AND STRANGERS FROM THE TELEPHONE! IT CAN NOT BE APPROPRIATE FOR YOU TO BE HERE! I'M CALL-ING THAT HOTLINE AND REPORTING YOU! This has been a very bad couple of weeks! What did I do?! I WAS A GOOD GIRL! SO WHY IS GOD PUNISHING ME NOW?—I may have killed some children yesterday, BUT THAT WAS NOT MY FAULT! IT WAS AN ACCIDENT!

SERGE: You're unbalanced.

AMANDA: OF COURSE I'M UNBALANCED!! I HAVEN'T EATEN IN A WEEK! FAGGOT!!

OTTO: Have a bagel.

BEA: Ya got a bialy?

OTTO: Let me look—

AMANDA: I WILL NOT BE REDUCED TO THIS GROVEL-ING, WHINING STATE! I WILL NOT BE MISS HAV-ISHAM!

SERGE *(To Ford)*: We could be fucking right now.

AMANDA: Otto!!! SHOOT HIM!!

BEA: STOP IT! God, stop it already with the shouting. Enough already. You're giving me a headache.

AMANDA: SHOOT HER! SHOOT ME! SHOOT SOMEONE!

BEA: You listen to me, darling. I have had extensive crises intervention training, and I *BELIEVE* I can be of some assistance.

AMANDA *(Collapsing in despair)*: I give up.

BEA: Ford, you haven't said much and it seems to me that you are the apex of this unfortunate pentagon. Now . . . I ask you. Look at Serge. Think before you answer. Would you say you had feelings for him? Would you say you cared for Serge? Would you say you loved him?

(Ford paces and thinks for a very long time before answering.)

FORD *(Nodding)*: Uh-huh.

AMANDA *(Under her breath)*: Shoot the fairy, Otto. Shoot the fairy.

BEA: Quiet! . . . Now, Ford. Look at Amanda.—Who, I'm assuming has looked better. Would you say you also had feelings for her? Do you love Amanda?

(Ford paces and thinks for a very long time before answering.)

FORD *(Nodding)*: Uh-huh.

BEA *(Sagely)*: I see . . . I see. . . . All right. If I were to ask you which one you preferred, what would you say? Let's imagine that the building is on fire and you can only get one of them out alive. Which one would you save? Which one do you love more?

(Ford looks at Amanda and Serge, respectively. He paces, thinks, tries to decide, then gives up.)

SERGE: What is the point of—

BEA: Listen to me. I spend all my time on the phones at the crisis center. I listen to hundreds of people. And they all got a different story. But it's only the details that are different. Basically, they all got the same story: they're alone. They've got nothing. They never found someone who made them feel, something. I never found someone. Well, I let someone slip through my fingers, but that's another story. You are all so lucky. Why choose? Can't you all just love each other? Must you condemn yourselves to lives of regret and resentment?

　　(She seems to step out of the play for a moment to make a grand point) These are miserable times for the artist in America, spiritually and economically. It seems to me you should be banding together, not pulling apart.

AMANDA *(Pause, then grudgingly)*: I must admit, Serge, I enjoyed kissing you. Although I found your tongue hyperactive.

SERGE: My apartment is tiny really and it's terrifically over-priced. A few years ago it went co-op and I didn't buy in. Now I regret it.

BEA: There are seven days in the week and only three of you.

SERGE *(To Amanda)*: I like the way you smell.

AMANDA *(To Serge)*: I can tell you have a big penis.

(Ford smiles at that.)

SERGE: Thank you.

BEA: That all right with you, Ford?

(Ford shrugs "sure.")

OTTO: WHAT ABOUT MEEEEEEEE!!!!!!!!

AMANDA: Aw, poor Otto.

OTTO: It's all very fine for the three of you to realize you're shallow to the point of convex, but where does that leave me in your polygamist equation?!

SERGE: Out in the cold.

AMANDA: Sorry.

BEA: Don't binge.

OTTO: Where's the justice?! Fuck justice, where's the symmetry?! I HATE ALL OF YOU VERY MUCH!!—I don't mean that—YES I DO MEAN IT!! I AM SO UNHAPPY! I HATE MY BODY! My skin is so stretched out of whack it's all different textures! Everything shakes! I'm afraid to let people see my feet! I have the ugliest feet in the world! I have no nail on my pinkie toe! I'M A FREAK! I hate the smell of me! My teeth are rotting in my mouth! I have to put antiperspirant on ALL over my body because there's no telling where some new fold of flesh is going to POP up spontaneously! I wish I could hope for a change, but at this point I consider it a triumph just getting through the day! I WILL NOT GO ON LIKE THIS! I CAN NOT GO ON LIKE THIS!!

(Otto inserts the gun into his mouth. There is a long moment during which the others put their hands over their ears and squint, awaiting the bang, terrified only of the noise. Then Bea steps forward and yanks the gun from Otto.)

BEA: MUST YA PUT EVERYTHING IN YOUR BIG FAT GREASY MOUTH!?

OTTO: Gimme the gun!

BEA *(Pointing it at Otto)*: You're outa control, Otto. I should never a' let you get your own apartment. Look at yourself! Ya look like sumthin' got loose from the Macy's parade!

OTTO: Give me that—

BEA: LISTEN TO ME! From now on you don't leave my sight!

OTTO: But—

BEA: Not for a minute! Startin' tomorrow: sit-ups before breakfast! Push-ups before lunch! Five-mile walks twice a day and no more mayonnaise! Low-fat foods and Diet Coke!

OTTO: But—

BEA *(Marching Otto to the door at gunpoint)*: MOVE! MOVE IT, YA TUB A' GUTS! I'll have ya looking like a HUMAN BEING in a year or two! We'll wire your jaws shut! We'll get ya to a gym. Ya need aerobics—Step aerobics! Jazzercize! We'll get ya one of them "Sweatin' to the Oldies" tapes! And a treadmill, and a stationary bike and a Nordic Track and a Soloflex and a ThighMaster! And no snacks! GREENS! GREENS AND COLONICS TWICE A WEEK! GREENS, COLONICS and for God's sake—VERTICAL STRIPES! Everyone looks one hundred percent better in vertical stripes!

(Otto and Bea are gone. Amanda shuts the door. There is a pause.)

AMANDA *(Disturbed)*: He should've killed himself.

SERGE: I would've.

FORD: Hmmm.

AMANDA: What time's your appointment?

SERGE: Ten.

AMANDA *(Rushes to the bedroom)*: That gives us twenty minutes. . . . Come on!

(She goes into the bedroom, followed by Serge. Ford sits and eats Otto's groceries. We hear Serge and Amanda's lovemaking at once.)

AMANDA *(Offstage)*: Oh God.

SERGE *(Offstage)*: Oh Christ.

AMANDA *(Offstage)*: Oh God.

SERGE *(Offstage)*: Oh Christ.

AMANDA *(Offstage)*: Oh God!

SERGE *(Offstage)*: Oh Christ!!

(There is a pause.)

SERGE *(Offstage)*: Ford!!

AMANDA *(Offstage)*: We're waiting!

(There is a violent knocking at the front door.)

OTTO *(Offstage)*: Serge! IF I SIT, QUIET IN THE CORNER . . . COULD YA LOVE ME!!?

(Blackout.)

END OF PLAY

This is the ending of the play as it was performed at the Woolly Mammoth Theater in Washington D.C. The text is essentially the same to the point where Ford shrugs in acquiescence to Bea's suggestion that he live with both Amanda and Serge. Otto's reaction, you will see, is quite different.

OTTO: WHAT ABOUT MEEEEEEEE!!!!!!!!

AMANDA: Aw, poor Otto.

OTTO: It's all very fine for the three of you to realize that you're shallow to the point of convex, but where does that leave me in your polygamist equation?!

SERGE: Out in the cold.

AMANDA: Sorry.

BEA: Don't binge.

OTTO: Oh, I don't care! I just don't care anymore! I've had it. I AM SO UNHAPPY!! I've always been unhappy! You say they're lucky to feel something? Well, I'm not so sure. I feel plenty. I feel everything. And it feels pretty goddamn terrible!

BEA: Here he goes!

OTTO: Where's the justice! Fuck justice! Where's the symmetry?! . . . No one ever liked me. Mother, you carry pictures in your wallet of people you never met, instead of pictures of me! . . . When I was a child, I was in the sixth grade, I think, we had a dance at my school on the first day of May, a Sadie Hawkins dance. It was silly, it was nothing—is it hot in here as Buchenwald, or what?—Anyway, the girls were supposed to ask the boys to dance. And I was not an unattractive child! Tell them, Mother. I wasn't fat then. I didn't have clubbed feet or dandruff or anything. I was quite normal looking, and maybe even a little better than normal looking. But NO ONE asked me to dance . . . no one. The entire dance went by and not one little girl ever came over and asked me to dance. I went to the cloak room and cried and cried. The teacher, Miss MacFarland, I'll never forget her, Miss MacFarland heard me. She came to the cloak room, drawn there by my hideous, shrieking sobs. And she knelt down, next to me, down to where I'd curled myself into the fetal position, on the floor, buried under a mountain of coats. She uncovered me and said . . . "Otto? Otto, why are you crying?" I could barely talk. But I spoke in that spastic, convulsive way children do when they're sobbing. I said, "No one will dance with me." She nodded very sagely, the chain that held her glasses around her neck bobbed up and down. And then she said, "Oh." I wasn't satisfied. That wasn't the comfort I needed. I asked her, "Why?" She thought for a very long time. And then she answered me . . . "No one likes you, Otto. No one likes you and no one ever will. . . ." Well. It's hard to argue with a figure of such authority as Miss MacFarland. But I knew she was wrong. Or lying. Sometime, somewhere, someday, someone would! I thought Serge did. For a moment—I mean people have pretended to like me, when it suited their needs, if there was something they wanted—help with their homework. But, I thought, Serge . . . I thought . . . well, it doesn't really matter what I thought at this point, does it?

SERGE: Not really.

OTTO: I HATE MY BODY!!! My skin is so stretched out of whack it's all different textures! Everything shakes!! I'm afraid to let people see my feet! I have the ugliest feet in the world! I have no nail on my pinkie toe! I'M A FREAK!! I hate the smell of me! My teeth are rotting in my mouth! I have to put antiperspirant on ALL over my body because there's no telling where some new fold of flesh is going to POP up, spontaneously! I wish I could hope for a change, but at this point I consider it a triumph just getting through the day! I HATE ALL OF YOU VERY MUCH!! I don't mean that! Now none of you are ever going to like me— YES I DO MEAN IT! None of you are ever going to like me anyway! I gave up on you, Mother, a long time ago! And at this point, Serge, I realize, yes, that YOU are NEVER GOING TO LOVE ME AGAIN! WELL FUCK YOU! That's all I can say! Because I'm never going to love you again either! And THANK GOD! I AM SICK OF YOU! I AM TIRED OF WEARING THIS UNREQUITED LOVE, LIKE A YOKE AROUND MY NECK! I HOPE YOU DIE! . . .

(With great dignity) Now, if you'll excuse me, I'm going to the bathroom, because I FEEL SICK!

(Amanda points, indicating the powder room. Otto exits, grandly and shuts the door behind him.)

AMANDA: He's unbelievably loquacious.
BEA: You have no idea.
SERGE: I hope he leaves soon.

(There is a gunshot from behind the powder-room door. Amanda, Serge, and Bea rush to the door and open it. Amanda screams in terror and the three of them stand, frozen, horrified, in the powder-room doorway. Ford stands where he was, eating Otto's discarded groceries. The lights fade, slowly, to darkness.)

END OF PLAY

PTERODACTYLS

Pterodactyls premiered at the Vineyard Theatre (Douglas Aibel, Artistic Director; John Nakagawa, Managing Director), in New York City, in October 1993. It was directed by David Warren; the scene design was by James Youmans; the costume design was by Teresa Snider-Stein; the lighting design was by Donald Holder; the sound design was by Brian Hallas; the fight director was Rick Sordelet; the production stage manager was Karen Loftus. The cast was as follows:

TODD DUNCAN	T. Scott Cunningham
EMMA DUNCAN	Hope Davis
TOMMY MCKORCKLE	Kent Lanier
GRACE DUNCAN	Kelly Bishop
ARTHUR DUNCAN	Dennis Creaghan

CHARACTERS

TODD DUNCAN, 23.
EMMA DUNCAN, 20. Todd's sister.
TOMMY MCKORCKLE, 22. Emma's fiancé.
GRACE DUNCAN, 45-50. Todd and Emma's mother.
ARTHUR DUNCAN, 45-50. Todd and Emma's father.

PLACE

The elegant living room of the Duncan family
of Main Line, Philadelphia.

TIME

ACT I
Is It Any Wonder I Can't Remember a Thing?
Summer

ACT II
SCENE 1: *An Appropriate Gift*
Autumn
SCENE 2: *A Walk in the Park*
Winter

Pterodactyls is a play about, among other things, systems of denial and the price they carry in the world today. As such, most of the characters have a specific method of denial (memory loss, alcoholism, abstraction, etc.) and, as a group, the Duncan family lives in a grand mechanism of denial: farce. Drawing freely from theatrical worlds suggested by Philip Barry and Kaufman and Hart, the Duncans muddle along, never noticing a threat until it's too late. This is not to suggest that the actors can perform even the silliest-seeming moments with anything less than the strongest commitment. No matter how manic or absurd the action, it is based in real need. If it is not, the moments when a darker truth pokes through will fall flat. And the ending, when all efforts to maintain a bright facade have passed, will seem to come from nowhere. We were very blessed in the original production with actors who instinctively understood this juxtaposition of broad comedy and utter despair. What matters is that these conflicting spirits not become muddy. The hard-edged humor should not be softened, nor the rage diluted to achieve a homogenous texture. The texture is not intended to be homogenous. It should be disturbing, and even shocking when harsh reality intrudes.

It is also very important that the character of Todd, who has no comically exaggerated denial mechanism, *not* be portrayed as "better" than the others. His actions are, objectively, amoral. He may be our way into the play, but he must not be interpreted as superior in any way. That approach would instill an atmosphere of righteousness and throw the play out of balance. Only when Todd is sufficiently cruel will we feel for those he victimizes. Mind you, his cruelty need not be overt; I simply want to indicate that Todd is no more heroic than the other characters.

ACT I

IS IT ANY WONDER
I CAN'T REMEMBER A THING?

The stage is dark. A pool of light comes up on Todd Duncan. Dressed casually, in clothes obviously much, much too big for him, he stands at an easel on which is propped a map of the earth. He carries a pointer. He addresses the audience.

TODD: In the beginning, there were dinosaurs. Lots of dinosaurs. And they were big. They were very, very large—in comparison to man they were. They were huge. And there were many different kinds. There were ceratops and stegosauruses. There was the tyrannosaurus and the pterodactyl. And they lived, not in harmony, roaming the earth at will, raping, as it were, the planet and pillaging without regard. And, and um . . . uh . . . *(He loses his place and quickly checks his pockets for notes)* Um, I seem to have forgotten my notes. I'm sorry. I thought I left them in my pocket. Maybe I wasn't supposed to wear this. Maybe I left them on the table. Maybe I—oh well, it doesn't matter now. I don't have them. That's the point. I think I remember most of it.—Maybe I left them—it doesn't matter.

Where was I? Oh, yes. It got cold. That's right, it got very, very cold and all the dinosaurs died. They all died. At once. It got cold and they died. And the land masses shifted and arranged themselves into the pattern we see now on the map. Basically. I think. There weren't any divisions for countries or states or anything, and I'm sure California was bigger, but it resembled what's on the map. During the cold spell, which is generally referred to as "the ice age"—or maybe it was before the ice age, or after it—I can't remember—but life started spontaneously. In a lake. Here, I think. *(He indicates the Sea of Japan)* And amoebas multiplied and became fish—don't ask me how—which evolved into monkeys. And then one day, the monkeys stood up, erect, realized they had opposing thumbs and developed speech. Thus, Mankind was born. Here. *(He indicates Africa)*

Some people liked Africa, so they stayed there and became black. Some people left, looking for something, and became Europeans. And the Europeans forgot about the Africans and made countries and Queen Elizabeth executed her own half-sister Mary Queen of Scots. Some Europeans were Jewish, but most were Christians of some kind, Jesus having been born some time prior—oops, I forgot that. I'm sorry. Jesus was born. And there were other religions too, but I can't remember much about them, so I'm sure they weren't very important. During the Renaissance people got very fat. Picasso sculpted *David*, Marco Polo invented pizza, Columbus discovered the New World and Gaetan Dugas discovered the Fountain of Youth. Europeans imported tea, to drink, and Africans, to do their work. Edison invented the telephone. Martha Graham invented modern dance. Hitler invented fascism and Rose Kennedy invented nepotism. Orson Wells made *Citizen Kane* and mothers loved their children, who rebelled, when the sun shined most of the time, except when it rained and there was a rhythm to our breathing. There was an order to the world. And I was born here. *(He indicates Philadelphia)* I give you this brief summary of events, this overview, so you'll have some perspective. I'm sure I got some of it wrong, I've lost my notes, but it's basically the idea. And I wanted you to have, I think, some sense of history.

(He picks up the easel and exits. The lights come up on the living room of the Duncan family. The decor suggests not just money, but breeding. There is a sofa, end tables, wingback chairs, fresh flowers and four exits. One to the outside world, one to the kitchen. French doors reveal a terrace and the yard beyond. Stairs lead to the second floor. Tommy is standing behind Emma, kissing her.)

EMMA: I'm nervous.

TOMMY: Don't be.

EMMA: I don't feel well.

TOMMY: You smell like wet feathers.

EMMA: I can't breathe.

TOMMY: Your neck tastes like licorice.

EMMA: I'm going to suffocate.

TOMMY: Your hair tastes like marzipan.

EMMA: Don't eat my hair.

TOMMY: Say that again.

EMMA: Don't eat my hair.

TOMMY: Your voice is like Mozart!

EMMA: I feel like there's a brick behind my eyes.

TOMMY: Your voice is Ravel.

EMMA: Do you have a decongestant?

TOMMY: It's Wagner!

EMMA: Some VapoRub?

TOMMY: You are the Venus vomited forth by the sea on the shell of a clam.

EMMA: Ick.

TOMMY: Have I upset you?

EMMA: Oh no. Although I do find the use of the word "vomit" disturbing.

TOMMY: I'm sorry.

EMMA: In a romantic setting.

TOMMY: I can't do anything right. I don't know why I try.

EMMA: Do you have an antihistamine?

TOMMY: I'm a dope.

EMMA: Now I've depressed you.

TOMMY: You haven't.

EMMA: I have. I can tell.

TOMMY: It's not you. It's not your fault. I get depressed a lot.

EMMA: Do you have a Drixoral?

TOMMY: Almost anything can set me off. If my coffee's too hot or too cold. If the sky is cloudy or the sun is too bright. Sometimes I just slip into an uncontrollable funk for no reason at all.

EMMA: I never noticed.

TOMMY: I've hidden it. I thought you'd find it unattractive.

EMMA: How long does it last?

TOMMY: A moment.

EMMA: Oh. *(Pause)* How are you now?

TOMMY: I'm fine.

EMMA: That's good.

TOMMY: But my tooth—

EMMA: What?

TOMMY: I've got a terrible toothache.

EMMA: That's too bad.

TOMMY: It's nothing.

EMMA: Do you think there's something caught?

TOMMY: I floss.

EMMA: Just decay.

TOMMY: I think it's a wisdom tooth.

EMMA: I have some Darvon in my purse.

TOMMY: Why?

EMMA: I get leg cramps.

TOMMY: I never noticed.

EMMA: I suffer in silence. How's your toothache?

TOMMY: Spreading down my arm.

EMMA: I've lost sensation in my hip.

TOMMY: From what?

EMMA: I don't know.

TOMMY: My hand is twitching, isn't it?

EMMA: No.

TOMMY: It's nerves.

EMMA: It's not twitching.

TOMMY: You just can't see it.

EMMA: If it were twitching I could see it.

TOMMY: It's twitching internally.

EMMA: If you say so.

TOMMY: Don't patronize me.

EMMA: I wouldn't. I love you.

TOMMY: Really?

EMMA: Yes. I think about you all the time. I try to read, or brush my hair but all I think about is you. Sometimes I say your name over and over again, under my breath. No one can hear me, but I don't care. It just feels good to say it.

TOMMY: Thanks.

EMMA: Try it sometime. You'll see.

(Grace enters, carrying shopping bags.)

GRACE: Flo!

EMMA: Mother. I'm so glad you're home—

GRACE: Help me with these, would you? It's hot as an oven and my arm's asleep. *(Emma takes Grace's bags. Seeing Tommy for the first time)* Oh. Hello.

EMMA: Mother, I'd like you to meet—

GRACE: I must look unbearable. The sidewalk is melting and I would swear that I actually saw someone fry an egg.

TOMMY: It's very warm.

GRACE: Goodness, I'm exhausted. I've had the most horrible day.

EMMA: Mother—

GRACE: I've been to the city—I picked up the most cunning little black sheath, Dolce & Gabbana, and a sweet suit, so Issey Miyake!

EMMA: Mother—

GRACE *(Adjusting her hair and makeup)*: I used to enjoy shopping. When I married your father it was a real event to go into the city, have lunch in the sunshine, in Rittenhouse

Square. Everyone was well mannered and well groomed. People wore hats. Now. Now, the Square is filled with hobos needing a bath and a companion. Really. They just stagger about in the sunlight, dirty and talking to themselves about the fall of communism and whatnot. I don't know. I tried, but I couldn't follow a word of it. They all just want money, anyway. You can't encourage them. Give them a coin, they talk your ear off.

EMMA: Mother.

GRACE *(Finally looking up)*: Yes, dear?

EMMA: This is Tommy McKorckle—*(To Tommy)* stand up straight.

TOMMY: How do you do?

GRACE: It's nice to meet you. Emma so seldom brings around boys.

EMMA: Mother.

TOMMY: The pleasure is mine.

GRACE: Isn't that charming? He's charming. You're charming.

TOMMY: I like your dress.

GRACE *(Ringing a small bell on an end table)*: Thank you. I need a hot drink and a cold bath—or vice versa.

TOMMY: It suits you.

GRACE: "A+" for charm.

EMMA: Mother, I'd like to talk to you.

GRACE: Oh, Emma. This may not be the day. I'm exhausted.

TOMMY: Maybe we should wait.

EMMA: Tommy.

GRACE: Look at me—if you dare—I've perspired through my clothing. I'm a wreck.

TOMMY: Not at all.

GRACE: You're sweet. I need a quick drink and a long bath, or the other way around—*(She rings the bell again)* Where's Flo?

EMMA: Who?

GRACE: Flo, dear. Where is she?

EMMA: I don't know anyone named "Flo." Is she with you?

GRACE: The maid. Flo, our maid.

EMMA: Flo?

PTERODACTYLS

GRACE: Flo. Florence. You remember Flo. Wears wigs, walks with a limp.

EMMA *(Discouraged)*: Oh I don't know.

GRACE: You must excuse my daughter, Mr.—

TOMMY: McKorckle.

GRACE: Yes. She forgets things.

EMMA: I write things down. I try to concentrate. But facts run through me like Chinese food.

TOMMY: I think it's sweet.

GRACE: Do you. Really? Lord, I'm thirsty. *(She rings again)* Where could she be? I hope she's all right. I hope nothing's happened to her.

EMMA *(Asserting herself)*: We have to talk, Mother.

GRACE: Can't it wait?

EMMA: No.

GRACE: I'm exhausted and I seem to be without a staff.

TOMMY: Maybe tomorrow.

EMMA: We have to assert ourselves.

GRACE: Oh what is it?

EMMA: Well, I wanted you to meet Tommy—

GRACE: And I have. May I bathe now?

EMMA *(Blurting it out)*: Because we're going to get married!

(Pause.)

GRACE: Pardon me?

EMMA: That's it. That's what I wanted to say. That's what I've said. We're getting married.

TOMMY: Assuming you approve, and Mr. Duncan too, of course.

EMMA: Tommy?

GRACE: I see.

EMMA: And, well, that's what I wanted to tell you.

(Grace sits.)

Well?

GRACE: Well what?

EMMA: What do you think?

GRACE *(After a moment)*: How long have you known my daughter, Mr.—

TOMMY: McKorckle.

EMMA: Call him Timmy.

TOMMY: Tommy.

EMMA: Sorry.

TOMMY: Three weeks.

GRACE: That's not very long.

EMMA: It's long enough.

GRACE: I see. Do you drink?

EMMA: Mother.

GRACE: I don't trust a man who drinks. My father's brother drank and suffered fits of kleptomania.

TOMMY: I don't drink.

GRACE: Emma? Have you been doing things you oughtn't?

EMMA: Of course not.

TOMMY: Socially, sometimes.

GRACE: You wouldn't remember if you had.

TOMMY: Wine with dinner.

GRACE: Let me see your hands.

TOMMY: Pardon me?

GRACE *(Inspecting Tommy)*: You don't wear jewelry, do you? No necklace under your shirt?

TOMMY: No ma'am.

GRACE: I don't trust a man with a necklace.

EMMA: He doesn't wear jewelry, Mother.

TOMMY: Does a watch count?

GRACE: Men who wear jewelry are repulsive. It's a sign of weakness. It's not natural. Wouldn't you agree?

TOMMY: I never thought about it.

GRACE: Some men have to wear medic-alert necklaces. That's understandable. They're epileptic, or allergic to penicillin. But beyond that, men in jewelry are aberrations, criminals against nature. They're freaks and we want nothing to do with them.

TOMMY: I don't wear any jewelry.

GRACE: Thank goodness.

EMMA: Why aren't you happy for me Mother?

GRACE: I am. This just comes as a shock. One day you're sitting in your room, all by yourself, not a friend in the world, and the next you're getting married—*(To Tommy)* tell me something about yourself.

TOMMY: I think I can make Emma happy. I know she makes me happy. From the moment I saw her—

GRACE: Tell me about your family.

TOMMY: I have no family.

GRACE: Oh. Why's that?

TOMMY: I'm an only child.

GRACE: Oh?

TOMMY: And my parents died when I was six.

GRACE: That is too bad. An accident?

TOMMY: Heart attacks.

GRACE: How odd.

EMMA: He was raised by acrobats!!

GRACE: I'm only taking an interest.

EMMA: What difference does it make about his family?

GRACE: Please. I'm not judging. I'm only asking. You tell me you plan to marry this young man. Now, what kind of mother would I be if I showed only a cursory interest?

TOMMY: It's all right. I was raised by nuns at the orphanage on City Line.

GRACE: How cunning of you.

EMMA: Must you be so condescending?

GRACE: I have no idea what you mean. Do you know what she means?

TOMMY: I lived with the nuns for twelve years.

GRACE: Were they kind?

TOMMY: Not really.

GRACE: I'm so sorry.

TOMMY: But the priests were giving.

GRACE: I bet they were.

EMMA: What do you mean?

GRACE: I've heard stories.

EMMA: What stories?

TOMMY: The nuns kept mostly to themselves.

GRACE: And now?

TOMMY: I'm sure they're still involved. They had inseverable ties.

GRACE: No, no. You.

EMMA: What kind of stories?

TOMMY: I've broken off completely. Although I still get letters from Father O'Hara, who seems fixated.

GRACE: That's not what I meant.

EMMA: My stomach hurts.

GRACE: What do you do now?

EMMA: There's something in my stomach.

GRACE: You *do* work?

TOMMY: I'm a waiter.

GRACE *(As if she does not recognize the word)*: A waiter?

TOMMY: At Salad City.

GRACE: I'm unfamiliar.

TOMMY: On Suburban Square.

EMMA: That's where we met.

GRACE: How touching.

TOMMY: It's very nice, really. We do a big lunch trade. Salads mostly.

GRACE: I assumed.

TOMMY: I was just a busboy then.

EMMA: He scratched and clawed his way to waiter.

TOMMY: I have ambitions.

GRACE: It's obvious. You have winning ways.

EMMA: You may not be able to tell by looking at him now, Mother, but Tommy's going to be very important.

GRACE: Head waiter?

TOMMY: There are *no* head waiters in Salad City.

GRACE: I don't mean to be unenthusiastic. Really, I don't. I've no intentions of squashing your romance, but Emma, I have to say, I have my doubts.

EMMA: Why can't you be supportive?

GRACE: I just don't think a waiter is for you.

EMMA: I hate you!

GRACE: My daughter is used to the finer things. Godiva chocolates. Prescription pills.

TOMMY: I won't be a waiter forever.

EMMA: You just don't want me to be happy!

TOMMY: I have plans.

GRACE: Thank goodness. What are they?

TOMMY: I'm thinking of going into law. Or medicine. Or maybe banking.

GRACE: Mr. Duncan is in banking.

TOMMY: But what I really want to do is direct.

EMMA: Tommy's a genius.

TOMMY: I love the movies.

GRACE: I never go.

TOMMY: You're kidding!

GRACE: Sex and violence, violence and sex. Bare breasts and imitation butter.

TOMMY *(Passionate)*: Have you ever seen *Hiroshima, Mon Amour*?

GRACE: I missed it.

TOMMY: I have vision!

EMMA: Mother. I love Tommy. And I intend to marry him.

GRACE: I see. *(Pause)* Well, first thing we'll have to do is get you out of that restaurant. It really won't do. Where do you live?

TOMMY: When I left the orphanage, I took a furnished room on Market Street.

GRACE: I see.

TOMMY: But I had to give it up, tips not being what I'd hoped for.

EMMA: They expect him to wear tight jeans and keep his shirt unbuttoned.

TOMMY *(Ashamed)*: Did you ever see *The Night Porter*?

GRACE: No. And now?

TOMMY: I have a lean-to on Lancaster Pike.

GRACE: Oh.

TOMMY: It's not bad. It's nice really—except when it rains.

GRACE: Hmmmm. *(Pause)* I know! You'll stay here! With us!

TOMMY: Well—

EMMA: That's a wonderful idea!

TOMMY: I'm afraid I couldn't do that.

GRACE: Why not?

TOMMY: I have my pride.

EMMA: Tommy!

TOMMY *(Proud)*: Did you ever see *The Grapes of Wrath*?

GRACE: I'll tell you what—you can earn your keep!

TOMMY: Doing what?

GRACE: Well, Flo seems to be *in absentia*. You can be the maid!

TOMMY: I don't know—

EMMA *(To Grace)*: You're a genius!

TOMMY: I don't think—

GRACE: Perhaps Mr. Duncan could find you something at the bank, but I hate to ask him—he's been so overwrought lately. If you prove yourself as the maid then he'll have to give you a job!

TOMMY: Couldn't we just—

GRACE: It's settled. You need a job and I need a servant!

TOMMY: But—

GRACE: No, no! I've decided. And when I decide something I decide it. Now, come along with me and we'll see if that old Flo left any uniforms in her closet—you'll love the servants' quarters. Pale blue with little ducks on the baseboard—then you can draw me a bath!

TOMMY: Emma!

GRACE *(Ushering Tommy off)*: You can have Mondays and every other Sunday off. Unless of course we're entertaining. Can you make Bananas Foster? Flo made a divine Bananas Foster!

TOMMY: Of course not.

GRACE *(Exiting)*: It's easy! You take several ripe bananas and a bottle of brandy, sauté in butter, halve the bananas, flambé and serve, at once, à la mode.

(Grace and Tommy are gone. Emma goes to her purse and takes a pill. She addresses the audience. As she speaks, Todd enters, unnoticed by her, through the terrace doors.)

EMMA: I know I shouldn't. But one can't hurt, and dear God, I'm in continual pain. My skin is killing me. I feel as if this weren't my skin at all. It's someone else's skin. It's the skin of a tiny child and it's been stretched over my body. I'm sorry, I'm Emma Duncan. Welcome. I don't mind telling you I'm glad that's over. Mother can be so overbearing. I know she means well. I know she loves me. I know it, I know it, I know it, I know it. But that doesn't make her any easier to take and Tommy doesn't have much self-confidence. But he does have beautiful hair and lips like pudding. Doesn't he? I think I love him very much. I dream about him every night—

TODD: Hello.

EMMA *(Startled)*: What?!

TODD: I said hello.

EMMA: Where did you come from?

TODD: I walked from the train station.

EMMA *(Nervous and afraid of him)*: How did you get in here?

TODD: I just want to lie down.

EMMA: I asked you a question!

TODD: The door was open.

EMMA: That door is locked!

TODD: No, it's not.

EMMA: What do you want?

TODD: I need a place to live. I need a place to sleep. I've been traveling so long. I've been walking forever.

EMMA: Don't sit down!

TODD: Everything's different.

EMMA: What are you talking about?

TODD: The furniture's different.

EMMA: Different from what?

TODD: The sofa is new.

EMMA: Do you want money? Is that what you want?

TODD: I don't want any money.

EMMA: Why are you staring at me?!

TODD: You look so different.

EMMA: Don't come at me—

TODD: You look beautiful.

EMMA: Get out of here!

TODD: Don't you recognize me?

EMMA: Just go, please!

TODD: You don't remember me?

EMMA: We've never met—

TODD *(Approaching her)*: Of course we have.

EMMA: Stay away!

TODD: Don't be afraid.

EMMA: Stay where you are!

TODD: I'm your brother.

EMMA: I don't have a brother!

TODD: I've been away a long time.

EMMA: My stomach hurts.

TODD: But I'm back.

EMMA: My skin is too tight.

TODD: What's wrong with you?

EMMA: I don't have any brothers or sisters!

TODD: Look at me!

EMMA: My father'll be home soon! If you touch me, he'll kill
    you!

TODD: Look at me Emma!

EMMA: He's the chief of police! He's a Nazi! He'll kill you!

TODD *(Grabbing her)*: Think!

EMMA: Let me go!

TODD: Remember growing up!

EMMA: You're hurting me!

TODD: We played games!

EMMA: Oh God! You're going to rape me, aren't you! GOD!
    DADDY! GOD! HELP ME!

TODD: Think!

(She breaks free.)

Emma!?

EMMA *(Threatening him with a letter opener)*: I don't know who you are, but get out of here or I'll kill you myself! I WILL!

TODD: I just needed a place to stay—

(Grace rushes on.)

GRACE: Emma! What on earth's going— *(She sees Todd)* Todd?

TODD: Mother.

(Grace and Todd embrace.)

EMMA *(To herself)*: There's something wrong with me. There's something very wrong.

GRACE: Let me look at you!

TODD: How are you Mother?

GRACE: Emma, why didn't you tell me your brother—

EMMA: I don't have a brother!!

TODD: I'm home Mother.

EMMA: Who is this person?

GRACE: She forgets things.

EMMA: I'd remember a brother.

GRACE: Well, you'd think so—Todd, let me look at you.

EMMA: What's going on here?

GRACE: Oh think, Emma. You remember Todd. Think! He went away five years ago to study sculpting?

EMMA: I don't think so.

GRACE: Think back. When you were twelve we went to Washington? We had a picnic. We sat on the lawn and ate sandwiches and grapes. You got amebic dysentery.

EMMA: Who did?

TODD: When you were ten we all went to London, for Christmas.

GRACE: We ate lard and salty beans.

TODD: We walked the bridge in the cold dank mist.

EMMA: I don't know what anyone's talking about!

GRACE: She represses.

TODD: She's lucky.

GRACE: What an ironic remark. Isn't your brother ironic?

EMMA: Who?

GRACE: Skip it—You look thin. Are you eating?

TODD: You mean right now?

GRACE: I meant in general.

TODD: Oh.

GRACE: It's wonderful to see you.—How long can you stay?—
Your father'll be thrilled!

TODD: He will?

GRACE: He'll be home soon. He's at the bank.

TODD: On a Sunday?

GRACE: Is it Sunday?

EMMA *(Out)*: Who are these people!?

GRACE: I was just saying to Nina Triten how I wish you'd come
home for a visit. I was beginning to think you didn't like us.
And now, here you are! You're a man! A grown up! Do I
look different? I've just lost five pounds. I eat lemon zest
and bib lettuce! Prisoners on death row eat better than I!—
I've stopped smoking. That was three years ago. When
Bunny Witton died of emphysema, I took it for a sign—You
look well. Your clothes don't fit and I must admit they're
dirty.

TODD: They're comfortable.

GRACE: We'll get you some new clothes. We'll go shopping first
thing in the morning. Remember how we used to go shopping? You'll need a blazer. I saw a beautiful Byblos at Plage
Tahiti.—Where are my manners!? You must be starved!
How did you get here? Would you like a drink?

TODD: No thank you.

EMMA: I would.

(Grace rings bell.)

GRACE: Be honest. I look older, don't I? I shouldn't. I had my eyes done last August, but one's tighter than the other and now everyone thinks I'm winking at them all the time—I know! We'll have a party! How long can you stay!

TODD: I don't think that's—

GRACE: It's decided! I have decided. You'll be the guest of honor!

TODD: I have AIDS.

GRACE *(After a moment)*: We'll have a buffet, that'll be nice. You give me a list of what you'd like. Or we could barbecue. That'd be sweet. I don't have any idea what you like anymore.

TODD: I have AIDS. I need a bed and a place to live. I have AIDS.

GRACE *(Falling apart, plowing ahead)*: Your father can string up those paper lanterns. The ones we used at your sister's sweet sixteen. We still have them, I think. I think they're in the attic. We packed them away, I think, with the Christmas ornaments.

TODD: I need a pillow and some peace and quiet.

EMMA: Who are you?

GRACE: We'll serve champagne or punch, or something to drink.

TODD: I have—

GRACE *(Her despair now shows)*: And the Beekmans'll come! Essie was always fond of you. She's married now. Gotten fat. Don't be shocked when you see her.

TODD: I said—

GRACE: I don't think she's happy really. She married a nice enough man. Very attractive. In real estate.

TODD: I have AIDS.

GRACE: I think he beats her.

TODD: I have AIDS.

GRACE: And the Plimptons.

TODD: Listen to me.

GRACE *(Rather frenzied now)*: And the Weathertons—maybe we should cater! I don't know—I love planning a party! I feel I'm really in my element when I'm planning a party! We'll have music on the terrace! I'm most alive planning a party! You'll see, Todd, it'll be wonderful! It'll be beautiful! You're going to love it! You're just going to love it!

TODD: I have AIDS.

(Blackout. Grace steps into a pool of light and addresses the audience.)

GRACE: We were always very close and I thought Todd extremely gifted. He sculpted the gargoyles on the terrace, of course that was later. We didn't need to speak. Sometimes, we would just sit in the garden, reading, not needing to speak. We would watch the leaves change color.

(Arthur joins her in the pool of light.)

It's Todd, Arthur.

ARTHUR: Who?

GRACE: Buzz. Talk to him.

ARTHUR: What's wrong?

GRACE: He's dying.

(Grace turns and exits. After a moment, Arthur addresses the audience.)

ARTHUR: When he was a boy, Buzz wanted to be a sports announcer on the radio. He loved the Philadelphia Phillies. He talked about them all the time. He said their names over and over again: Nick Etten and Danny Litwhiler, Eddie Waitkus and his favorite, Granville Hamner. Buzz worshipped him. He saw the poetry in his name. Oh, that was me. Not Buzz. I liked the Phillies. Buzz drew a lot. I think. Buzz was born a month after my father died and I was a little distracted. He never liked the Phillies, I did. But later, we had catches, on the yard. And like all little boys, Buzz looked up to me and idealized me. He admired me. He loves me and I love him. He's my son and my world and the most important thing in my life—did I say thing? I mean person. And I would do anything for him. Take any suffering. I would cut off my arm. I wouldn't cut off my arm. I know it's a figure of speech, but I wouldn't. I need my arms. He's not the most important person in my life. I do love him, but I said that, didn't I?

(The lights come up. Todd is dragging a large sack in from the terrace.)

Buzz?

TODD: Yes?

ARTHUR: What are you doing?

TODD: I've been in the yard.

ARTHUR: What?

TODD: I fell asleep on the sofa, I thought I'd never wake up. But I had strange dreams, so I went out for some air. *(He spills the contents of the sack onto the floor. It is dozens of bones)*

ARTHUR: What is that?

TODD: There was something sticking up, out of the ground. I dug it up.

ARTHUR: This is garbage.

TODD: These are bones.

ARTHUR: So, a dog buried bones.

TODD: We don't have a dog.

ARTHUR: Maybe your sister.

TODD *(Sorting through the bones, on the floor)*: I think this house was built on a burial ground.

ARTHUR: So what?

TODD: Or maybe there's been a murder.

ARTHUR: What are you talking about?

TODD: Or maybe these are fossils.

ARTHUR: Put them away.

TODD: I'm going to find out. I'm going to put them together.

ARTHUR: I'd like to talk to you.

TODD *(Fitting the bones together)*: Talk.

ARTHUR: Your mother tells me . . .

TODD: What?

ARTHUR: She says you're dying.

TODD *(Ignoring Arthur, pulling more bones from the sack)*: Does she?

ARTHUR: She's very upset.

TODD: Is she?

ARTHUR: Of course.

TODD: She registers it oddly.

ARTHUR: Listen to me.

TODD *(Not looking)*: I am listening.

ARTHUR: She says you're going to die.

TODD: We're all going to die.

ARTHUR: Is it true?

TODD *(Looks at Arthur)*: Is what true?

ARTHUR: Are you dying?

TODD *(Returning to his work)*: No.

ARTHUR: Is this a joke? I don't find it funny.

TODD: I never said I was dying.

ARTHUR: Your mother said—

TODD: I have AIDS. So what? I have no symptoms. I am asymptomatic. I'm healthy. I'm strong. I'm not dying.

ARTHUR: Is there something you want?

TODD: I'd like a Diet Coke.

ARTHUR: I'd like us to be close.

TODD: Uh-huh.

ARTHUR: I'd like us to be friends, Buzz. I'd like us to share things.

TODD: Such as?

ARTHUR: I don't know. You're my son.

TODD: Uh-huh.

ARTHUR: Buzzy, do you remember when you were ten? Your sister was eight. She was very sick, in the hospital. You were in a play in school. Do you remember that, Buzzboy?

TODD: What was the play?

ARTHUR: *Oliver.*

TODD: It was *The Birthday Party*, by Harold Pinter.

ARTHUR: Is that a musical about British pickpockets and lovable street urchins?

TODD: It's about a man pursued by mysterious strangers on his birthday until he's driven to rape.

ARTHUR: Really?

TODD: Yes.

ARTHUR: I remember urchins.

TODD: You're mistaken.

ARTHUR: Who did you play?

TODD: The rapist.

ARTHUR: You were ten.

TODD: It was a private school.

ARTHUR: I never cared for Pinter. I like *Oliver*. I like a nice story with a song. Don't you?

TODD: What's the point.

ARTHUR: I left the hospital the minute your sister was out of surgery. The minute they said she'd be okay I rushed to your school to see the second act. I'd missed the first . . .

TODD: Thus your confusion as to the subject matter.

ARTHUR: You played a rapist?

TODD: In the sixth grade.

ARTHUR: That can't have been healthy. But I remember, you looked so cute. I was standing in the back and I was so proud.

TODD: I raped with aplomb.

ARTHUR: Don't sully the story—I remember it so clearly. I thought, "My daughter is safe, and my son is up there, on that stage, with all the other fathers looking and watching." I felt we were close. It was a wonderful moment. Can't we be again?

TODD: What?

ARTHUR: Close.

TODD: We're close.

ARTHUR: No, we're not, Buzzy.

TODD: Todd.

ARTHUR: Not really.

TODD: I don't know what you want.

ARTHUR: I'm your father.

TODD: So?

ARTHUR: We should do things together. Why can't you just try? Why can't you try to be my friend. Let me in? Confide in me.

TODD: I want to take a nap.

ARTHUR: How did you get this?

TODD: What?

ARTHUR: How did you get this disease?

TODD: That's none of your business.

ARTHUR: You can trust me, Buzz!

TODD: I don't think so.

ARTHUR: Try me!

TODD: I sat on a dirty toilet seat.

ARTHUR: I'm asking.

TODD: I ignored a chain letter.

ARTHUR: I want some rapport. When you were little we had catches, we had fun. Remember Sundays? They were your day. They were Buzz-day. Let me in.

TODD: I fucked men.

ARTHUR *(After a moment)*: Why?

TODD: It feels good.

ARTHUR *(Hopeful)*: But they didn't fuck you?

TODD: It feels great. It feels better than great.

ARTHUR: It's all right. I'm not shocked.

TODD *(As he continues, he speaks without anger)*: I fucked prostitutes I picked up on the street.

ARTHUR: That can't have been healthy.

TODD: I fucked women and men in bathrooms. In beds. On rooftops, in subways and basements and attics.

ARTHUR: I understand.

TODD: I took their fists up my ass and their cum down my throat. I gave blow jobs to people I never met, in dark rooms crowded with strangers. I buried my face in their asses, suffocating. I jerked off strangers, and wiped their cum on my face. And I knew what I was doing. I knew it was "not safe." And knowing drove me on. I was killing myself night after night. You want some rapport? Well, I can do nothing more to please you.

(Pause.)

ARTHUR: Why are you here, Buzz?
TODD: This is my family.
ARTHUR *(After a moment)*: I feel good about our talk.

(Todd reaches into the sack and pulls out a dinosaur skull.)

TODD: Look.
ARTHUR: What?
TODD: It's a dinosaur! *(He holds the skull up to show Arthur)*
ARTHUR: I'll see you at dinner. *(He exits)*
TODD: *(Addressing the audience)*: I was ten and, the night before the play, my mother came to see me.

(The lights shift, in either angle or color. Todd lies down on the sofa. Grace enters. She carries a drink.)

GRACE: Todd? *(No response)* Todd, are you sleeping? *(No response)* Todd!
TODD *(Groggy)*: What?
GRACE: Are you sleeping?
TODD: Mommy?
GRACE: Are you?
TODD: No.
GRACE: That's good. I didn't want to wake you.
TODD: What time is it?
GRACE: Two-thirty.
TODD: What do you want?
GRACE: Would you like me to run your lines?
TODD: I want to sleep.
GRACE: Are you nervous about tomorrow?
TODD: No.

GRACE *(Sitting)*: You're going to be wonderful. I was in plays when I was a girl. You and I are just alike. I'm sorry I won't be there. You know what's going on, don't you?

TODD: I think so. You've crept into my room in the middle of the night.

GRACE: I meant with your sister.

TODD: Oh yes. She ate a shoe.

GRACE: That's right. And it's stuck in her stomach. It's stuck in her bowel, and they have to operate to get it out.

TODD: Why'd she eat it?

GRACE: I have no idea. I don't understand anything she does. She's five.

TODD: She's eight.

GRACE: There were beets in the fridge. Perfectly good, delicious beets.

TODD: I hate beets.

GRACE: Me too. We're just alike.

TODD: They make me sick.

GRACE *(After a moment)*: I'm so scared.

TODD: What of?

GRACE: Your sister's going to die.

TODD: No she's not.

GRACE *(Weeping)*: I know she is! They're going to cut her open and she's going to die! God! Don't let her die!

TODD: Can I have her records?

GRACE: God is punishing me.

TODD: There is no God.

GRACE: There is and he punishes bad people—I dreamed I held a pillow over her face.

TODD: I dreamed I was you.

GRACE: If I was a good mother, I would've stopped her! I turn my back for a minute.

TODD: Please cheer up.

GRACE: You're so good. I can't cry—don't want to cry in front of your father. He needs me to be strong. He's frightened. He loves Emma. He prefers her to you, you know.

TODD: I know.

GRACE: I prefer you to me though.

TODD: What?

GRACE: I mean you to her. What did I say?

TODD: Me to you.

GRACE: Hold me.

TODD: How?

GRACE: Like this. *(She embraces him)* I don't want Emma to die! I'll try to love her!

TODD: Sssshhh. Sssshhh.

GRACE: Play with my hair—I want to start over! I want her to be a baby again! I want to try again! I want another baby! I want to be a baby!

TODD: Mommy.

GRACE *(Rising)*: Oh, I'm sorry. I'm sorry, it's late. I shouldn't burden you.

TODD: It's all right.

GRACE: I'm sorry. I just wanted to say good luck tomorrow.

TODD: Thanks.

GRACE *(Cheery)*: Sleep tight. *(She exits)*

TODD: And I did.

(The lights return to normal. Todd exits onto the terrace. As he does, Tommy enters carrying a feather duster and wearing a maid's uniform: black dress and apron. Emma descends the stairs.)

EMMA: Tommy, what are you doing?

TOMMY: Dusting and waxing.

EMMA: Can't it wait?

TOMMY: This wood is parched.

EMMA: You have all day.

TOMMY *(Paying no attention, happily cleaning)*: And a hectic schedule! I have to dust and polish, fetch your father's pinstripe from the cleaners, dip the silver and select a menu for dinner.

EMMA: I'm having an asthma attack.

TOMMY: And to tell you the truth, I'm out of ideas.

EMMA: I'm running out of oxygen.

TOMMY: Do you prefer Veal Diana to venison crêpes?

EMMA: I'm suffocating.

TOMMY: Of course everyone loves poultry.

EMMA: The room is spinning.

TOMMY: Except some people.

EMMA: I'm going to faint.

TOMMY: I could try a soufflé.

EMMA: Everything is going black.

TOMMY: I know! Fondue!

EMMA: I'm not happy!!

TOMMY: Don't you like fondue?

EMMA: I don't think I've ever had it—

TOMMY: Oh, you'll like it. It's fun. You take bread and very long forks and a pot of boiling cheese—

EMMA: You've been here three weeks and everything's falling apart!

TOMMY *(Insulted)*: This place's never been so tidy!

EMMA *(Sadly)*: How can you wear that?

TOMMY: Am I showing too much leg?

EMMA: It's grotesque!

TOMMY: I look good in black.

EMMA: Something's very wrong here.

TOMMY: I realize some men would find this getup degrading and an insult to their masculinity, but I have to admit I find it liberating . . . and oddly titilating.

EMMA: I thought you'd rescue me. I never even see you.

TOMMY: You're seeing me now.

EMMA: You used to talk to me. You used to want me. You used to kiss me.

TOMMY: I don't have time.

EMMA: How long does it take?

TOMMY: I have cheddar to melt.

EMMA: You used to tell me I was beautiful. Don't you think I'm beautiful?

TOMMY *(Cleaning)*: Yeah, yeah, you're beautiful. Your hair's like candy, your eyes like diamonds.

EMMA *(Brightly)*: Let's discuss the wedding!

TOMMY: You talk. I'll dust.

EMMA: Do you hate me? Is that it?

TOMMY: I love you.

EMMA: I don't think so! You never even look at me! And aren't we ever going to have sex!?

TOMMY: Someone will hear you.

EMMA: I don't care! I don't want to die a virgin!

TOMMY: Hans Christian Anderson died a virgin.

EMMA: How do you know that?

TOMMY: I read it.

EMMA: Where?

TOMMY: In a book. And he brought happiness to millions of children all over the world.

EMMA: I don't want to bring happiness to millions of children all over the world!

TOMMY: Don't you like children?

EMMA: I want to experience sex! I'd like to have an orgasm. Is that so hard to understand.

TOMMY: It's a little self-centered.

EMMA: I'm a woman! I have breasts. I have a vagina. I want to use them.

TOMMY *(Dusting)*: I see.

EMMA: Make love to me! Kiss me and kiss me in private places and make me forget that my skin is too small and every pore shrieks! Take me by force right here and now!

TOMMY: You're asking an awful lot.

EMMA: You say you love me. You know I love you—

TOMMY: You criticize me continually. You hate my outfit. How do you think that makes me feel? How do you expect me to have a healthy self-image if I don't feel good about the way I look?

EMMA: It's not bad really.

TOMMY: You don't mean that.

EMMA: Yes. I do. I like it. I'd like to borrow it.

TOMMY: You hate my cooking.

EMMA: That's not so. I loved last night's banana nut loaf.

TOMMY: You ate your eggs through a straw!

EMMA: Well they were raw.

TOMMY: They were soft.

EMMA: They were liquid—

(Todd enters from the terrace, carrying two dinosaur skeleton legs.)

TODD: Look what I found!

EMMA and TOMMY: More bones.

(Todd sits and tries to piece the legs together with the other bones.)

TODD: Oh, Tommy, I meant to tell you how much I enjoyed breakfast—

EMMA: I HATE YOU. I HATE EVERYONE! *(She exits)*

TOMMY: I don't know what's gotten into her lately.

(Todd, distracted, pulls a book out from under the sofa and refers to it as he works with the bones.)

TODD: She was always high-strung.

TOMMY: We're growing apart.

TODD: It happens to everyone.

TOMMY: It's happened to you?

TODD: Of course.

TOMMY: What did you do?

TODD: Watch.

TOMMY: That's all?

TODD: You can't fight the inevitable.

TOMMY: But I care about Emma! I love her! If anyone harmed her I'd kill them. We belong together.

TODD: And sex?

TOMMY *(Casual)*: No thank you, I've just eaten.

TODD: I mean are you sexually compatible?

TOMMY: Well . . . I don't know.

TODD: What do you mean?

TOMMY: We haven't actually had "sex."

TODD: Are you Mormon?

TOMMY: No.

TODD: Do you find her attractive?

TOMMY: She has beautiful eyes.

TODD: So do you.

TOMMY: Beautiful legs.

TODD: So do you.

TOMMY: Beautiful lips.

TODD: So do you.

TOMMY: Beautiful breasts!

TODD: So do— *(Pause)* Then what is it?

TOMMY: Well, we've necked . . . and so on.

TODD: Yes?

TOMMY: But the fact is—No, I'm sorry, I'm too embarrassed.

TODD: You can tell me. What is it? Trust me.

TOMMY: You see, I'm a little insecure.

TODD: What about?

TOMMY: Well, for one thing I don't think my penis is very big.

TODD *(Sadly)*: Oh, I see.

TOMMY: But isn't that part of the human condition? I mean aren't all men, on some level, insecure about the size of their genitalia?

TODD: No.

TOMMY: I'm so humiliated!

(Todd places his hand on Tommy's crotch.)

TODD: It feels . . . big.

TOMMY: That's the feather duster.

TODD: I'm sorry.

TOMMY: But it's not just that. You see, I've never really had a woman.

TODD: Surely at the orphanage.

TOMMY: Just the priests. And they tied me up so all I had to do was shout the occasional "Hail Mary." They were easily satisfied. I never had to do anything. Now, I'll have to do something!

TODD: You have nothing to worry about. I'll help you.

TOMMY: How can you? No one can. Sex is the loneliest arena.

TODD: Pretend I'm Emma.

TOMMY: Pardon me?

TODD: Pretend I'm Emma, I'll talk you through it.

TOMMY: Do you think we should? It might not be safe.

TODD: I'll be careful.

TOMMY: I don't know. I've tried to forget my past and this seems oddly redundant.

TODD: Just come here.

TOMMY *(Crossing to Todd)*: This won't involve harnesses or holy water?

TODD: Give me your hand.

TOMMY *(Doing so)*: All right.

TODD: Put your hand on my waist.

TOMMY *(Doing so)*: Like we're dancing?

TODD: And your other hand . . .

TOMMY: Yes?

TODD: On my breast.

TOMMY: What breast?

TODD *(Forceful)*: Imagine!

TOMMY *(Placing his hand)*: It's nice.

TODD: Grab my nipple.

TOMMY: Like that?

TODD: Harder.

TOMMY: Like that?

TODD: Harder. Just rip that motherfucker off!!

TOMMY: Doesn't that hurt?

TODD: YES! YES! YES!

TOMMY: It seems like a fetish.

TODD: It's not! Women love this!

TOMMY: What's next?

TODD: Don't rush. Do this for a long time.

TOMMY: How long?

TODD: You'll know. And trade off, don't ignore the other one!!

TOMMY: And then?

TODD: Just shove her down on all fours like a dog and degrade her!!

TOMMY *(Shocked)*: No!

TODD: Yes!

TOMMY: Shouldn't I build up to that?

TODD: If you want.

TOMMY: I do.

TODD: All right, tell her she's pretty.

TOMMY: You're pretty!

TODD: Thanks.

(With that, Tommy clubs Todd to the floor with a grunt. Blackout. Emma rushes into a pool of light and addresses the audience.)

EMMA: I've had a memory! I don't think I saw it in a movie or a photograph. I think I remember it. Yes. It's my birthday. I'm seven, or twelve and it's a school day, so I have to go to school. But all the children have to make me a card in art class, and I get a cake in the cafeteria. I blow out my candles and I wish I were someone else. I wish I lived on a farm. I wish I were Pippi Longstocking.

(Arthur enters her pool of light.)

ARTHUR: Emma?

EMMA: Hello, Daddy. I've had a memory!

ARTHUR: Don't dwell.

EMMA: Do you like Tommy?

ARTHUR: Not very much.

EMMA: Oh.

ARTHUR: But if you love him, I—love him.

EMMA: Is there something in your throat? You sound like you're choking.

ARTHUR: I'm going to miss you very much.

EMMA: You have a picture in your wallet.

ARTHUR: It's not the same.

EMMA: I'll miss you too, Daddy.

ARTHUR: I have a wedding gift for you. *(He hands her a piece of gum)*

EMMA: It's a piece of gum.

ARTHUR: When you were little you loved a piece of gum.

EMMA: I did?

ARTHUR: You were my little girl. *(He embraces her)* When I came home from work, I'd give you some gum and you hugged me.

EMMA: I did?

ARTHUR: And I stroked your hair.

EMMA *(A little sick)*: You did?

ARTHUR: And I whispered your name, and I loved you, and I kissed—

(Emma pushes away.)

EMMA: Is it any wonder I can't remember a thing!

(Emma's light goes out. A light comes up on Grace.)

GRACE: My children were good children. Always well behaved and beautiful. When I had Emma, I had what's called a post-partum depression, so my mother came to stay with us and got on my nerves. Arthur and I were devoted parents. I read all the books on child rearing. Todd cried a lot, and it upset me very much. We had an instant rapport. He had no right to get this disease. Who exactly does he think he is?

(Grace's light goes out. A light comes up on Todd.)

TODD: It was not uncommon to see my mother in her girdle and bra. This was a natural thing. The bra was translucent and I could see her nipples through the fabric. This was considered dressed. Or maybe it was just okay to see my mother's nipples. I never saw Emma's nipples. I saw my father's nipples plenty of times. I assume my mother did. And when he saw my nipples, it was strictly by chance, and not very often . . .

(Todd's light goes out. A light comes up on Tommy, carrying a polishing rag.)

TOMMY: I didn't grow up with these people. I'm not part of this family and I think any memories I'd have of the nuns and priests at the orphanage would be inappropriate.

(General light comes up. Tommy goes to the dinosaur skeleton, now one-third finished and standing on a platform. He polishes it. Emma enters.)

EMMA: Stop that!
TOMMY: I promised your brother—
EMMA: How can you touch it! It's a carcass!
TOMMY: Think of it as sculpture.
EMMA *(Going to him)*: Take me away!
TOMMY: What?
EMMA: Let's run away. We can go to Las Vegas! They have chapels in malls.
TOMMY: What are you talking about?
EMMA: I don't want to live here anymore!
TOMMY: What about my job?
EMMA: Quit!
TOMMY: Your mother's been so good to me.
EMMA: You won't help me. I hate you.
TOMMY: I thought you loved me.

EMMA: I do—I mean—I want to get away! We don't have to get married. We'll live in a field!

TOMMY: There are bugs.

EMMA: We'll eat them! We'll make them into a paste and spread them like jam!

TOMMY: I don't care for bugs.

EMMA *(Losing control)*: I have to get away! There's a crack in the plaster over my bed, over my body and it's getting worse! One night it'll snap and I'll snap with it! We have to go! My parents are apes! They talk in code! In riddles! I hate my dress! It's either too big or too small! And I never seem to change it! I'm trapped in my dress! I'm a prisoner—

TOMMY: Shut up! *(He grabs her)*

EMMA: Help me!

TOMMY: You're pretty. *(He grabs her nipple)*

EMMA: OUCH!

(He clubs her to the floor with a grunt. Blackout. Todd rushes into a pool of light and addresses the audience.)

TODD: Earlier, when I gave my overview of life on the planet, I explained that I'd forgotten my notes. Now, it's been pointed out to me that I made some mistakes. But I'm not going to correct them, because I don't believe they were mistakes. I think the people who corrected me are idiots. The point is, I forgot my favorite part. The ten plagues. I love the plagues. They happened, as you know, or maybe you don't, after the Jews built the pyramids, or before it, or during. And God wanted to punish the Egyptians for being nasty to the Hebrews, so he tortured them with plagues. I don't remember them all. There was lice and vermin, which always seemed redundant to me. And frogs and blood and something else and something else. And my favorite, the slaying of the first born. It's my favorite because I am a "first born."

(Solemn) "And it came to pass at midnight, that the

Lord smote all the first born in the land of Egypt, from the first born of the Pharaoh that sat upon the throne unto the first born of the captive in the dungeon; and all the first born of the cattle. And Pharaoh rose up in the night, he and all his servants, and all the Egyptians; and there was a great cry in the land of Egypt; for there was not a house where there was not one dead. And he called for Moses and Aaron by night and said: 'Rise up and get you forth from among my people, both ye and the children of Israel; and go and serve the Lord as ye have said.' And the Egyptians were urgent to send them out of the land in haste; for they said ... 'We are all dead men.'"

(The lights come up. Everyone is present. Todd goes to work on the dinosaur. Arthur is reading the newspaper. Emma holds an ice pack on her breast. Tommy cleans windows.)

GRACE *(Blankly)*: Let's talk funerals.
ARTHUR: Grace!
GRACE: Well, since Todd is dying—
TOMMY: Did you ever see *Funeral in Berlin*?
ARTHUR: Buzz isn't dying.
TODD: I have no symptoms.
EMMA *(Raising her hand)*: I have symptoms.
GRACE: I thought he might want to have some say—come away from that thing.
ARTHUR: It's revolting.
TODD: It's our history.
GRACE: I want to talk to you.
TOMMY: I like it.
TODD: It's a stegosaurus.
EMMA: It's icky.
TODD: Or a tyrannosaurus.
EMMA: It's creepy.
TODD: Or a coelurosaurus.

EMMA: It's *Roget's Thesaurus!*

TOMMY: With a shade, in the corner, and a forty-watt bulb—

GRACE: Don't you want some say in what happens after you're gone?

ARTHUR: I find this inappropriate.

TODD *(Still working)*: In terms of what?

ARTHUR *(To Todd)*: Let's have a catch! Ya like that, Buzzboy?

TODD: No.

GRACE: In terms of who reads what, who wears what—

ARTHUR: We'll go in the yard. It's your day!

TODD: Did you know dinosaurs lived as families, traveling in packs?

ARTHUR: Who cares?

EMMA: The air is like sand.

GRACE *(To Todd)*: What would you like to wear?

TOMMY: I'd like to wear something simple with a—

ARTHUR *(To Tommy, hostile)*: Isn't it dinnertime?

TOMMY: Excuse me. *(He exits)*

ARTHUR *(Going to Emma)*: Let's plan the wedding!

EMMA *(Politely)*: Please don't touch me.

ARTHUR: I think that's a good idea! It's okay with you, isn't it, Buzzboy?

TODD: Todd.

GRACE: I'll wear my black Donna Karan.

EMMA: At my wedding?

GRACE: It's very simple. A black column. Very Greek. Very tragic. Very Medea.

ARTHUR: I don't think that's appropriate.

EMMA: It's my wedding.

ARTHUR: People will talk.

EMMA: I wish I were dead.

GRACE: I love planning a party!

ARTHUR: Grace.

GRACE: Or an affair.

EMMA *(To Todd)*: Can you breathe?

TODD: Yes.

GRACE: Emma, you wear that new black Romeo Gigli.

EMMA: I thought I'd wear white.

ARTHUR: And you'll look beautiful.

EMMA: What do you mean by that?

GRACE: How's "Oh, Promise Me"?

ARTHUR: At Buzz's funeral?

TODD: I'm not dying.

GRACE: At Emma's wedding.

TODD: Did you know all dinosaurs lived on land?

GRACE: I thought that's what you wanted to plan.

TODD: Pterodactyls, for instance, weren't dinosaurs. They lived in the sky. But they died just the same.

GRACE *(To Todd)*: Open casket?

ARTHUR: Stay on one subject Grace.

GRACE *(Out)*: I love planning a party! The occasion is piffle.

EMMA: The air is like halvah.

GRACE: Remember the party I threw for the new lawn jockey?

EMMA: Of course not.

ARTHUR: Remember that, Buzz?

TODD: Call me Todd.

ARTHUR: Remember that?

GRACE: I thought we might do something along those lines.

TODD: At her wedding?

EMMA: At his funeral?

ARTHUR: Grace! No one knows what you're talking about!

GRACE: Don't shout at me!

TODD: Don't bully her!

ARTHUR: Don't be fresh, Buzz.

TODD: My name is Todd!

EMMA *(Extending her hand)*: My name is Emma. Have we met?

TODD *(To Emma, hostile)*: Christ!

ARTHUR: It's all right, Emma.

EMMA *(Politely)*: Please don't touch me.

GRACE: What about entertainment?

TODD: I'll read poems by Brecht!

EMMA: At my wedding?

GRACE: Too downbeat.

TODD: His comic poems.

GRACE: I thought a sit-down dinner, on the lawn, under a tent.

TODD: I like this one:

> "I am dirt. From Myself
> I can demand nothing but
> Weakness, treachery and degradation."

ARTHUR: That's not comic. Not remotely.

GRACE: I thought squab or salmon, or both with pearl onions!

TODD: How about:

> "With arsenic: I had
> Tubes in my side with
> Pus flowing night and day—"

EMMA: Ick!

GRACE: Emma, if you have a hundred can Tommy make due with a hundred?

TODD: Should I continue?

GRACE, ARTHUR and EMMA: No!

EMMA: A hundred what?

GRACE: Guests. People. Friends. Family.

EMMA: Tommy has no family.

TODD: Lucky.

EMMA: And I have no friends.

TODD: What about Alice Paulker?

EMMA: Dead.

ARTHUR: I cannot afford dinner for two hundred people!

GRACE: How many weddings will you give?

EMMA: I don't need a wedding.

GRACE: Yes, you do.

EMMA: I don't I don't I don't.

GRACE: How many daughters do you have?

EMMA *(Panicked)*: Are there sisters I've repressed?

ARTHUR: Who are these two hundred people?

GRACE: There are the Beatons and the Litwhilers and the Hamners and the Seatons—

ARTHUR: I loathe Nora Beaton!

GRACE: You do not!

ARTHUR: She's a Buddhist!

GRACE: That's Cora Seaton!

EMMA: Coricidin is a cold medication.

GRACE: You like Nora Beaton.

EMMA: My sinuses hurt.

GRACE: You ought to. You slept with her.

ARTHUR: Grace!

GRACE: Think back. Eight years ago, Pearl Harbor day?

ARTHUR: What are you talking about?

GRACE: In the gardener's shed!

ARTHUR: I have no idea—

GRACE: I knew it! Everyone knew it!

TODD: I never knew.

EMMA: I might have known it.

GRACE: No one cared!

EMMA *(Out)*: I would have repressed it.

GRACE: I never cared.

ARTHUR: Because you were drunk!

TODD: Leave her alone.

ARTHUR: Be quiet Buzz.

GRACE: I don't get drunk!

ARTHUR: You don't even know it!

TODD: I said—

ARTHUR: Buzz!

GRACE: I've never been drunk!

ARTHUR: You get drunk and you forget!!

TODD: I said—

ARTHUR: Be quiet Buzz!!

(Todd explodes in a rage which shocks the others.)

TODD: MY NAME IS TODD!!!!!

GRACE: My God—

TODD: WHY CAN'T YOU CALL ME TODD!!!? WHY CAN'T
    YOU CALL ME BY MY NAME!!!?

ARTHUR: It's a nickname—

TODD: IT IS NOT!!!

GRACE: Your father doesn't mean—

TODD: IT IS SOMEONE ELSE'S NAME!! MY NAME IS TODD!!

EMMA: Means "death" in German.

TODD: BUZZ IS THE NAME OF AN ASTRONAUT! I DON'T KNOW ANYONE NAMED BUZZ OR BUZZY OR BUZZBOY!! MY NAME IS TODD!

ARTHUR: You're overwrought—

GRACE: MY SON IS DYING!!

TODD: I AM NOT DYING!!

ARTHUR: This can't be healthy—

GRACE: I'M BEING PUNISHED! GOD IS PUNISHING ME!!

TODD: I WILL NOT DIE! I WILL NOT! I WILL BE HERE FOREVER! WHEN YOU ARE DUST I WILL BE HERE! I WILL OUTLIVE THE TREES AND THE STARS AND THE SEAS AND THE PLANET! I AM DIRT AND FROM MYSELF I CAN DEMAND NOTHING! I AM THE AIR AND I WILL BE HERE WHEN THE AIR IS GONE! WHEN THE EARTH FALLS OUT OF ITS ORBIT I WILL GO ON! WHEN THE SEAS MERGE AND SWALLOW THE LAND I WILL GO ON! WHEN THERE IS NOTHING I WILL GO ON! I WILL GO ON I WILL GO ON I WILL GO ON I WILL GO ON I WILL GO ON!!!

(Tommy enters.)

TOMMY: Dinner is served!

(Blackout. We hear a bright, too-cheery song such as "Ac-Cent-Tchu-Ate the Positive.")

ACT II

SCENE 1

AN APPROPRIATE GIFT

A pool of light comes up on Grace, who addresses the audience.

GRACE: When Todd came home and told me what had happened to him, told me of his illness, I studied him. I watched him with the devotion of a Carmelite nun. I listened for any irregularity in my child's breathing. I scrutinized his diet. I made a job of noticing his weight, his mood and the way his clothes hung on him from one day to the next. Was he walking slower? Was his speech lethargic? Did he sleep enough? But . . . his gait was quick, his speech unchanged and he slept through the night.

(As she continues, a light rises on the dinosaur skeleton, upstage center. Now obviously a tyrannosaurus, more than half finished, it towers over the room.)

He devoted himself to his work. He was driven and I was glad, because it gave him a purpose. And I realized that my concern might be interpreted, by him, as panic. I was afraid he would hate me for having no faith, when he had so much. And there, as a tribute to his will, stood my child's grotesque monument to the transience of everything. So with the frenzy of a dervish, I threw myself into other things.

(The lights come up, revealing Emma on the sofa, writing thank you notes and wearing a cocktail-length wedding dress. Gifts are scattered about. Through the French doors we see that it is autumn. Grace fiddles with the place cards.)

EMMA: How do you spell "escargot"?

GRACE: All the place cards are out of order.

EMMA: You don't know how to spell escargot?

GRACE: Thirty-two is man heavy.

EMMA: What does that mean?

GRACE: It's all men. How did that happen?

EMMA: What difference does it make?

GRACE: Good God, Emma. It makes all the difference—who on earth sent you snails?

EMMA: Not snails, Mother. Forks. Escargot forks. Two dozen.

GRACE: From whom?

EMMA: Cousin Paul.

GRACE: Typical. Never marries. Sends forks.

EMMA: I like Cousin Paul. I think he's funny.

GRACE: Oh he's funny all right.

EMMA *(Writing)*: ". . . Love, Emma." Can I stop now?

GRACE: How many have you done?

EMMA: Forty-two. And I have writer's block.

GRACE *(Shuffling cards)*: You mean writer's cramp—If I put Louise at thirty-two, I can put David Comstock at eleven.

EMMA: Can I change please?

GRACE: Let me see the hem.

(As Emma rises, Tommy enters from outdoors.)

TOMMY: Has anyone called for me?

EMMA: Shut your eyes! Shut your eyes!

TOMMY: Have they?

EMMA: You're not supposed to see me before the wedding!

TOMMY: I see you when I shut my eyes.

GRACE: Isn't that sweet?

TOMMY: Has anyone called?!

GRACE: Tommy, would you mind not sitting with Emma tomorrow?

TOMMY: No.

EMMA: I'd mind.

GRACE: Have you tried on your tux?

TOMMY: Has anyone called!?

EMMA: No.

GRACE: You're going to look dashing in pants.

TOMMY: Thank you.

GRACE: And isn't Emma's dress beautiful? I'm so glad we decided
against the full-length. Is the hem straight?

TOMMY: The hem?

EMMA: I can't breathe.

TOMMY: I think so.

GRACE: I hope I ordered enough champagne.

EMMA: You did.

GRACE: Well, do me a favor and don't drink champagne.

EMMA: At my wedding?

GRACE: Drink Scotch.

EMMA: I don't like Scotch.

GRACE: You haven't given it a chance. Trust me, drink enough
of it, you'll like it.

(Phone rings. Tommy rushes to answer it.)

TOMMY: Hello. . . . It's for you. *(He hands the phone to Grace)*

GRACE: Hello? Oh, hello, Mr. Lavie.

EMMA: Where were you all morning?

TOMMY: Out.

EMMA: Out. Out? Out? Out where?

TOMMY: I had some errands to run.

EMMA: What does that mean?

GRACE *(Into the phone)*: Oh, that is too bad—

TOMMY: I had things to do.

EMMA: What kind of things?

TOMMY: Personal things. Private things.

GRACE *(Into the phone)*: No. I don't understand—

EMMA: You have secrets. I hate secrets.

TOMMY: I don't have secrets. I have boundaries.

EMMA: I hate them more. Boundaries make me feel insecure. They make me feel unworthy of being loved. Boundaries make me feel fat.

TOMMY: Don't be stupid.

EMMA: Name calling makes me feel needy and unwanted.

TOMMY: I'm sorry. I'm just nervous.

GRACE *(Into the phone)*: That simply won't do. *(Hangs up)* This is terrible!

EMMA: What is it Mother?

GRACE: That was Mr. Lavie. There's a problem with the rabbit pâté.

TOMMY: Rabbit pâté?

GRACE: For the cocktail hour—it seems all the rabbits had cervical cancer and the pâté is contaminated.

TOMMY: Ick.

EMMA: I don't like the idea of eating bunnies anyway.

GRACE: That leaves us short on hors d'oeuvres! What am I supposed to do? Pass out Ritz Crackers?

EMMA: I like Ritz Crackers!

GRACE: I hate Mr. Lavie! He wears a pinkie ring with a diamond in it. And did you see? The tent is mustard and navy! I specifically asked for burnt ochre and midnight!

TOMMY: What's burnt ochre?

EMMA: Mustard.

GRACE: The orchids are heliotrope!

TOMMY: What's heliotrope?

EMMA: Purple.

GRACE: They look like giant bruises! I ordered aubergine!

TOMMY: What's aubergine?

EMMA: Purple.

GRACE: It's all part of the harvest—the vegetable theme I'm doing. The ochre, the aubergine—it's a visual cornucopia—

(The phone rings; Grace answers it.)

Hello?

TOMMY: Is it for me?

GRACE *(Waving him away)*: Oh hello dear!

TOMMY: You were right. I'm sorry we didn't elope.

GRACE *(Into the phone)*: That is too bad. Of course I understand. I'll call you soon. Bye-bye. *(She hangs up the phone)* I hate her!!!!

EMMA: Who's that?

GRACE: Nina Triten!

EMMA: Who?

GRACE: You remember her, from the club.

EMMA: No.

GRACE: Well, she begs me to have her children at the wedding— you know I hate children, socially, at an affair—but she begs me. She plays the devoted mother, can't leave them home, can't leave them with strangers. So I acquiesce. And now, when it's too late to fill her table, she cancels! She and her six, screaming, sticky-fingered little brats!

EMMA: Why?

GRACE: Oh I don't know. I wasn't listening. Something about death, cancer, lymphoma, one of her children. Who cares? It was obviously an excuse!

TOMMY: Cancer?

GRACE: I should just throw the place cards in the air and start from scratch. Twenty-seven is empty! I could put your Father O'Hara there, and the Gideon twins—I know! Tommy, do you think if I called them right now, eight or nine of those nuns who raised you might be free tomorrow?

TOMMY: I don't know.

GRACE: Of course they are. What else do they have to do all day?

TOMMY: They supplicate.

GRACE: Oh, they can skip that for one day. This is an emergency, God won't mind—I better go through my address book—Oh why does everything happen to me? *(She exits up the stairs)*

EMMA: I have something to tell you.

TOMMY: Then just tell me! Do you have to narrate everything you do? Can't you just do things? It's not normal.

EMMA: I'm pregnant.

TOMMY: What?

EMMA: I'm going to have a baby.

TOMMY: Who's the father?

EMMA: You are of course! I knew something was happening to me. My colon wasn't hurting and my leg stopped cramping.

TOMMY: Those aren't signs.

EMMA: And I missed my last two periods. The doctor called this morning. Do you want to feel it?

TOMMY: No thank you.

EMMA: Your seed is growing inside of me. I hope it's a boy. Or a girl! I love children. Don't you?

TOMMY: No.

EMMA: What do you mean?

TOMMY: What could I mean by "no"?

EMMA: Children are nice.

TOMMY: Noisy, screaming bundles of goo.

EMMA: You'll come around. No one likes children until they have one.

TOMMY: We'll see.

EMMA: Tomorrow we'll leave here and never come back.

TOMMY: Don't you think we should stay until the baby comes.

EMMA: Why?

TOMMY: You don't know anything about babies.

EMMA: There's nothing to know. My breast'll make milk.

TOMMY: I just think—

EMMA: You promised me!

TOMMY: I know I did.

EMMA: I can't stay here! It's been all right! I've been all right because I knew I was escaping! I knew there was an end!

TOMMY: I don't want to go.

EMMA (Not listening to him): Todd scares me! He's creepy. He spends all of his time with the bones of dead things! And my father's possessed—I know it! He speaks in tongues!

TOMMY: Don't be dramatic.

EMMA: I don't let on because I don't want him to eat me! He comes to me at night. He wears a halo of fire. His feet are cloven, his hair is a tangle of snakes and his tongue is a mile long!

TOMMY: Your father?

EMMA: I can't breathe!

TOMMY: Mr. Duncan?

EMMA: You promised you'd save me!!

TODD (Offstage): Hello.

EMMA (To Tommy): CHEESE IT!

(Todd enters, carrying books on dinosaurs and a gift.)

(To Todd, cheery) Hello.

TODD: You look very beautiful in your dress.

EMMA and TOMMY: Thank you.

TODD: I meant Emma.

TOMMY: Oh.

EMMA: Thank you.

TODD: Although you look well too, Tommy.

TOMMY: This old thing?

EMMA: I had another memory today! We were in a beautiful hot-air balloon, with tiny twinkling lights on the basket, listening to "Moonlight Serenade."

TODD: That never happened.

EMMA: But I remember it.

TODD: I've never been in a hot-air balloon.

TOMMY: That's from the cult-favorite, much maligned, 1980 Woody Allen film, *Stardust Memories*.

TODD *(Out)*: Never saw it.

TOMMY *(Out)*: Self-indulgent.

EMMA *(Out)*: Guess I liked it.

TOMMY: How are you feeling?

TODD: Fine.

EMMA: It's remarkable that you have no symptoms.

TODD: I brought you a gift.

EMMA: I love presents! What's the occasion?

TODD: Your wedding.

TOMMY: It's very nice of you.

EMMA *(Unwrapping it)*: It's beautiful! It's . . . a gun.

TODD: Your pattern.

EMMA: It's sweet. It's a sweet-looking gun.

TODD: I hope you like it.

EMMA: It's lovely, but, do you really think a gun is an appropriate gift?

TODD: I didn't know what to get you.

EMMA: I like earrings.

TOMMY: Don't be ungrateful.

EMMA: It's pretty!

TODD *(Taking the gun, loading it)*: I thought you might need it.

EMMA: And we don't have a gun. Do we honey?

TODD: I thought since you're leaving—

EMMA: You told him?! I can't believe you told him!

TOMMY: I didn't mean to. It slipped out.

EMMA: We promised we wouldn't.

TOMMY: He won't tell anyone.

EMMA: That's not the point! We agreed!

TOMMY: Well I did it and I can't undo it!

TODD: You'll need it out there. Everything is ending. People are
corpses. They trample each other and never notice the cry
of sorrow. While mothers, doctors and civilized men practice their genocide.

EMMA *(Bewildered, retrieving the gun)*: Well . . . I'll just go toss
this in my hope chest. *(She exits)*

TOMMY: I'm going to die.

(Arthur enters and hangs his jacket on the dinosaur.)

ARTHUR: Grace! Where's Mrs. Duncan? Grace!

TODD: I've asked you not to do that!!!

TOMMY *(Removing jacket)*: I'll take it sir.

ARTHUR: How are you feeling Buzz-Todd?

TODD: Fine!

ARTHUR: No symptoms?

TODD: No!

(Phone rings. Tommy rushes to it, dropping Arthur's jacket on the floor. Todd goes to work on the dinosaur.)

TOMMY: Hello?

ARTHUR: Where's your mother?

TODD: Upstairs.

ARTHUR: Grace!

TOMMY *(Into the phone, irritated)*: Oh, just a minute.

(Grace enters.)

GRACE: Is that you Arthur? What are you doing home? Isn't it the afternoon? I've lost the thread of the day—

TOMMY *(Handing Grace the phone)*: It's for you.

GRACE: Thank you, Tommy. Hello?

TOMMY: Can I get you something, sir?

ARTHUR: Privacy.

GRACE *(Into the phone)*: You must be kidding me.

TOMMY *(Hostile)*: I'm just doing my job.

GRACE *(Hanging up)*: This is terrible!

TOMMY: What is it?

GRACE: Arthur, can you play the violin?

ARTHUR: Of course not.

GRACE: Viola?

ARTHUR: Grace!

GRACE: It seems our violinist was killed this morning by a stray bullet during a bank holdup.

TOMMY: Did he work at a bank?

GRACE: He was holding one up.

ARTHUR: Who cares? No one'll miss one violin from an orchestra.

GRACE: It's a string quartet.

TODD: Not anymore.

ARTHUR: I have to talk to you Grace.

GRACE *(Starting to rush off)*: Can't it wait? I have to locate a violin and practice like mad!

ARTHUR: No! Something terrible has happened.

GRACE: Oh I know it. The tent is wrong, the flowers are off, the rabbits malignant, and I've got a table full of nuns at twenty-seven.

ARTHUR *(Sitting)*: Get me a drink.

TOMMY *(Bitterly)*: Yessum Massa Duncan. *(He exits)*

GRACE: I wish, Arthur, you'd say please to the servants. Your curtness is read as ingratitude. You're the reason we can't keep good help.

ARTHUR: Don't criticize me. I've had a terrible day.

GRACE: So have I. See your setbacks as challenges. That's what I do.

TODD: I had a nice day.

GRACE: Did you?

TODD: But I see my setbacks as setbacks.

ARTHUR: Please. I don't know how to say this—

(Tommy enters with a drink.)

TOMMY: Here.

ARTHUR: Why are you still wearing that?

TOMMY: It's my uniform.

ARTHUR: I asked you to wear pants.

TOMMY: Mrs. Duncan said—

ARTHUR: It's awful.

GRACE: It's snappy.

ARTHUR: It's faggy.

GRACE: Arthur, please.

ARTHUR: Well, it is. It's the fruitiest thing I've ever seen.

GRACE *(Under her breath)*: You'll offend Todd.

ARTHUR: Oh, he doesn't care. Do you Buzz-Todd?

GRACE: Arthur, he's homosexual.

ARTHUR: That doesn't mean he's effeminate.

GRACE: He'll have another "fit."

ARTHUR: That's all behind ya, isn't it Buzz-Todd?

TODD: No.

TOMMY: I think I look like Tony Curtis in *Some Like It Hot!*

ARTHUR: I hated that movie.

TOMMY *(Hostile)*: It's a classic.

GRACE *(To Arthur)*: You never had a sense of humor.

TODD: I found it politically incorrect in it's portrayal of transvestites as buffoons.

GRACE: Didn't you have something to tell me? I left Emma on a
stool upstairs with pins in her hem.

ARTHUR: Don't look at me. I don't think I can say this if anyone
is looking at me.

(The others turn away from Arthur.)

GRACE: Oh my. Maybe I should have a drink too.

ARTHUR: What?

GRACE: It sounds as if I'm going to need one.

ARTHUR: Do you have to?

GRACE: Just one.

ARTHUR: It always starts with "just one" doesn't it?

GRACE *(Turning back to Arthur)*: What does?

ARTHUR: You know very well.

GRACE: I don't know what you're talking about—Tommy, a
Scotch.

(Tommy rises.)

ARTHUR: Sit down, Tommy.

(Tommy sits.)

I'm asking you not to.

GRACE: If I understood your implication, I'd be insulted. A drink, please.

(Tommy rises.)

ARTHUR: Sit Tommy.

(Tommy sits.)

GRACE: Stand Tommy.

(Tommy rises.)

ARTHUR: Grace, it's not even four.
GRACE: So what?
ARTHUR: If you start now, you'll be gone by dinner.
GRACE: Gone? Gone where? Try to avoid the vague euphemism.
TOMMY: Would you like me to leave?
ARTHUR: That would be best.

(Tommy starts to exit.)

GRACE: Stay put Tommy.

(Tommy sits.)

If Mr. Duncan wishes to hurl ugly accusations, let him do so in public. What are you trying to say, Arthur?
ARTHUR: You're an alcoholic, Grace.
GRACE *(Very still)*: What did you say to me?
TODD: He called you an alcoholic.
ARTHUR: I wish you wouldn't drink so much!
GRACE: What's "so much"?

ARTHUR: You drink yourself blind every night.

GRACE: You call that "so much"? Please.

ARTHUR: Your drinking is out of control!

GRACE: I don't have a problem! Todd! Am I an alcoholic?

TODD: Of course.

GRACE: Speak up.

TODD: Yes. You're an alcoholic.

GRACE: Oh piffle! I don't have a problem! You're the one with the problem, Arthur!

ARTHUR: I know this is a difficult time. We're all under a lot of strain. Buzz-Todd's sick. There's a big dead thing in the living room—

GRACE *(Snapping)*: You wouldn't know if I were drinking or dying—*(To Todd)* Sorry.

ARTHUR: Fine! I don't want to discuss it!

GRACE: I could have left you years ago and you'd never know it! You're never here!

ARTHUR: I'm always here—

GRACE: Were you home for dinner last night? Or the night before?

TOMMY: I slave and slave over a hot stove.

ARTHUR: Well, why bother! You'd be passed out in the tub!

GRACE: Were you!

ARTHUR: I was working!!

TOMMY: Likely excuse.

ARTHUR: Night and day! To satisfy your insatiable need for "things!"

GRACE: You delude yourself, Arthur! You always have. Justify your philandering! I'm a drunk so you can assuage your guilt over being less than a father and less than a husband. But I've told you, Arthur, your indiscretion is immaterial to me. I learned a long time ago to replace you in my affections, as you had me in yours. Now. What did you want to tell me?

ARTHUR *(Sweetly, cruel)*: It pains me to say this, Grace. But the fact is, I no longer have a job.

(Pause.)

GRACE: Pardon me?

ARTHUR: That's it. That's what I wanted to tell you. It's over. It's all over. Finished. Done.

GRACE *(Still stunned)*: What are you talking about?

ARTHUR: I have been asked to step down.

GRACE: Well, decline politely!

ARTHUR: It's not that simple.

GRACE: You're the president, Arthur!

ARTHUR: Was dear. Was the president. Past tense.

GRACE: You're lying.

ARTHUR: Why would I lie about a thing like this?

GRACE: This is a dream. I'm living a dream—

ARTHUR: It's no dream. It's over. And I must say, I feel so free. I feel comfortable for the first time.

GRACE *(Simply)*: What happened?

ARTHUR: It's complicated.

GRACE: Explain it to me!

ARTHUR: In time.

GRACE: Now!

ARTHUR: I feel as if a terrible burden has been lifted. I feel lighter.

GRACE: How dare you?

ARTHUR: It wasn't my choice Grace.

GRACE: Women I could tolerate. Not poverty!

ARTHUR: We can spend more time together.

GRACE *(After a moment, a threat)*: What did you do?

ARTHUR *(Not recognizing the word)*: Do? I'm sorry.

GRACE: You were at that bank for thirty years!

ARTHUR: Good years.

GRACE: You were president for ten!

ARTHUR: Wonderful years.

GRACE: Things don't just happen—you did something!

ARTHUR: I did my best.

GRACE: Did you steal? Did you embezzle?

ARTHUR: I feel positively liberated.

GRACE: STOP SAYING THAT.

ARTHUR: So sorry. Buzz-Todd, a catch?

TODD: No, thank you.

ARTHUR: Aw.

GRACE: You did something! I know it! You did this on purpose! This has been a terrible goddamn—did you see that tent!!?—EXCUSE ME!! *(She runs off)*

ARTHUR *(After a moment)*: I think that went very well.

TODD: What did you do?

ARTHUR: I didn't do anything.

TODD: Don't lie to me. I can tell.

ARTHUR: I need some air.

(Arthur exits onto the terrace. Todd turns to the dinosaur.)

TODD: I'm almost finished.

TOMMY: I'm going to die.

TODD: You said that.

TOMMY: I'm scared!

TODD: Everybody dies. Grow up.

TOMMY: I've been to the doctor.

TODD: Doctors are sadists.

TOMMY: I've had a blood test.

TODD: Doctors are idiots.

TOMMY: He should call.

TODD: What difference does it make?

TOMMY: It makes a difference to me!

TODD: You blame me, don't you?

TOMMY: I want to.

TODD *(Working on the dinosaur)*: Do you realize some species of dinosaur cannibalized themselves?

TOMMY: But I love you.

TODD: Did you know the brachiosaurus ate the eggs of its young?

TOMMY: No I didn't! I said I love you!

TODD: Lower your voice. Someone'll hear you.

TOMMY: I don't care! I'm going to die, what do I care who hears me? You're the only thing that matters to me now.

TODD: That's extremely flattering.

TOMMY: Look at me!

TODD *(Does so)*: You can live a long time. You can live forever with this disease.

TOMMY: I dreamed, last night, that I was dying.

TODD: Me too.

TOMMY: You dreamed you were dying?

TODD: No. I dreamed you were.

TOMMY: Creepy.

TODD: You were in a forest.

TOMMY: That's right.

TODD: You were choking. You were drowning. You were coughing. It was awful.

TOMMY: And you held me.

TODD: No. I wasn't there.

TOMMY *(Grabbing Todd)*: Don't do this to me!

TODD: Let go of me!

TOMMY: I need you! It's my own fault, I knew what I was doing, and I didn't care! I wanted it. Every night, I decided. But please, say I matter. Stay with me.

(Tommy is distraught. In a rare moment of softness, Todd comforts him.)

TODD: All right. It's all right.

(They embrace.)

TOMMY: My life was a series of random accidents. Now everything seems ordered.

TODD: Avoid clichés.

TOMMY: You make me happy?

(They kiss. Emma rushes down the stairs.)

EMMA: Mother, are you ever—oh my.

(Tommy and Todd break their embrace. Phone rings. Emma answers it.)

Hello?

TOMMY: Is that for me?

EMMA *(Into the phone)*: No, this is her daughter.

TODD: I'll leave the two of you alone.

TOMMY: Don't!

EMMA *(Into the phone)*: Yes, I'll tell her, crab claws. Thank you. *(She hangs up)* Tommy? What, um, was going on, before, when I came down the stairs? What was happening?

TOMMY: Well, Emma, I was kissing your brother. And I'm glad you came in. I don't want to hurt you—but I have to be honest. And the truth is, I love Todd. I'm in love with Todd.

EMMA: What? Huh? What? What?

TOMMY: I said I'm in love with Todd.

EMMA *(After a moment, gaily)*: I'M DEAF!

TOMMY: What?

EMMA: I AM! I'M DEAF! I'M STONE-COLD DEAF!

TOMMY: Don't play games.

EMMA: I KNOW YOU'RE TALKING. I CAN SEE YOUR LIPS MOVING AND YOUR CHEST IS GOING UP AND DOWN—

TODD: Let me try.

EMMA: FUNNY HOW IT JUST COMES OVER A GIRL.

TODD: EMMA! EMMA! CAN YOU HEAR ME? CAN YOU HEAR ME EMMA?

EMMA *(Banging her ears)*: HUH? HUH? WHAT? WHAT? WHAT?

TODD: She's faking.

TOMMY: Really?

TODD: She hears you. She's faking.

TOMMY: What should I do?

TODD: Just talk. She hears you.

EMMA: WHAT? WHAT ARE YOU SAYING? ARE YOU TALKING TO ME?

TOMMY: EMMA. I'M SORRY.

EMMA: WAIT! WAIT! WAIT!

TOMMY: SAY YOU UNDERSTAND.

EMMA: I HEAR SOMETHING!

TOMMY: SAY YOU FORGIVE ME.

EMMA: I HEAR A SONG!

TODD: SHE HEARS YOU.

EMMA: A Johnny Mercer song. Or Hoagy Carmichael! I ALWAYS GET THEM CONFUSED.

TOMMY: I CAN'T MARRY YOU. BUT I'LL ALWAYS CARE ABOUT YOU. YOU'RE A KIND SWEET INSANE PERSON AND I HOPE YOU FIND WHO YOU'RE LOOKING FOR.

EMMA *(Continuing in good cheer)*: I HOPE YOU DON'T MIND THAT I'M DEAF. I KNOW SOME MEN WOULD BUT SOME WOULD LIKE IT. IT WON'T MATTER. KNOW WHY? BECAUSE WE LOVE EACH OTHER AND OUR LOVE CAN SUSTAIN DEAFNESS! WE'RE GOING TO BE SO HAPPY!

(Grace enters from the kitchen, drink in hand, wickedly bright.)

GRACE: LET'S REHEARSE!

(Emma doesn't respond. She is deaf.)

TOMMY: We've got to talk, Mrs. Duncan—

GRACE: Tomorrow you travel from servant to son, call me Grace—

TOMMY: But—

GRACE *(To Todd)*: Where's your father?

TODD: Out there.

GRACE: Be a cherub and get him. Go, go, go, go, go.

(Todd exits onto the terrace.)

TOMMY: You don't understand Mrs. Duncan.

GRACE: Grace means beauty of form, proportion and movement, please address me thus.

TOMMY: All right, Grace, it's about the wedding—

GRACE: Which needs the nurturing and attention of a hothouse orchid.

(Todd and Arthur enter from the terrace.)

ARTHUR: What is it?

GRACE: We're going to rehearse!

ARTHUR: Rehearse what, for God's sake?

GRACE: The wedding, you squid.

ARTHUR: Have you been drinking?

GRACE: I am naturally gregarious!! Now, tomorrow morning—

TOMMY: Listen to me!

GRACE: We'll talk later.

TODD: There's no judge.

GRACE: He can wing it—

TOMMY: MRS. DUNCAN!

GRACE: Oh what is it!?

TOMMY: There's not going to be a wedding.

GRACE: What?

ARTHUR: Thank God.

TOMMY: I'm sorry, but the wedding is off.

GRACE: Emma! What do you have to say about this?

(In response, Emma stands and bursts into a grotesquely cheerful performance of "Skylark" by Hoagy Carmichael and Johnny Mercer. She continues to sing under the dialogue until her exit.)

What? What does that mean?

ARTHUR: What's wrong with her?

TOMMY: She seems to be deaf.

ARTHUR: Oh my God! My baby!

TODD: She hears music.

TOMMY: Johnny Mercer.

ARTHUR: Pumpkin.

GRACE: Oh that's nothing. That's hysterical deafness. I had it on my wedding day.

ARTHUR: Can you hear me?

GRACE: It's nothing!—Now, Emma you go upstairs and come down during "Here Comes the Bride," Todd, you be the judge over there by the terrace, Emma go upstairs, Arthur you stand on the stairs and take Emma when she passes, Emma go now, I'll have come down first in my Christian Lacroix and I'll join Todd, by the judge at the door—Arthur just push her, she'll go—

(Arthur starts Emma with a push. She exits upstairs. Grace continues her high-speed directions.)

Tommy, you enter from the kitchen, with your best man, that Father O'Hara, and go directly to the judge, who's Todd, and Todd, and myself.

TOMMY: I don't love your daughter! I can't marry her! The wedding is off!

GRACE *(After a moment)*: There will be a wedding. You listen to me: Two hundred and fifty people—eight of them nuns— are descending on this house tomorrow, and you can trust me, they will be treated to a wedding! A beautiful, expensive and excessive affair! Thirteen kinds of hors d'oeuvres! Aubergine orchids, burnt ochre stripes and a string trio playing "La Vie en Rose"!!

TOMMY: But I don't love her—

GRACE: So what!! As you may or may not have heard, for reasons passing understanding, I am about to be stripped of the amenities to which I've grown accustomed! Plunged into poverty! And this wedding, this social event, this bacchanalian carnival of rapacious consumption, shall be my last hurrah! My fond farewell to all I care about, need, love

and have worked for all my life! So mark my words, there
will be a wedding!! PLACES!!!!

*(As they scatter to their places in fear, Grace maniacally
sings Mendelssohn's "Wedding March.")*

Da da da da! Da da da—

(The phone rings.)

TOMMY: I'll get it!!!
GRACE: STAY. *(She answers the phone)* Hello?
TOMMY: Is that for me?
GRACE *(Into the phone)*: He can't. I'll take a message.
TOMMY *(Kneeling at her feet)*: Give me the phone!
GRACE *(Into the phone, cheery)*: Blood test positive. Thank you
doctor, okeydoke. *(She hangs up the phone)*
TOMMY: Oh my God.
GRACE *(Turning to the stairs)*: EMMA! *(Singing)* Da da da da!
Da da da da! Da da da da da da da—

*(There is a gunshot. Todd steps out of the scene into a pool
of light.)*

TODD: And then it got very, very cold.

(Lights shift as Todd and Tommy exchange a look of farewell.)

SCENE 2

A WALK IN THE PARK

*The lights come up on Todd and the dinosaur, now com-
plete—a giant skeleton towering over the room. Todd
addresses the audience.*

TODD: And it was a tyrannosaurus rex. Named from the Latin, meaning king lizard. And it was the largest land-living car-nivore who walked the earth. And it was beautiful. He lived in the Cretaceous period of the Mesozoic era, one hundred and fifty million years ago. He is recognized by his large head, small forelimbs, and dagger-like teeth. He started life at fifty pounds and grew to sixty tons, unless he died, as mine, a child, for reasons no one can remember, because no one was alive.

(Todd curls up under the dinosaur. The general lighting comes up, revealing the room, no longer grand, but gray and dreary. Outside it is winter. There is a bottle of Scotch and a glass on the end table. Grace enters from the kitchen; her dress is now threadbare. She wears an afghan around her shoulders. Her high-flown chatter has been replaced with an alcoholic snarl. She carries a bowl of cereal and a spoon. She sits. She holds the bowl to her ear and listens.)

GRACE: Damn. I've been robbed.

TODD: What?

GRACE *(To the dinosaur)*: What?

TODD: You said something.

GRACE *(To Todd)*: I didn't know you were there.

TODD: What'd you say?

GRACE: You want to keep me company?

TODD: What did you say?

GRACE: I asked if you want to keep me company.

TODD: Before that.

GRACE: Oh. I said, "I've been robbed."

TODD: What are you talking about?

GRACE: My cereal is supposed to make noise.

TODD: Like music?

GRACE: Like popping or something.

TODD *(Going to her)*: You're eating Cornflakes.

GRACE: So?

TODD: Rice Krispies make noise. Cornflakes are silent.

GRACE: Oh . . . how's your fever?

TODD: Normal.

GRACE: Is it cold in here?

TODD: No.

GRACE: Check the thermostat.

TODD: The thermostat's broken.

GRACE: Maybe I'm going through the change.

TODD: If you were going through "the change" you'd have hot flashes, not cold flashes.

GRACE: Are you a gynecologist?

TODD: No.

GRACE: You're a woman then?

TODD: No.

GRACE: Then what would you know about menopause?

TODD *(Starting to exit)*: I'm going upstairs.

GRACE: No don't. Keep me company. I miss everybody.

TODD: You never liked them to begin with.

GRACE: I like you.

TODD: Thanks.

GRACE: We're so much alike.

TODD: So you say—

GRACE: We have the same interests—

TODD: So often.

GRACE: We have the same temperament. We like the same things.

TODD: Stop saying that.

GRACE: The same music. The same kind of people.

TODD: I'm not you. I'm me. I'm not like you. I'm like me.

GRACE: You see? It would drive me crazy too—if someone kept saying I were like them.

TODD *(Snapping at her)*: Can we talk about something else?

GRACE: I always change the subject. Typical.

TODD *(Going up the stairs)*: I'm going upstairs.

GRACE: I go upstairs! See? You see?

TODD: Mother!

GRACE: I'm sorry. I won't do it anymore. I'll just sit and eat my Cornflakes.

TODD: Good.

GRACE *(After a moment)*: I miss Emma.

TODD *(Returning)*: Did you like her?

GRACE: Of course. What do you mean?

TODD: I don't.

GRACE: Don't what?

TODD: Miss her.

GRACE: She was your sister.

TODD: I know that. How long have you been drinking?

GRACE: Twenty years.

TODD: I meant today.

GRACE: So did I.

TODD: You better eat your Cornflakes.

GRACE: I hate them.

TODD: Well, you're supposed to add milk.

GRACE: We didn't have any.

TODD: Well, no wonder you can't eat them.

GRACE: Why don't you miss your sister?

TODD: I don't know—

GRACE: Do you miss Tommy?

TODD: Who?

GRACE: Tommy. Tommy. The maid. Tommy.

TODD: Oh. I suppose.

GRACE: Me too.

TODD: He was a good maid.

GRACE: We'd have milk.

TODD: It's true.

GRACE *(Going to the French doors)*: He went so fast. It was sad. It's good he choked, drowned. He got so ugly, all purple and swollen. *(She turns and looks out at the yard. She focuses on something specific, then quickly turns back to Todd)* We should bury him, Todd.

TODD: The ground is frozen.

GRACE: Come look at him.

TODD: I'd rather not.

GRACE: He looks so sad.

TODD: Naturally he looks sad. He's dead.

GRACE: We should bury him.

TODD: The ground's too hard.

GRACE: It's not right.

TODD: Who sees him?

GRACE: That's not the point!

TODD: If no one sees him, it doesn't matter!

GRACE: It's not right—

TODD: What does that mean?!

GRACE: You know what I mean!

TODD: You think God cares?

GRACE: He shouldn't just be lying there.

TODD: You want him buried?! You bury him!

GRACE: Don't shout at me!

TODD: Don't nag me!

GRACE: Leave me alone!

TODD: I'm going upstairs.

(Todd starts to exit, but stays on the stairs and sits. Grace pours herself a drink. Emma enters from the terrace and addresses the audience.)

EMMA: Hello everybody. I'm dead. How are you? I'm glad I killed myself. I'm not recommending it for others, mind you—no Dr. Kevorkian am I. But it's worked out for me. Looking back, I don't think I was ever supposed to have been born to begin with. Of course the idea that anything is "supposed to be" implies a master plan, and I don't believe in that kind of thing.

When I say I shouldn't have been born, I mean that my life was never all that pleasant. And there was no real reason for it. I was pretty. I had money. I was lucky enough to be born in a time and into a class where I had nothing but opportunities. I look around and there are crippled people and blind people and refugees and I can't believe I had the gall to whine about anything! I had my health—oh sure, I complained a lot, but really I was fine. And I had love! Granted the object of my affections was a latent, or not-so-latent homosexual as it turned out, who was infected with the HIV virus, who in turn infected me and my unborn baby—but isn't that really picking nits?

I can never thank Todd enough for giving me the gun, because for the first time, I'm happy. The pain is gone and I remember everything. Tommy is here, but we're not speaking. He spends all his time with Montgomery Clift and George Cukor talking about movies. I assume.

And I've been reunited with Alice Paulker. We went to school together. She was shot last year by a disgruntled postal worker. She has long, wavy brown hair and skin so pale you can see right through it—I don't mean it's really transparent and you can see her guts and organs and everything. It's just pale. And she has very big eyes, green. And we listen to music and go for walks. We take turns reading aloud to each other. She reads poems by Emily Brontë and I read chapters from *The Tropic of Cancer* by Henry Miller. She was always classier than me. And sometimes, we don't read. Sometimes, we just hold each other. And I run my fingers through her hair and she touches her lips, gently, along my cheek. She makes soft sounds, comforting sounds and she takes her time and she runs her tongue along the edge of my ear. We take off our clothes and just look at each other. I was shy at first, but Alice helped me and never rushed me. She held my breasts in her hands and ran her lips between them, down my stomach. I touch her eyelids and her forehead and her hair and her fingers and the back of her neck. And she enters me and I am everywhere at once and nowhere at all. And I remember everything and find that nothing matters. And for a moment, for a moment or two that lasts forever, we become one person. And I forget, we forget, that we were ever alive. And everything makes perfect sense.

(Emma joins Todd on the stairs. Arthur enters from the terrace, wearing a winter coat, which he quickly removes.)

ARTHUR: It's freezing in here.

GRACE: Where've you been?

ARTHUR: I went for a walk.

GRACE: Why?

ARTHUR: I wanted to.

GRACE: You know you're not supposed to.

ARTHUR: Supposed to?

GRACE: You want to catch pneumonia?

ARTHUR: Just for you. This year, for Christmas.

GRACE: Very funny.

ARTHUR: I wore a coat.

GRACE: It doesn't matter. It's zero out. It's zero degrees.

ARTHUR: I didn't notice.

GRACE: You wander around outside in the zero degrees like some kind of goddamn polar bear—

ARTHUR: I thought it was warm.

GRACE: What?

ARTHUR: I was warm.

GRACE: Did you eat today?

ARTHUR: Of course I ate—

GRACE: You forget to eat and—

ARTHUR: I'm perfectly fine. I ate! It's warm out.

GRACE: It's freezing.

ARTHUR: It's spring.

GRACE: It's December.

ARTHUR: It can't be.

GRACE: It is.

ARTHUR: But the sun was hot. The birds are crying for water.

GRACE: There aren't any birds, Arthur.

ARTHUR: You're lying.

GRACE: Birds go south in the winter, Arthur. God, where were you in the third grade?

ARTHUR: Don't be snide with me Grace.

GRACE: I give up.

ARTHUR: I accept that birds go south in the winter. I know that. I'm not a child. What I do not accept, is your basic premise that it *is* winter. How could it be? I was just outside on the steaming lawn. You're trying to drive me insane!

GRACE: And doing very well.

ARTHUR: It's obviously spring or, at the very latest, summer.

GRACE *(Starting to exit)*: I'll fix you something to eat.

EMMA *(From her place)*: I love you Daddy.

ARTHUR: Wait a minute, Grace.

GRACE: What is it?

ARTHUR: We should talk about the wedding.

GRACE: What do you want to eat, Arthur?

EMMA: I don't need a wedding.

ARTHUR: Is everything ready?

GRACE: Do you want a sandwich? Do you want some eggs?

ARTHUR: It has to be beautiful.

GRACE: What does?

ARTHUR: The wedding.

GRACE: It was months ago—or actually, it wasn't.

ARTHUR: It'll be nice, on the lawn—

GRACE: I mean it would have been.

ARTHUR: Under the trees. Under a tent.

GRACE: There was no wedding, Arthur. You know that.

ARTHUR: Is everything ready?

GRACE: I told you yesterday. I told you this morning.

ARTHUR: Everything should be perfect.

GRACE: I told you at lunch.

ARTHUR: Every detail.

GRACE: Emma is gone, Arthur.

EMMA *(Out)*: Death is a walk in the park.

ARTHUR: What do you mean. Did she run away?

GRACE: No. I mean she's dead.

ARTHUR: Pardon me?

GRACE: She was dead yesterday. Dead this morning. Dead last night and she'll be dead tomorrow.

ARTHUR: Don't be ridiculous—*(He calls upstairs)* EMMA!

(Emma would respond, but Todd stops her.)

GRACE *(After a moment)*: You see?

ARTHUR: Maybe she's out?

GRACE: She's not.

ARTHUR: She's napping.

GRACE: She's not.

ARTHUR: She's sleeping.

GRACE: She's dead.

ARTHUR: Very deeply?

GRACE: She shot herself.

ARTHUR: I don't feel well.

GRACE: I'll get you an aspirin.

(Grace exits. Arthur addresses the audience.)

ARTHUR: When she was a girl, Emma wanted to be a sports announcer on the radio. She loved the Philadelphia Phillies. She talked about them all the time. She said their names over and over again.

EMMA *(Out)*: I wanted to be a ballerina.

ARTHUR: Nick Etten, Danny Litwhiler, Eddie Waitkus . . .

EMMA *(Out)*: Or a nurse.

ARTHUR: And her favorite, Granville Hamner.

EMMA *(Out)*: Or a wife and mother.

ARTHUR: She worshipped him.

TODD *(Standing)*: That's not true.

ARTHUR: What?

EMMA *(Out)*: But I don't really like children.

TODD: What you're saying isn't true.

EMMA *(Out)*: So it's for the best.

ARTHUR: What would you know about it?

143

TODD *(Descending the stairs)*: That's what you say about me.

ARTHUR: I have a headache.

TODD: But it's not true.

ARTHUR: Let's have a catch? Would you like that?

TODD: About anyone.

(Grace reenters with an aspirin.)

GRACE: Here you are—Todd, what are you doing up?

TODD: I couldn't sleep.

ARTHUR: We're going to have a catch.

TODD: We'd die from the cold.

EMMA *(Out)*: I hate crowds.

GRACE: Take a pill Arthur.

ARTHUR: I don't want to take a pill.

GRACE: Too bad.

TODD: He was saying how Emma liked the Phillies.

GRACE: You liked the Phillies, Arthur.

ARTHUR: I did?

GRACE *(To Todd)*: Maybe you should lie down.

TODD: I don't want to lie down.

ARTHUR: *(To Todd)*: Did you like the Phillies?

TODD: I hate baseball.

EMMA *(Out)*: Me too.

GRACE: No one likes baseball, Arthur.

ARTHUR: What are you talking about? Lots of people like baseball! It's the national pastime!

GRACE: No one in the room.

ARTHUR: Who are you people?

GRACE: I'm your wife.

TODD: And your son.

ARTHUR: I miss Emma.

GRACE: Well, too bad. She's gone.

TODD: Say dead.

ARTHUR *(To Todd)*: And it's your fault!

GRACE: He didn't kill her!

ARTHUR: He gave her the gun!

GRACE: Leave him alone—

ARTHUR: Why should I?

GRACE: Because he's sick!

TODD: I'm fine!

GRACE *(To Todd)*: Go to bed!

ARTHUR: Someone has to be responsible!

GRACE: She's responsible. She did it.

ARTHUR: She wouldn't.

EMMA *(Out)*: I did.

TODD: But she did.

GRACE: She did it herself.

ARTHUR *(To Todd)*: I blame you!

GRACE *(To Todd)*: Go. To. Bed.

EMMA *(Out)*: To get away.

ARTHUR: I hate you!

GRACE: Arthur!

TODD: I know.

GRACE *(To Todd)*: He doesn't mean that—

ARTHUR: I do!

GRACE *(To Arthur)*: He's sick!

TODD: I'M NOT!

ARTHUR: She wouldn't leave me all alone!

EMMA: Sure, I would.

GRACE: You're not alone Arthur! What the hell's the matter with you? I'm here—

TODD: Me too.

GRACE: I was here in the beginning, I'm still here! I will always be here!

ARTHUR: But I don't love you Grace.

(A long pause.)

GRACE: Oh.

ARTHUR: I loved Emma. She was beautiful.

EMMA: Thank you.

ARTHUR: She was perfect.

TODD: And you wanted to fuck her.

ARTHUR: NO!! THAT IS NOT TRUE!!

GRACE *(Panicked)*: Let's talk about dinner.

TODD: You killed her. Leering at her, staring at her, touching her—

GRACE: Is anyone hungry?

ARTHUR: I NEVER DID ANYTHING WRONG!!

EMMA: That's debatable.

TODD: Kissing her—

ARTHUR: WHY ARE YOU HERE!

TODD: I have no one—

GRACE: He's our child!

TODD: I belong here.

ARTHUR: YOU DO NOT BELONG HERE!

GRACE: Of course he does!

TODD: Where then?

ARTHUR: I DON'T CARE. I'M SORRY, BUT I DON'T!

GRACE: Stop it, Arthur! Stop this!

ARTHUR: I DO NOT WANT YOU HERE! I DON'T KNOW YOU AND YOU DON'T BELONG! MY LIFE WAS GOOD—MY LIFE WAS—I DON'T WANT YOU HERE!

TODD: Too fucking bad! Too bad for you! What do you want?! Some pretty family! Pretty wife! Pretty daughter! Pretty son named BUZZ! TOO FUCKING BAD! BUZZ IS GONE! BUZZ IS DEAD! BUZZ NEVER WAS!

ARTHUR: I don't care what happens! Where you go—I do not care! I DON'T! YOU'RE NOT MY CHILD! GET AWAY! STOP IT! STOP IT! STOP IT!

(Arthur attacks Todd. There is a struggle. Arthur is strangling Todd.)

GRACE and EMMA: Stop!

(Arthur stops, realizes what he's done. He walks away, slowly.)

EMMA *(Out)*: Death is a day at the beach.
GRACE *(At Todd's side)*: Are you all right?
TODD: I'm fine.
ARTHUR: I'm sorry.
TODD: I'm fine.
ARTHUR: I don't know . . .
GRACE *(To Arthur, stunned)*: What's wrong with you?
ARTHUR: I don't know.
TODD: He tried to kill me.
ARTHUR: I lost control.
GRACE *(Standing)*: I think you should go.
ARTHUR: What?
GRACE: I think you should leave.
ARTHUR: I'm your husband.
GRACE: Just go.

(Arthur starts to exit, then pauses.)

ARTHUR *(After a moment, to Todd)*: You're to blame. *(He exits)*
GRACE: You're all right?
TODD: Yes.
GRACE: You want to lie down?

(Todd shakes his head "no.")

TODD: You don't believe him, do you?
GRACE: What about?
TODD: I'm not to blame.
GRACE: Of course not. You're my baby.

(Todd pours Grace a drink.)

Thank you.

TODD: It'll be dark soon.

GRACE: Are you hungry?

TODD: No.

GRACE: You have to keep up your strength.

TODD: I'm not hungry.

GRACE: Let me know. I'll cook you something. *(She downs her drink)*

TODD: You can't cook.

GRACE: I know it. Do you remember, when you were little? We'd have canned carrots for dinner. That was it. On cook's day off, we'd have carrots and I'd call that dinner.

TODD: I remember.

GRACE: You didn't mind. Never cared about food. Really. Just like me. You and I are just alike.

TODD: I suppose.

GRACE: Always were.

TODD: And it's a shame.

GRACE: What is?

TODD: You made me just like yourself, when you hate yourself to begin with.

GRACE: You'll give me a headache.

TODD: Sorry.

(He fills her glass. A light goes out, then another, reducing their playing area. Grace is very tired and somewhat drunk.)

GRACE: It's so cold.

TODD: It'll be dark soon.

GRACE: Are you hungry?

TODD: No.

GRACE: You have to keep up your strength. *(She drinks)*

TODD: I feel fine.

GRACE: You are amazing. You are so strong. My baby . . . how long has it been?

TODD: Since what?

GRACE: Since your father left?

TODD: I don't know. Two weeks. A month.

GRACE: Really?

TODD: Why'd you marry him?

GRACE: I hate it when it's dark in here. At night.

TODD: I like it.

GRACE: It gets so dark. I feel like I'm floating in space. I feel completely alone. Like I was the last living thing on earth.

TODD: That's why I like it.

GRACE: Play with my hair.

TODD: No.

(He fills her glass. Another light goes out, reducing their playing space further. Grace is groggy and quite drunk, very broken and disoriented.)

GRACE: It's so cold. *(She downs her drink)*

TODD: It's almost dark.

GRACE: Let me look at you.

TODD: What do you want?

GRACE: I just want to look at you. I want to look at my baby. I hate your disease.

TODD: I don't.

GRACE: You're so beautiful.

TODD: I have no symptoms.

GRACE: I'll cook you something. *(She tries, unsuccessfully, to rise)*

TODD: Sit down.

GRACE: I got dizzy.

TODD: Lie down.

(She does so.)

GRACE: I'm so sleepy.

TODD: Take a nap.

GRACE: You have to eat. Can't let you die.

TODD: I think I died a long time ago.

GRACE: What does that mean?

(Todd puts the afghan over her.)

TODD: Take a nap.

GRACE: Some mothers don't love their children. But you know I do, don't you?

TODD: Yes.

GRACE: Love me?

TODD: Of course.

GRACE: Talk to me. Maybe I'll sleep if you talk to me.

TODD: What about?

GRACE: I don't care. Dinosaurs.

TODD: Two hundred and twenty million years ago the dinosaurs came to be. And they were large. In comparison to man they were. And they lived not in harmony, roaming the earth at will, raping, as it were, the planet. But they cared for their young and they flourished as no creature before or since, for one hundred and fifty million years before dying out completely. And no one knows why. Why they lived. Or ceased to. Some people think there was a meteor. Perhaps volcanic ash altered the atmosphere. Some think they over-populated and the shells of their eggs became too thin. Or they just ran their course, and their end was the order of things. And no tragedy. Or disease. Or God.

(He looks at Grace. He covers her face with the afghan. She is dead.)

It's so dark.

(He exits up the stairs. When he reaches Emma, they embrace. Then they walk together up the stairs. Once they are gone, the lights dim, but for the light on the skeleton, which grows brighter and brighter.)

END OF PLAY

FREE WILL & WANTON LUST

Free Will & Wanton Lust premiered in 1991 at the Sanford Meisner Theater. It was produced by the Vortex Theater Company; it was directed by the author; the set design was by MyKeal Kearny; the lighting design was by Jan Bell; the costume design was by Ruth Parsons; the stage manager was Lizze Fitzgerald. The cast was as follows:

CLAIRE	Stephanie Correa
TONY	Charles Derbyshire
AMY	Debra Riessen
PHILIP	Chuck Coggins
VIVIAN	Deb Snyder

In 1993, the play was produced by the Woolly Mammoth Theatre Company (Howard Shalwitz, Artistic Director, Nancy Turner Hensley, Producing Associate). It was directed by the author. The set design was by James Kronzer; the lighting design was by David Zemmels; the costume design was by Rosemary Ingham; the sound design was by Hugh Caldwell; the stage manager was Scott Hammar. The cast was as follows:

CLAIRE	Kerry Waters
TONY	Christopher Lane
AMY	Audrey Wasilewski
PHILIP	Jason Kravits
VIVIAN	Naomi Jacobson

CHARACTERS

CLAIRE, An attractive, witty,
glamorous woman in her mid-forties.

TONY, An opportunistic Adonis in his early twenties.

AMY, Claire's daughter, fifteen. A wilted flower, a sad madcap.

PHILIP, Claire's son, twenty.
A mass of nerves, gaunt and hostile, a drug addict.

VIVIAN, Philip's fiancée, late twenties.
A creature of pure intellect.

TIME AND PLACE

ACT I
Reckless Abandon
The living room of a Manhattan duplex,
furnished in art-deco style. Late afternoon.

ACT II
Etiquette & Vitriol
Claire's bedroom. Fifteen minutes before the end of Act I.

Free Will should be approached as a conflict of theatrical styles. Claire is written as a character from Noël Coward, a character from *The Vortex*. Philip is depicted in Brechtian terms. Act I belongs to Claire and is intended to be played very slickly. Philip, eventually, takes over Act II. There the tone shifts, becomes more aggressive. The final scene is a battle between these two aesthetics (as well as between characters). These dueling theatrical genres should be reinforced with design elements. The more severe the contrast between Claire's glamorous and Philip's proletarian worlds, the better.

ACT I

RECKLESS ABANDON

As the audience enters, "Love Is Good for Anything that Ails You" is playing. The stage is obscured by a chiffon drape. During the song, Amy enters and opens the drape to reveal the set. The room is slick and lavishly designed. There is a curved staircase, leading to nowhere, which diminishes as it spirals. A deco, asymmetrical couch, an ottoman and a bar. The effect of the room is glamour, an elegance one associates with a long-ago era. Amy pours herself a drink, and having downed it, exits. The lights dim out. As the song ends, Claire, wearing an elegant dressing gown, strolls into a pool of light and addresses the audience.

CLAIRE: I have lived, a long time, alone. Always really. I was a girl and I was alone. I was married and I was alone. I had two children, and they are darling, don't mistake me, but I was still alone. And it's true. I have taken many lovers to my bed, but I was still, and always, alone. . . . Until now.

(As she continues, the lights come up, revealing the living room. Tony is languishing luxuriating on the sofa, perhaps asleep.)

This morning I went to the dressmaker, where I had a fitting for Melanie Winslow's party on the eighth, celebrating her first year of sobriety. And there, I ran into my old friend, Phoebe Potter. At first, I didn't recognize her. My goodness, she's gotten old. Her skin just hangs from her bones like a weeping willow. Tragic. Phoebe hugged me and we reminisced, briefly, about our days as schoolgirls together. I told her she looked marvelous, which was a lie. She looked ghastly. Her hair is going gray, or she's finally letting it go gray. She has liver spots on her hands like tweed gloves. And she was being pinned into the *most* matronly chiffon Herrara. And, truth be told, it made me sad to see her. And a little happy. . . . Then it was my turn. And as I stood there, as I was being pinned, as I looked into the mirror, I was startled. I was honestly surprised. I am getting younger! It's an absolute fact. Irrefutable. I get younger and younger with every day and every hour. My skin gets firmer and my hair grows thicker. And where Phoebe has the beginnings of a cataract or two, I've the mischievous glint of youth and possibility. It's miraculous really. It's unbelievable. *(She goes to Tony)* Should this keep up, I'll soon take to jacks and hoops. And by year's end, I'll be in a crib. I mean, I've always had a spirit for living, but this is really new. . . . And I know you're to blame. You're responsible. I was aging, until I met you, and now, it's reversing. My God, I am lucky.

(Tony squirms, barely awake, at her touch.)

TONY: I'm the lucky one.
CLAIRE: Make love to me.
TONY: Again?
CLAIRE: Ravish me on the sofa. I'll reupholster in the morning.
TONY: You'll wear me out.
CLAIRE: I'd love trying.

(They kiss.)

I adore your lips. If you were nothing more than a pair of lips, I'd still love you.—Have me in the broom closet! We've never done it in the broom closet. It's a room, I feel, that's been ignored.

TONY: Later.

CLAIRE: Oh all right. Then get me a drink, would you darling?

TONY *(Doing so)*: You talk so much about your age, and you know, I don't know how old you are.

CLAIRE *(On the floor)*: We've never made love on *this* spot! We must.

TONY: How old are you?

CLAIRE *(Taking the drink)*: Thank you—I am thirteen.

TONY: I know that's not true.

CLAIRE: And a half.

TONY: How old is your son?

CLAIRE: Philip? Twenty.

TONY: So you must be—

CLAIRE: Ten years younger than when we met and five years younger than this morning. You are Ponce de Léon!

TONY: All right.

(They kiss.)

Did you look at the slides?

CLAIRE: I couldn't—

TONY: I worked very hard.

CLAIRE: I meant to, darling, honestly. But that idiotic Hillary Beekman kept me on the phone all morning. The poor wretch is suicidal. She says her marriage is over. Her husband's left her. And you know, she just had her face done, for him really, and now he's walked out. But her face is so tight she looks happy about it.

TONY: I think this series is my best work.

CLAIRE: I couldn't hang up.

TONY: She's a horrible person.

CLAIRE: You mustn't judge people.

TONY: She's always drunk.

CLAIRE: You've only met her twice.

TONY: She was drunk both times.

CLAIRE: No, no. That's a speech impediment. She can't say her
S's.

TONY: You promised you'd look at them.

CLAIRE: I know I did, and I am sorry. But I couldn't abandon
her. Hillary is absolutely my best friend in the whole world.

TONY: You never say anything nice about her.

CLAIRE: Exactly. *(Changing the subject)* Now tell me. What are
you going to wear tonight?

TONY: This.

CLAIRE: Oh Tony, be serious.

TONY: I am.

CLAIRE: You just can't wear jeans to an opening at the Met.

TONY: Why not?

CLAIRE: I'll know everyone there. What will they say?

TONY: You've taken a handsome young lover with bad taste in
clothes?

CLAIRE: You delight in tormenting me.

TONY *(Out)*: It is fun.

CLAIRE: I loathe you. I absolutely abhor you. I'll never speak to
you again as long as I live.

TONY: That's a relief.

CLAIRE: You're evil.

TONY: You adore me.

CLAIRE: Say you'll dress.

TONY: We'll see.

(They kiss.)

CLAIRE: Don't you understand? This is an opportunity. It's a
place to meet people. You never know where you're going
to sell a painting. Please don't argue about it. And besides,
I want tonight to be special. My husband comes home
tomorrow and I'll have to spend some time with him.

TONY *(Getting a drink)*: I don't see why.

CLAIRE: Because I have to. He's my husband.

TONY: I don't believe you are married. I've never met this phantom husband. I think he's a figment.

CLAIRE: I'm married and he returns tomorrow, so this is our last night of reckless abandon. For a while at least—I want to make love in the fountain at Lincoln Center! We've never done it in the fountain at Lincoln Center!

TONY: And you want me to dress?

CLAIRE *(Coy)*: I'll buy you a suit in the morning.

TONY: Promise?

CLAIRE: Anything.

(They kiss and hold their embrace. Amy enters, unnoticed by them.)

AMY: I'm going to kill myself. I want to die.

(They ignore Amy. As a result, she becomes highly dramatic.)

I said, I'm going to kill myself!!—Mother?

CLAIRE *(Looking about)*: Amy?

AMY: I don't want to live any longer. I want to die!

TONY *(Turning Claire toward him)*: Darling?

CLAIRE: Pet.

(Tony and Claire resume necking as Amy tries, vainly, to gain Claire's attention.)

AMY: What is life anyway but a hollow, sinking sham? I'm so tired of everything: the random absurdity, the bleak hopelessness, the utter despair. What's wrong with me? I'm so pretty. Men are nothing but genetics gone mad! I'd like to take a gun and kill them all—I know! I'll become a lesbian! I don't mind women. I find women appealing. I enjoy looking at myself.

CLAIRE *(Turning her head)*: Did you—
TONY: Your tongue tastes divine!
CLAIRE: I've had a mint!

(Tony and Claire resume necking.)

AMY: Although a bullet to my head would be quicker. Mother, do you have a gun?
CLAIRE *(Turning her head)*: I've no idea. Look in my purse.
TONY: You smell like fresh bread.
CLAIRE: You lynx!

(Tony and Claire resume necking.)

AMY: I WOULD LIKE SOME ATTENTION PLEASE!!

(All three are shocked by Amy's force.)

Thank you.
CLAIRE: Did you say something?
AMY: I announced my imminent suicide.
CLAIRE: Don't be rude, dear. Greet your uncle Tony.
AMY: He's not my uncle.
CLAIRE: Good enough.
AMY: I'm not stupid. I have no uncles. You and Daddy have no siblings and I won't pretend you do.
TONY: She seems disturbed.
AMY: I'm right here in the room. Don't discuss me in the third person!
CLAIRE: Tony, you are pathologically sensitive to my daughter's moods.
TONY: Thank you.
AMY: It's over!
CLAIRE: What's over?
TONY: Should we guess?
CLAIRE: Ooooo, what fun!

AMY: Everything is over. My youth, my life, my relationship with Maxwell.

TONY *(To Claire)*: You smell like Hershey's Kisses.

CLAIRE: And you've a thrilling profile. You should be on a coin.

(Tony and Claire resume necking.)

AMY: As you know, Maxwell and I have been seeing each other steadily for several months. I thought he loved me. I thought he cared about me. But everything is transient. After every summer dies the swan!

CLAIRE: Maxwell? Maxwell? Was he that young man with the prosthetic limb?

AMY: No, Mother! That was Anton! Don't you care about me at all?

CLAIRE: Did you want honesty, or support?

AMY: Maxwell is beautiful, inside and out. He's a poet. He burns with the adolescent rage of alienated youth. He tattooed my name on his private parts!

TONY: Ick.

AMY: You are so bourgeois. He's completely in touch with the collective unconscious. He writes sonnets from the bowels and colon of his soul.

CLAIRE: My.

TONY: You smell like glass.

(As Amy speaks, Tony kisses Claire, working his way down her body. Claire attempts to conceal her growing frenzy by pretending to listen to Amy. Amy gets a drink as she speaks.)

AMY: The point is, I told Maxwell that I'm carrying his child inside me, growing in my uterus as a tribute to our love. And you know what he said to me? He said, "Amy, how do I know it's my child?" "I know," I said, "because I haven't been with anyone else since that perfect night we met at Cynthia Tipton's house." And he said, "Really?" Because he didn't think we had that kind of relationship. And besides, he told me, everyone knew I'd had a tryst with Roul Bender—or did he mention Daryl Smyth? One night at Felix Omar's house, I'd had too much to drink and was passed from hand to hand, like a dish of salted nuts. "But Maxwell," I begged, "I was blotto!" And he responded, "Were you drunk with Xavier Sutton?" *(She sips her drink)* Is this Scotch? I don't like Scotch. Oh well. *(She downs her drink and pours another)* "That was one night. It was nothing. You're my life and my breath!" He grew very cold and informed me that any one of those men could be the father of my child and he was going away with this person named Sherri, whom, I might add, is as fat as a mule and as dumb as a post. How could he prefer her to me? "Can't we discuss this? Find a solution?" But he said he had to go, and he withdrew from me. Off he went . . . out of my life . . . to social studies. So here am I, left with child to lick my wounds. I just want to die! *(She down her drink)*

I know! I'll drink myself to death. I don't mean the slow way where the liver fails. I mean, I'll just stand here and drink and drink, until my guts explode!

CLAIRE *(On the verge of ecstasy)*: I'm sorry, what?

AMY: I'm in trouble. What kind of mother are you? What's wrong with you?

CLAIRE: I'm in love!

AMY: I'm in pain!

TONY: I'm running late.

CLAIRE: No!

TONY: I have to go.

CLAIRE: Don't leave me with her. She's creepy.

AMY: Do we have any gimlet mix?

TONY: You want me to change my clothes?

CLAIRE: Oh yes, that's right. It slipped what I laughingly refer to as my mind. Dash home and throw on a blazer or something.

AMY: Vermouth?

CLAIRE: But do hurry back. We'll have a cocktail before we go.

TONY: Of course.

(Tony and Claire kiss.)

Charming as always, Amy.

CLAIRE: Are you back yet?

TONY: I'll fly! *(He exits)*

CLAIRE: I feel flushed. Do I look flushed?

AMY: How do you make a vodka collins?

CLAIRE: Isn't Tony darling? I could drown myself in his eyes!

AMY: Have you gone suddenly deaf?

CLAIRE: I don't think so. Say something.

AMY: You're a maggot-ridden crust of a woman with the morals of a tiger slug.

CLAIRE: No, no. I heard that.

AMY: My God. *(She drinks)*

CLAIRE: Have you ever seen shoulders like his?

AMY: Like whose?

CLAIRE: Like Tony's.

AMY: Yes, as it happens, I have.

CLAIRE: What do you mean?

AMY: Skip it.

CLAIRE: I think you could be more gracious to Tony, dear.

AMY *(Panicked)*: Don't call me dear.

CLAIRE: Pudding?

AMY: No. You only call me dear when you can't remember my name.

CLAIRE: Don't be absurd. You're my daughter.

AMY: All right. What is it?

CLAIRE *(Panicked)*: I'll not be cross-questioned like this.

AMY: You can't remember, can you?

CLAIRE: I think you're drunk. Have you been adding soda water?

AMY: My name, Mother.

CLAIRE: I don't want to play this game. I don't care for it. Let's play another—I spy something taupe! You guess!

AMY: I don't want to.

CLAIRE: Canasta? Bridge? Quick round of freeze tag?

AMY: I can't believe you've forgotten my name!

CLAIRE: I haven't!

AMY: Prove it.

CLAIRE: Oh, all right . . . Gertrude?

AMY: Oh my.

CLAIRE: Well, it could be. You've been drinking more than you ought.

AMY: I'm living a nightmare.

CLAIRE: Don't tell me! Sheila?

AMY: You're insane.

CLAIRE: I was never good with names. Good with faces, bad with names.

AMY: But you named me!

CLAIRE: All right, all right! . . . What does it start with?

AMY: A.

CLAIRE: A? A. A. A. A? A. A, huh? Alice? Alex? Allison?

AMY: No.

CLAIRE: Anita? Abigail? Arthur?

AMY: Arthur?

CLAIRE: Axle? Algenon! Albatross!

AMY: Dear God.

CLAIRE: Algebra!

AMY: Amy! Amy! My name is Amy!

CLAIRE: No, no. That's not it.

AMY: I should know my own name.

CLAIRE: Produce identification.

AMY: My name is Amy.

CLAIRE: Well, fine. If you say so. I believe you're mistaken, but I've no wish to quarrel.

AMY: Oh Mother, why did you adopt me?

CLAIRE: I didn't adopt you. I had you myself.

AMY: This comes as a grave disappointment.

CLAIRE: I remember it distinctly. It hurt quite a bit.

AMY: I loathe you.

CLAIRE: Hand me my purse, would you darling? I feel pale.

(Amy does so.)

I have to fix my face. I'm using a new rouge: adobe brick.
Isn't it cunning?

AMY: I'd like to see you suffer.

CLAIRE: Tony has the most perfect complexion! And he doesn't
wear any make-up at all—at least I don't think so.

AMY: I could douse you with gas and set you on fire.

CLAIRE: He has arms like mighty oaks!

AMY: He's repulsive.

CLAIRE: You haven't seen his pelvic girdle.

AMY: Thank God.

CLAIRE: He's divine.

AMY: He's insincere.

CLAIRE: I can't imagine why you'd say such a thing.

AMY: And it's humiliating, the way you carry on about him.

CLAIRE: Your bitterness will age you prematurely and give you
feather-like lines around your eyes.

AMY: How can you let him touch you?

CLAIRE: He makes love like an Olympic swimmer!

AMY: I don't want to hear this part.

CLAIRE: His semen is a youth serum!

AMY: I'm going to hum.

CLAIRE: He penetrates me and I am prepubescent!

AMY: *Frère Jacques, Frère Jacques, dormez-vous?*

CLAIRE: I am a fetus in utero when we make love!

AMY: Daddy would be so hurt if he knew.

CLAIRE: Oh, your father doesn't care.

AMY: He will! I'll tell him tomorrow and he'll leave you. And
I'll live with him. And we'll go to the park every day, except
when it rains, when we'll go to the movies. And once a year
we'll go to visit you. I promise. No matter where you're living, after Daddy's gone, no doubt, a cold-water flat. But
we'll bring scones and day-old bread. You can get a job like

Grandma at the end, tearing sheets of foam rubber into chunks for stuffing pillows, until your hands become gnarled with rheumatoid arthritis! Tony could support you, but he'll be dead after Daddy kills him!

CLAIRE *(She has been applying lipstick)*: Do you like my lips? They're Bakolite.

AMY: What's wrong with you? Can't you see you're throwing your life away on that two-faced, foul-breathed sycophant?

CLAIRE: He worships the ground, over which I glide.

AMY: He's twenty-four!

CLAIRE: And I am sixteen.

AMY: He thinks you can help him.

CLAIRE: We can help each other.

AMY: You buy him things.

CLAIRE: Tokens.

AMY: You feed him.

CLAIRE: Snacks!

AMY: He thinks you can introduce him to people.

CLAIRE: I can. I'm poised. I say, "Tony, this is so and so. So and so, this is Tony."

AMY: People who can help him. He's a struggling artist. You're a wealthy woman with wealthy friends. You're completely blind.

CLAIRE: I'd just as soon you refrain from innuendo.

AMY: I'll say it directly.

CLAIRE: If I didn't assume you were completely drunk, I'd send you to your room.

AMY: I'm trying to help you!

CLAIRE: Don't bother.

AMY: I shouldn't.

CLAIRE: I think you're jealous!

AMY: What?!

CLAIRE: It's as plain as my nose on your face. You have some nitwit, school-girl crush on Tony yourself! Well, I saw him first and you can't have him!

AMY: I don't want him!

CLAIRE: Of course you do. Your affair has ended badly so you've affixed your emotions to Tony. You're in love with him, aren't you? Well, young lady, I forbid it!

AMY: I am not in love with him. I'm a lesbian! I told you that. As of today, I never want to see another man, let alone sleep with one!

CLAIRE: Oooo! Don't be ridiculous! You'll sleep with lots of men. Scores!

AMY: I will not.

CLAIRE: Hundreds!

AMY: I won't!

CLAIRE: You're being childish.

AMY: Well, I am, Mother, after all, fifteen.

CLAIRE: Years old?

AMY: Yes.

CLAIRE: Really?

AMY: Yes.

CLAIRE: I would've sworn—why aren't you in school?

AMY: I left school two years ago.

CLAIRE: I should've noticed.—Where was I? Oh yes. You'll sleep with hundreds of men if I have to tie you down myself!

(Philip enters, unnoticed.)

AMY: You can't make me!

CLAIRE: Just watch.

AMY: I'm a lesbian. I'm a lesbian. I'm a lesbian!!

CLAIRE: You will be heterosexual, young lady, and promiscuous at that! Now! I'll have no more of this discussion!

AMY: I hate you! I hate you! I hate you!

(Amy runs off, but collides with Philip.)

Philip!

CLAIRE: Darling! What are you doing here?

PHILIP: I live here. This is my home. I live here.

CLAIRE: Welcome home!

AMY: Does this mean I lose his room?

CLAIRE: Yes, it does.

AMY: I hate everyone everywhere.

CLAIRE: Don't be silly. You don't know everyone everywhere.

AMY: I don't care. I hate them anyway.

CLAIRE: Dear Philip, you remember your sister, the cherub who oozes graciousness like musk?

PHILIP: How are you, Amy?

AMY: Pregnant, bitter and hell-bent on revenge.

CLAIRE: That's right dear. Let out the poisons.

AMY: No one takes me seriously. Beauty is no passport to success.

CLAIRE: Philip, angel, what are you doing here? Not that I'm not happy to see you, because I am. I'm always happy to see you. I'm delighted! What a joy to have my children around me.

AMY: You look sick, Philip. I'm a lesbian now.

PHILIP: That's nice.

CLAIRE: She's not. You're not. She's not. I've forbidden it.

AMY: Do you mind if I wear your old clothes?

CLAIRE: A lonely life of emotional stoicism and hip-hugger trousers, you're bound to regret.

AMY: I like lesbians. I always have. I find them direct. What do you think of lesbians, Philip?

PHILIP: I don't know. They have their place.

CLAIRE: Why didn't you write that you were coming home?

AMY: Mother, we haven't settled the question of my sexual identity yet.

CLAIRE: Oh go to New Jersey, have your child, and fornicate with sheep for all I care.

AMY: I know what you're up to. You think I just want attention, don't you? You think I'm acting out of some infantile, neurotic need, don't you? You think if you ignore my rebellion, it'll pass, don't you?

CLAIRE: Frankly, no. That hadn't occurred to me.

AMY: Oh.

CLAIRE: My indifference was sincere.

PHILIP: I meant to write, but I didn't want to write my news. I mean, I didn't want to write it. That's the same thing, isn't?

CLAIRE: Watch how I dote on your brother.

PHILIP: I wanted to tell you in person. I hope you'll be happy. I hope we can be a family again.

AMY: Again?

CLAIRE: How was London, dear?

PHILIP: Foggy.

CLAIRE: So they say.

AMY: It's degrading, what passes for conversation in this house.

CLAIRE: Can I get you a drink?

PHILIP: That would be nice. I mean, that would be nice.

AMY: I'd like a drink.

CLAIRE: You've had enough. In your absence, your sister has lapsed into a state of adolescent alcoholism.

AMY *(Swiping the bottle)*: Don't be silly. I'm too old to be an adolescent.

CLAIRE: Your father returns tomorrow, so the house will be full.

AMY: You look rather ghastly, Philip. And you keep repeating yourself.

CLAIRE: I do wish I'd known you were coming. I'd've planned a party. I've missed you so.

AMY: I said, "You look rather ghastly and you keep repeating yourself—"

CLAIRE: I could've invited all your old friends!

AMY: I said—Oh I give up.

CLAIRE *(Handing him his drink)*: Do you remember Skipper Thompson?

PHILIP: I'm afraid not.

CLAIRE: Of course you do. He was a charming boy. Red hair.

PHILIP: No.

CLAIRE: Cherubic face and sinewy forearms?

PHILIP: I'm blank.

CLAIRE: Think, think, think. Large, blue-green eyes and freckles on his buttocks?

PHILIP: I-I-Nothing.

CLAIRE: Come, come, come. Strong trim thighs and *equine* genitalia?

PHILIP: I DO NOT REMEMBER HIM!

CLAIRE: Oh well. He killed himself anyway.

PHILIP: What?

CLAIRE: So I couldn't've invited him even if I'd had a party to welcome you home. Or I could've invited him, but he wouldn't have come. Let me look at you. You look well. A little pale, perhaps. And thin, and you have black rings under your eyes. But then I like that in a man. Who doesn't? You do, don't you Amy?

AMY: He looks like death.

CLAIRE: You didn't address the question so you get ignored again.

AMY: I'll drink.

PHILIP: I have some news.

CLAIRE: Still, I could've invited little Arthur Dewmerry. You do remember him?

PHILIP: Of course not.

CLAIRE: Think back. All stamina, with no finesse?

PHILIP: No, Mother.

CLAIRE: Donny LaFette! Raven tresses and a premature ejaculator?

PHILIP: I said I had some news.

CLAIRE: Oh you did, didn't you. Please forgive me. I'm adrift in memories of your lost youth.

AMY *(Slightly drunk)*: After a while Scotch tastes like pudding.

PHILIP: I've met someone.

CLAIRE: That's good dear. Bound to happen when you leave the house.

PHILIP: I mean, I've met someone. That's the same thing, isn't it? I mean, I've met someone.

CLAIRE: Repeating the same phrase, over and over again, is not elucidating.

PHILIP: I mean, I've met someone!

AMY: Oh God.

CLAIRE: I know! I'll ask yes or no questions to fill in the narrative gaps!

PHILIP: I've met a girl.

CLAIRE: Oooo, I didn't ask that yet. Living or dead?

PHILIP: Her name is Vivian.

CLAIRE: Oh, you're not playing at all.

PHILIP: A beautiful girl. A wonderful girl. The answer to my prayers.

CLAIRE: Imagine.

PHILIP: We're engaged to be married.

CLAIRE: What!?

PHILIP: I mean, we're engaged to be married.

AMY: She said, "What?" That time I heard her.

CLAIRE: Isn't this wonderful! Now I'll have to plan a party! We'll have seafood salad and eight different kinds of pâté— I adore pâté! This is too, too marvelous! Tell me all about her! I want to know everything—skip the ugly parts— where did you meet her? Is she British? I adore the British! I love their manners. I love their crooked rotting teeth and their receding chins!

PHILIP: Actually, no. She was raised just around the corner.

CLAIRE: From here?! Right here? Isn't that a coinkidink? Don't you think so, Amy?

AMY: What? Oh yes, sure, whatever.

CLAIRE: You had to go halfway around the world to meet someone from around the corner! Why it's just like that song— whatever it's called. Who cares really? I've always hated that song. You know the one I mean. That Italian girl sings it—what's her name? Judy Garland's daughter—have you seen her lately? I don't understand her hairdo at all—But isn't this something! At long last, I'll have a daughter!

(Amy takes a swig from her bottle.)

I'll have to invite all your old school chums to your party! The living at any rate. There's been a rash of suicides among your peers. Who can explain it? *Not I!* But I'm so happy for you!—By the way, where is your luggage? Oh you young people lead such rag-tag lives—I feel like celebrating! I feel like renting a piano, just so I can sit on top of it and mouth the words to Bea Lillie recordings! Do you think that's extravagant? I don't care! I'm thrilled for you! I don't mind telling you, I was beginning to think you were a tad socially retarded, but now!! I'm beside myself! I wish I could take you out tonight for a steak bernaise and some pâté, but I'm committed to taking Tony to the Met—

PHILIP: Tony?

CLAIRE: I know! You'll join us!

PHILIP: But, Mother—

CLAIRE: I won't discuss it. You're coming along!

PHILIP: But, Mother, Vivian is here.

CLAIRE: What? What? Where? *(She looks under the furniture)* Vivian? Vivian? Where is she? Is she tiny?

PHILIP: I mean, she's here.

CLAIRE: Your new verbal tick is grating.

PHILIP: She's in the hallway. I brought her here to meet you.

CLAIRE: What? She's been out there all this time? Why didn't you say something?

PHILIP: I did. I mean, I did.

CLAIRE: Look at me. I'm not dressed! I can't meet anyone like this. I look a fright.

PHILIP: It doesn't matter. She won't notice. She's not concerned with vanity.

CLAIRE: We can't leave her loitering in the hallway. What must she think of us? She'll think we've no manners at all. I feel just awful. Bring her, Philip.

PHILIP: VVVVVIIIIVVVIIIIAAAANNNNN!!!!!

CLAIRE: I could've done that dear.

PHILIP: Sorry.

CLAIRE: This is so exciting! I'm a-tingle—AMY!! STAND UP STRAIGHT!! And should you succumb to a fit of DTs, excuse yourself, and I'll explain you're epileptic.

(Claire turns her back, pinches her cheeks to raise color and adjusts her hair. Vivian enters, wearing glasses and a shroud.)

VIVIAN: Yes, Philip?
PHILIP: Come here.
VIVIAN: Yes Philip.
PHILIP: I'd like you to meet my mother.
VIVIAN *(Extending her hand)*: It's a pleasure.

(Claire turns and is stricken by the severe sight of Vivian. She recovers at once.)

CLAIRE: She's sweet! You're sweet. She's sweet, Philip!
VIVIAN: I've heard so much about you.
CLAIRE: Then you've the advantage, as I've only just heard your name.
VIVIAN: You have a lovely home.
CLAIRE: But you've only seen the hallway.
VIVIAN: It's a lovely hallway.
CLAIRE: Is it?
VIVIAN: The wallpaper has a print of tiny pineapples.
CLAIRE: I never noticed that . . . I adore your hair. Does it hurt?
VIVIAN: No—
AMY: Excuse me! I'm another person in the room.
PHILIP: Oh yes. Vivian, that's my—
CLAIRE: That's Amy. She's soused.
VIVIAN: It's nice to—
CLAIRE *(Crossing to the bar)*: Now Vivian, I'll fix you a drink while you tell me all about yourself, in short, information-packed sentences, as I must fix my hair and change my clothes. We're all going out tonight, you're included, of course, to celebrate your engagement—AMY! You've finished all the liquor.—Oh no. Here's something.
VIVIAN: What would you like to know?
CLAIRE: Oh I don't care. What do you do?

VIVIAN: What do you mean?

CLAIRE: What do I mean?

VIVIAN: What do I do?

CLAIRE: That was it!

VIVIAN: For a living?

PHILIP *(Scolding)*: Mother.

CLAIRE: Hush dear. Drink quietly. I'm getting to know Vivian.

VIVIAN *(Taking her drink)*: Thank you. Well. I've been working in London's West End. In an occult bookstore.

CLAIRE: Is that your vocation?

VIVIAN: I used to study art.

CLAIRE: I love art! I don't know a thing about it, but I made some dandy macaroni sculptures when I was a girl.

AMY: Do you believe in witchcraft?

VIVIAN: I don't know. Witchcraft, per se, seems to me, to be the refuge of frustrated thinkers. But I certainly believe there's a spirit world.

CLAIRE: Do you?

VIVIAN: So much of the occult literature is powerful and persuasive. You need only to open your eyes to see that the tangible world is a thin veneer. I've personally had experiences that shake my faith in the concrete.

CLAIRE: What are you talking about, dear?

PHILIP: Spiritual enlightenment.

CLAIRE *(Dismissive)*: A different kind of Catholicism.

VIVIAN: I don't believe in Catholicism.

PHILIP: I believe in reincarnation. I mean, I believe in reincarnation.

CLAIRE: Do you? And what do you think you were in a former life?

PHILIP: I think, before I was me, I was my father.

CLAIRE: He's still alive dear.

PHILIP: Oh yes. Damn!

CLAIRE: I believe in what I can see, hear, taste and smell. The rest is just a crutch that weak people use to distract themselves from the arbitrariness of their lives.

VIVIAN: You forgot touch.

CLAIRE: I didn't forget it dear. I don't believe in it.

PHILIP: What do you mean?

CLAIRE: I've no idea. Don't interrupt.

AMY: I don't believe our lives are remotely arbitrary. And I certainly don't believe our fates lie in the mystic hands of unseen forces.

VIVIAN: What *do* you believe?

AMY: We control our lives. We make our destinies as if from mounds of clay. If you ask me—

CLAIRE: I didn't. Did you?

AMY: I have the power to create my future. We can make ourselves over in our own images. There is no power of the cosmos, but that which is inside of us. Or me, at any rate.

CLAIRE: Thank you for the view from the bottom of the bottle.

AMY: I'm going to lie down now. *(She collapses behind the bar)*

CLAIRE: She's epileptic!! . . . Do you still paint?

PHILIP: Don't cross-examine her, Mother.

CLAIRE: Was I?

VIVIAN: I don't.

CLAIRE *(Condescending)*: I'm so sorry. Why's that?

VIVIAN: I find, as I mature, the physical simply holds no allure. Wouldn't you agree?

CLAIRE: Convince me.

VIVIAN: I regret, now, the wasted years of my childhood, I spent believing beauty was something you could see, developing my senses, instead of my intellect.

CLAIRE: Imagine!

VIVIAN: Have you ever read Nietzsche? Or Schopenhauer? Ideas are the true aphrodisiacs. Don't you find?

CLAIRE: It's over my head. I enjoyed *a* book—

VIVIAN: Who can fail to be thrilled by the light breaking, as you expand yourself to embrace the metaphysical realities of the universe? I stopped painting, because I saw, all at once, with a gestalt-like clarity, the sham of the physical, the lie of the literal, the falseness of the tangible. I have been trying, since the moment I last laid down my brush, to embrace, to understand, to become one with the all-encompassing apothegms of the unfettered mind and spirit! The world isn't something you can *see and paint*!! The vicissitudes of human development lay in the air around us and the atoms within us and cannot be made two-dimensional, or easily digestible!!!

CLAIRE *(After a moment)*: My.

VIVIAN: I'm afraid I've oraculated.

CLAIRE: Not at all.

VIVIAN: I'm sorry.

CLAIRE: To the contrary. I am absolutely fascinated, but I have to—brush my hair.

PHILIP: You haven't understood at all.

CLAIRE: I find her charming! I find you charming. But I have to sit in a hot tub, or I'm not worth as nickel.

VIVIAN: I understand.

CLAIRE: You must continue, later, to *enlighten* me: once I'm bathed and dressed. The most evolved of holy men could have no objection to a quick bath, I'm sure. And please, *do* promise that you'll come tonight. If you're worried that you've nothing—suitable to wear. You mustn't. I'm sure I have lots of dresses I'm sure you'd like. And now, you must excuse me. My head is throbbing! *(She exits)*

VIVIAN: I'm afraid I didn't make a very good impression.

PHILIP: You were brilliant.

VIVIAN: I gave her a migraine.

PHILIP: She's shallow and condescending.

VIVIAN: I'm not very charming or witty.

PHILIP: You have ten times her intellect.

VIVIAN: Do you think so?

AMY *(Rising, behind the bar)*: I think you're a vile bore and you drone on and on ceaselessly.

PHILIP: AMY! How dare you!?

AMY: I'm sorry . . . I thought I was unconscious.

VIVIAN: Oh, she's right. At least that's what your mother thought.

PHILIP: Who cares what she thought?

VIVIAN: You do. I know how much you like her. I just wanted to make a good first impression. Oh I'm a mess. Philip? Where's the powder room?

PHILIP: Through there.

VIVIAN: Thank you. Excuse me. I'm going to wash my hands and face in an effort to become more vain and shallow. *(She exits)*

PHILIP: AMY! I wish you wouldn't talk to my fiancée like that!

AMY: I said I was sorry.

PHILIP: You have no business! I mean, you have no business!

AMY: That's the same thing.

PHILIP: What's the same thing?

AMY: Skip it. Philip, you're not really going to marry her, are you?

PHILIP: Of course I am!!

AMY: But why?

PHILIP: I LOVE HER! YOU KNOW I HAVEN'T ALWAYS BEEN A HAPPY PERSON! I'VE NEVER BEEN THIS RELAXED! I'VE NEVER BEEN SO EASYGOING!

AMY: But she seems so dreary and serious. Completely lifeless. How old is she?

PHILIP: You know, I don't know. I never thought to ask.

AMY: I think she's a hundred. She's not very fun loving. Really, *I'm* fifteen and I'm pregnant.

PHILIP: It's perverted that you should measure her merits by the standards of your mistakes.

AMY: It's just so sad to see you settle. We're too young to settle.

PHILIP: I think you're jealous!

AMY: What!?

PHILIP: I think you're jealous.

AMY: THAT'S THE SAME THING!

PHILIP: You've always been jealous of me—don't bother to deny it! You resented that mother preferred me to you!

AMY: Ridiculous.

PHILIP: No matter what I had, you wanted it! My God! When I had the chicken pox you were pea-green with envy! And now I think you're jealous of Vivian! You said you were a lesbian. It's only natural that you would be attracted to her. She's so winning! You have some nitwit, schoolgirl crush on Vivian! Your catty remarks and condescension are a thin veneer for your wanton lust!!

AMY: That's sick!

PHILIP: It's obvious!

AMY: I'm not jealous of anyone! What's wrong with you people? Is it possible that I'm the last human being who cares for someone else?! You're my brother!

PHILIP: Your perversion is bottomless!

AMY: STOP IT!!

(All lights go out, but for a special on Amy, who addresses the audience.)

What's wrong with everyone? This morning, I was in bed, with Maxwell, whom you didn't get to meet, but he's beautiful. His skin is soft and his hair is long. It's loose and down to here, and he tightens it around my throat. He was holding me against his stomach and I couldn't move or catch my breath and I felt free, because I was safe. And I rose up, out of myself, off the bed, and watched him, and me, as we dissolved. I heard him whisper, until his voice divided and became three voices, like the Holy Trinity, making confession and promise after promise. . . . And then I woke up . . . and came home.

(General light returns. Tony, having donned a blazer, has joined them.)

TONY: I'm back!

AMY: Hello, Tony.

TONY: What's this?

AMY: This is my brother, Philip.

TONY: Oh yes. I've heard about you. The musician, right?

PHILIP: Not exactly.

TONY: Been in England?

PHILIP: Yes. I have.

TONY: How'd you find it?

PHILIP: They don't put ice in their drinks and there's not enough television.

TONY: I've heard that. Never been abroad myself, but I'd like—

PHILIP: Who are you?

TONY: I'm Tony.

PHILIP: I know your name. I mean, who are you? I mean, who are you?

TONY: Pardon me?

AMY: He repeats things.

TONY: I'm a friend of your mother's. You can call me "Uncle Tony."

PHILIP: I don't think so.

AMY: Tony is Mother's lover.

TONY: AMY!

AMY: Oh who cares? Who cares? He knows. Everyone knows. Mother's indiscretion is common knowledge.

PHILIP: You seem awfully young.

TONY: I work out. Free weights and StairMaster.

PHILIP: How old are you?

TONY: How old do you think?

PHILIP: I don't know.

TONY: What would you say?

PHILIP: I have no idea.

TONY: Guess.

PHILIP: I don't want to.

TONY: Go on, guess.

PHILIP: I don't care to!

TONY: I won't be offended. Guess.

PHILIP: No!

TONY: How old do I look?

PHILIP: I DON'T WANT TO GUESS! I DO NOT WANT TO! I ASKED A SIMPLE QUESTION! IF YOU DON'T WANT

TO ANSWER ME, FINE! SAY SO! BUT, DEAR GOD! DON'T MAKE ME PLAY GAMES!

TONY: Can't tell, can ya?

AMY: He's twenty-four.

TONY: Amy!!

AMY: He obviously doesn't want to guess.

TONY: I hate is when people won't guess.

PHILIP: I don't like to guess!

AMY: No one does.

TONY: I hate that!

AMY: Who cares?

PHILIP: I hate guessing.

TONY: I don't look it, do I?

AMY: And then some.

TONY: I think I look older in some ways and younger in others. I'm in very good shape—I don't have any lines at all, not even around my eyes. Work out twice a week, and I run too. It's invigorating. Do you run? No. I don't guess you do. I think you look older than me, in some ways, and younger in others. Some sun wouldn't kill you. How old are you again? No, no. Don't tell me. Let me guess.

PHILIP: Twenty! Twenty! I'm twenty!

TONY: I would've enjoyed guessing.

AMY: Pity.

TONY: Where's your mother?

PHILIP: She's dressing.

AMY *(Pouring a drink)*: Tony, have you got a pearl onion?

TONY: Of course not.

PHILIP: We're all going out tonight. I'm joining you.

AMY: An olive?

TONY: No.

PHILIP: What does someone your age see in someone her age?

AMY *(Drinking)*: Oh well.

TONY: I like older women. They're more grateful and less demanding.

PHILIP: Do you love my mother?

TONY: Guess.

PHILIP: Don't make me!

AMY *(Examining the bottle)*: All gone.

TONY: I adore her.

PHILIP: Thank you.

TONY: And she's mad about me.

AMY: For the moment. *(She hiccups)*

PHILIP: What could you possibly have in common?

TONY: What'd you mean by that, Amy?

AMY: Oh nothing. I'm pregnant, so I babble.

TONY: You said it so you must've meant something.

AMY: Really? Did I? Must I?

PHILIP: What do you do?

TONY: Why did you say that? Are you trying to make me insecure?

AMY: Guess.

PHILIP: What do you do for a living? Do you work? Do you have a job? Do you *do* anything??

AMY: Oh you know Mother. She talks nonstop. Of course she's said something.

TONY: About me?

AMY: She doesn't have to. Mothers and daughters have a special kind of nonverbal communication.

PHILIP: I feel suddenly dizzy. I—light-headed.

TONY: What did she say?!

AMY: It doesn't matter.

PHILIP: I feel faint!

TONY: It does to me!

AMY: Forget it.

TONY: You're trying to tell me something. Come out with it!

PHILIP: I feel nauseous. My hands are shaking.

AMY: Really, Tony. You didn't think you were the first, did you?

TONY: No. . . . She's married. She has children.

AMY: I mean the first young lover she's taken to her bed.

TONY: Well, I did.

AMY: Then you are.

PHILIP: I feel sick!

TONY: You're hiding something!!

AMY: Tony, I'm sorry. But for as long as I can remember, Mother has taken men half her age to bed with her. And I can remember very far back. This bordered on the perverted when I was younger and was against the law in several states.

TONY: I don't believe you.

AMY: I don't want to hurt you. I'm only telling you this because I care about you—deeply. You have no idea how deeply. You see, this is a pattern: She finds some vulnerable young thing, and convinces herself—she actually believes she cares for these beautiful, tight-buttocked creatures. But she doesn't. Not in any lasting way. She builds them up for a couple of months. Taking them places and buying them things. Why, I remember one boy named Sloppy, or Skippy or something. She carried on with him for months! He was twelve. Then, once she grew bored with him, or used him up like the rest, she dismissed him. Skippy was crushed and he drowned himself in our tub, which she had a terrible time explaining to my father. But the point is, for your own good, don't delude yourself into thinking that your passion is returned, or that you'll get anything out of this affair. I'm afraid you're just one more in a long line of nameless, faceless bodies.

TONY: Oh my God!

AMY: I'm so sorry.

TONY: Is that true?!

AMY: I can say no more.

TONY: She lied to me!?

AMY: I'm going upstairs now, to induce a miscarriage. *(She curtsies and seems to exit, but instead hides, out of Tony's sight and watches the scene)*

TONY: Philip!!

PHILIP: What!?

TONY: Is what she said true?!

PHILIP: I have to go! I have to leave! I HAVE TO GET SOME AIR! *(He rushes off)*
TONY: I'LL KILL HER!

(Vivian enters, her head in a towel.)

VIVIAN: I feel better now, although I should have removed my glasses. *(She lowers her towel)* Who are you?
TONY: Guess.
VIVIAN: I don't want to.
TONY: There's no sense of adventure in people anymore. I'm Tony.
VIVIAN: It's nice to meet you.
TONY: Who are you?
VIVIAN: My name is Vivian. *(Pause)* Where's Philip?
TONY: He went out.
VIVIAN: Really?
TONY: Yes.
VIVIAN: That's odd. He just left me here?
TONY: He wasn't feeling well.
VIVIAN: Oh.
TONY: He'll be back.
VIVIAN: I hope so. We're engaged.
TONY: I'm sure he hasn't gone for good. This is his home.
VIVIAN: Where's Amy?
TONY: Upstairs.
VIVIAN: Oh.
TONY: Aborting her child.
VIVIAN: Oh?
TONY: I expect we'll here blood-curdling screams soon.
VIVIAN: I hope she knows what she's doing.

(Pause. Tony looks at Vivian for the first time. An idea occurs to him and his demeanor changes.)

TONY: What did you say your name was?

VIVIAN: Why?

TONY: You look familiar to me. Do I look familiar to you?

VIVIAN: No. But then I'm astigmatic.

TONY: What was it?

VIVIAN: Vivian.

TONY: Vivian what?

VIVIAN: Vivian Hammer.

TONY: That's it!

VIVIAN: Yes, thank you. I know. I know my name.

TONY: Vivian, don't you remember me?

VIVIAN: From what? Have we met?

TONY: We were at the Art Students League together.

VIVIAN: Really?

TONY: You don't remember me? I'm insulted.

VIVIAN: That was five years ago.

TONY: Exactly right!

VIVIAN: Yes, I know.

TONY: You look—well, changed.

VIVIAN: Were we friends? Did we speak?

TONY *(Lewd)*: Not exactly.

VIVIAN: Either we did or we didn't.

TONY: I used to watch you all the time.

VIVIAN: Pardon me?

TONY: I stared at you. I thought you were beautiful.

VIVIAN: Me?

TONY: Didn't you realize?

VIVIAN: You're embarrassing me.

TONY: I undressed you with my eyes.

VIVIAN: That was hardly necessary. I posed nude quite often.

TONY: Yes, I know. I remember that.

VIVIAN: May we talk of something else? Did you vote this year?

TONY: I saw you in every mirror and young girl that I looked at.
    You became my obsession. You were, every night, in my
    dreams. I remember how you glided through a room. You
    seemed so superior. And your paintings! You were a won-
    derful painter.

VIVIAN: Thank you.

TONY: So violent and full of rage. It was as if you lived in a serene world and poured all your rage into your work.

VIVIAN: I've stopped painting.

TONY: That's terrible. Why?

VIVIAN: I'd rather not go into it.

TONY: Oh.

VIVIAN: I had a bad year.

TONY: What happened?

VIVIAN: I had a twin sister who was raped and murdered by a young man she met at a church social.

TONY: I don't believe in religion.

VIVIAN: It was a tragedy and I was thrown into a depression.

TONY: You were thrown?

VIVIAN: I found I could no longer paint. I could no longer see the beauty in a grotesque world. I wanted to disappear. My friends tried to console me, but they just got on my nerves. So I left the country. I wandered the continent, ending up, finally, in England, where I was alone. I tried to become a prostitute, but I lacked the confidence. I lived, for a while, in doorways, and ate scraps from the dustbin. One day, a kindly old woman took pity on me and brought me to her house. When I told her I could no longer see the order of the universe, she mistook my insight for a literal complaint and took me to the eye doctor, where I received my glasses. She was an idiot.

TONY *(Advancing)*: They suit you . . . sort of.

VIVIAN *(Withdrawing)*: I don't care! I don't care to be attractive any longer. I've moved beyond the pursuit of physical perfe— *(She looks at him as a sexual being, for the first time really)* Where was I?

TONY: At the ophthalmologist.

VIVIAN: Yes. That's right. My glasses were symbolic. I saw then, that I had to go on living. It was not time for me to resign myself. And so, I got a job and found new peace. Shortly after that, I met Philip.

TONY: And does he satisfy you?

VIVIAN: What do you mean?

TONY: He looks sickly. He looks like death.

VIVIAN: Oh. You mean physically.

TONY: What else is there?

VIVIAN: You mean sexually.

TONY: Yes.

VIVIAN: We don't have sex.

TONY: Pardon me?

VIVIAN: I don't see how it's any of your business, but we have a spiritual bond. We don't have to have sex.

TONY: No one *has* to.

VIVIAN: We don't choose to.

TONY: How can you love someone without sex?

VIVIAN: Must everything be physical? We're human beings, not gorillas.

TONY: I think so.

VIVIAN: You're standing too close to me.

TONY *(Not moving)*: I'm sorry.

VIVIAN *(Escaping)*: You sicken me.

TONY: For someone so enlightened, you're awfully quick to judge.

VIVIAN: I'm not judging. I'm just feeling queasy.

TONY: You wouldn't be so cruel, if you knew me better.

VIVIAN: We'll never know.

TONY: I wasn't always this Adonis women swoon over.

VIVIAN: I'm not swooning.

TONY: I've had a terrible life.

VIVIAN: I can only imagine.

TONY *(Obviously lying)*: You may not believe this, to look at me now, I know it's hard to believe, but . . . I was very unattractive as a child.

VIVIAN: Oh really?

TONY: Yes. Yes, I was. I was, I was . . . fat! I was very, very fat. I was huge! And I was covered with moles and warts and birthmarks! And I was bowlegged!

VIVIAN: I find this hard to believe.

TONY: I was grotesque and friendless.

VIVIAN: I'm sure you were friendless.

TONY: I spent my days in my room eating cookies and reading Spinoza.

VIVIAN: Then what happened to you? How did you accomplish this "transformation"?

TONY *(Stalling)*: I can't tell you.

VIVIAN: Fine.

TONY: It's too painful to relive.

VIVIAN: If you don't want to tell me.

TONY *(Making this up as he goes along)*: One day, I was driving along with my parents—who were also very ugly—I was driving with them to church. It was a Sunday, and I believed in God then. It was very foggy. And then . . . out of nowhere, out of the bushes by the side of the road, this very little boy . . . who was also very ugly, appeared on a little red tricycle. My father, who was a bad driver, as well as being ugly, swerved to avoid him. . . . The next thing I remember, we were very still. Somehow the car was upside down and my father's eyes were looking at me, but there was blood all over his face and my mother's head was turned in a way that I knew her neck was broken.

VIVIAN *(Weakening)*: My.

TONY *(Believing it himself at this point)*: I thought I was dead. I assumed it. And I think, maybe, for a time, I was. The next thing I knew, I was in the hospital. I was covered with bandages. They told me my parents were killed. But I couldn't cry. Or move. Or see. . . . Or feel!

VIVIAN *(Going to him)*: I'm so sorry.

TONY *(Retreating behind the sofa)*: Don't patronize me!

VIVIAN: I'm not.

TONY: I was in the hospital for months. I had surgery after surgery. They fixed my bones and my flesh and my face. But I was sick with something more than just my injuries. I was guilty because I had lived and my parents had died. . .

After a year, they removed my bandages to reveal what they'd made. And I saw the new me. And I saw that I was beautiful. So I set out to remake myself and discover the world. I resolved to live for pleasure at all costs. To please myself, physically, and make use of the miracle to which I was a witness.

VIVIAN *(Joining him, behind the sofa)*: That's very touching.

TONY: There is nothing but physical pleasure.

VIVIAN: I disagree.

TONY: Because you haven't known any.

VIVIAN: But what about rational thought and ideology?

TONY: Abstractions!

VIVIAN: But don't you think a set of aesthetics and intellectual criteria—

TONY *(Taking her)*: They don't compare to two hot, sweaty bodies writhing and pounding away at each other in a fit of hot, wet, animal lust!

VIVIAN: Please!

TONY: Trust me!

VIVIAN: Your hot breath is wilting my resolve.

TONY: Take off your glasses.

VIVIAN: I won't be a cliché.

TONY: Then leave 'em on. What the hell.

VIVIAN: I'm engaged.

TONY *(Kissing her neck)*: You smell like Hershey's Kisses.

VIVIAN: I have some in my pocket, would you like one?

TONY: No!!

VIVIAN: What are you doing?

TONY: Licking your neck!

VIVIAN: I was afraid that was it.

TONY: Admit you enjoy it.

VIVIAN: I'm engaged to be married!

TONY: You said that.

VIVIAN: No I didn't. "To be married" was new.

TONY: Don't speak.

VIVIAN: Why are you doing this?

TONY: Don't think about why!

VIVIAN *(Writhing)*: Oh God.

TONY: You're a beautiful woman!

VIVIAN: Compared to what?

TONY: Others in the room.

VIVIAN: Please stop!!

TONY *(Kissing her repeatedly, lowering himself)*: You have beautiful shoulders.

VIVIAN: They hold up my arms.

TONY: What lovely breasts!

VIVIAN: They hold up my nipples.

TONY: And what perfect nipples!

VIVIAN: They don't hold anything up—well, occasionally, my blouse.

TONY: They're fantastic!

VIVIAN: They're fine. They're nice, they're fine. I've always liked them.

TONY: They're spectacular!

VIVIAN: The left one's nice. I hate the right.

TONY *(Lower)*: And a tiny waist!!

VIVIAN: Oh God! It's suddenly as warm in here as the ninth circle of Dante's inferno!

TONY *(Disappearing behind the sofa)*: AND A DELICIOUS—

VIVIAN: OH MY GOD!!!

TONY *(Out of sight)*: A banquet!! A feast!!

VIVIAN *(Sinking out of sight)*: AAAAHHHHHH!!!!!!!!

TONY: Let go! Just let yourself go!!

VIVIAN: OH GOD! WHAT'S HAPPENING TO ME!? IT'S SO WARM!! IT'S VERY, VERY—

(Tony's head pops up, Vivian's panties in his teeth. He spits them out.)

OH GOD—THERE! THERE! YES, RIGHT THERE! DON'T STOP! NEVER! NEVER STOP! MAKE LOVE TO ME! YES! YES! YES! MAKE LOVE TO MEEEEE!!!

(Amy is enjoying this very much. Philip enters.)

PHILIP: VIVIAN!!

(Amy draws the curtain on Act I. We hear "Let's Misbehave.")

ETIQUETTE & VITRIOL

SCENE 1

As the audience returns, we hear "Do, Do, Do," recorded by Gertrude Lawrence. As the song ends, Amy opens the chiffon drape, revealing Claire's bedroom. Claire is alone, seated at her dressing table, adjusting her hair and makeup. She addresses the audience. For Claire, only a moment has passed since she left the stage in Act I.

CLAIRE: I have, for a long time, been a person who *tries* to see the best in others. I have, always, tried to see the beauty in all things. No matter how *grotesque*. And I find, more and more, I live in a grotesque world. Isn't everything ugly all of a sudden? I do not understand, I must admit, what passes for music in this age. But then, I force myself to remember that my mother did not understand my music, and I try to see the beauty in giving in, giving way, like a weeping willow bending gracefully in the inevitable face of gravity. *(She glances into the mirror and is momentarily sidetracked)*
     My mother was a sad woman to begin with, and then, when I was eight years old, she lost a baby. And her sadness became exaggerated to the point of farce.
     (Returning to her point) This morning, I went to the

dressmaker, to be fitted for a dress. I walked to the shop, It's not very far and I enjoy what's left of the fresh air. And I enjoy seeing people. Or I did. You see, more and more people seem to feel it all right to behave anyway they choose. For instance, more and more people seem to be— How shall I put this?—*Spitting*. I do not approve of this. Sometimes they walk over to the curb and spit into the street, as if this were so much better than spitting in the middle of the pavement. It's not. And apparently plenty of people feel as I do and they spit right where they are. And not just men, but women too! With hairdos and skirts. Now, I want to see the beauty in all of this, but it's *very* hard. It is eight blocks from my door to the dressmaker's and I must've passed thirty-five people spitting in the first three. Is it something in the air? Is it a byproduct of auto exhaust that has everyone spitting so continually? Now, I am willing to blame an awful lot on the industrial revolution, but not this, this sudden spitting frenzy. No! *(She glances at her bed, and loses her train of thought)*

When my sister died in my mother's womb, my father buried his head in bottles and, I suspect, under the covers of strange beds.

(Returning) At any rate, after the third block of my walk, I started counting these people who committed what I considered were affronts against civilization. Have we learned nothing in the past five thousand years? Don't these *people*, these *spitters*, realize that we all have to live together, and I would no sooner want to see their *expectorations* as I would their *bowel movements*? You may think me silly, but I believe that all the wars and suffering and prejudice and hate come down to nothing more than an unwillingness to understand each other. If we would only allow each other the space of our dignity, we would save so much time and trouble, and the money that we spend on nuclear weapons could be given to the New York City Ballet, who really do lovely work, that no one could find fault with!

As I was saying, I started counting "spitters." And within the next three blocks, I counted thirteen more—well, actually I counted fourteen. But I allowed for one man who was also muttering to himself, and barking, from time to time, like a dog. I believe this man was suffering from, the once little-known, suddenly fashionable, disease called *"Tourette's syndrome."* I saw a story all about it on a television news magazine, and I was, therefore, in a position to be sympathetic. My aesthetic is not so rigid that it doesn't allow for legitimate illness. *I* have never been sick a day in my life— but when I was eighteen, my father developed cancer of the pancreas and died. And he left me a great deal of money.

I don't know why my mind keeps wandering back to my parents. It's not what I intended, because something happened this morning, and I'm trying to get to that. But my mind keeps wandering off in tangents. A dear friend of mine once told me I spoke in a *baroque* fashion. I've no idea what she meant, but I'm sure it wasn't a compliment. Oh well, I never liked her anyway!

Oh, I'll get to my point, the thing that happened. I will. But right now I can't help remembering my mother's face at my father's funeral. It was long. She had a long face. Like a Modigliani painting. I've *never* liked Modigliani, although I found the Off-Broadway play about him, several seasons back, mildly entertaining. Still, I thought Mother was lovely. She had more dimension than his paintings. And she moved. Slowly. She possessed the grace of a ballet dancer and the alacrity of a pachyderm—I'm using sarcasm to make a point. She was languid in an era when things considered beautiful actually were. Before minimalism creeped into our landscape, when we could see farther and were unhindered by the cataract of modernism. I seem to see her all the time as a ballet dancer, in a Degas painting. I've *always* liked Degas, and I feel badly that they never made a play about him. But Mother was lovely. And before "the baby," as we euphemistically referred to her miscarriage, she was melancholy, but serene. Her hands were white, and she never wore nail polish. Every year at Christmas she would tie bows on handmade presents, her fingers dancing 'round the ribbons. And she *worshipped* my father, who was enormous. He had to be six and a half feet tall, with feet as big as tennis rackets. He scared me, truth be told. He would be very quiet, but inside there was an anger, building up, building over something, it could be anything. And then all of a sudden he would explode! And fists went flying and plates and tempers.—But he never swore. Which is odd. And makes him seem, somehow, less masculine, in my mind. But after "the baby," things changed *drastically.*

Mother, whom I mentioned was laconic to begin with, became absolutely *inert.* I don't mean the days immediately following, which, of course, she spent in bed. But the days became weeks and she wouldn't budge. She *never* got out of bed of her own accord. After about three weeks, we, my father and I, foisted her into a sitting position and put a book in her lap. We tilted her head so she was in a position to read. But she didn't! I sat there and stared and stared, and her eyes never touched a word! I said to her, "Mother, why don't you read?"........ "I do not care to," she responded. Resolutely.

Oh. Well. If she didn't care to, she didn't care to. There was little arguing. So at day's end, we put the book on her nightstand and turned out her lamp. In the morning, we tried again. "Why don't you read, Mother? You might enjoy it." "I do not care to." Hmmm. After about a week of "the book game," I went with my father into her room. We tried to interest her in getting up, getting dressed. "I do not care to." This was a woman of definite likes and dislikes. But my father had decided this "bed-rest thing" had gone on long enough. Perhaps, being a woman himself and only recently having had an unborn baby die in his belly, he felt he was the best judge.—I'm using sarcasm to make a point. So, we lifted her out of bed. This was easy. He was

big. She was small. And he held her up, rather like a mari-
onette, while I dressed her. Now, I was eight, and naturally
jealous that I'd been replaced as the center of the house, so
I put her in a very ugly outfit! Plaid skirt, floral sweater, two
different earrings and so on. "We're going for a walk!" my
father informed her. And she responded—exactly right! "I
do not care to." But out we went and, flanked on either
side, she greeted the fresh air. We looked like Oscar Levant,
Fred Astaire, and a drug-ridden Nanette Fabray, three
strong in strides from *The Bandwagon*!

Now don't misunderstand me. She was not catatonic.
No. She was not a zombie. She just chose not to. From that
day on, she chose not to. We pretty much had to prop her up
all over the place. We'd stand her at the stove, and she'd cook
something—although her disinterest in the project usually
resulted in dinners of pudding and peas. Or my favorite:
Aspirin! She just reached up, into the cupboard and cooked
what she grabbed. *(She is really enjoying herself)*

Oh, we'd prop her up in front of the radio. We'd put a
vacuum in her hand and she's clean the same spot, over and
over again . . . until it was immaculate! At first, I didn't
mind at all. It was like having this huge doll that really did
wet herself. And I'd have my friends over after school to
play with her. But, before long, I grew bored . . . the way
children do. And as the years passed, my father came home
later and later, leaving her to me. And he never yelled anymore. And he never threw things.

By the time he died he seemed very sad. That was a terrible time, the time he died. I was eighteen.—Oh, I said that.
And although he left me ample money to have someone
take care of her, I didn't feel I could leave my mother.
Besides, I was still in high school, where I was considered
very pretty and everyone liked my stories. I was *always*
charming, even then. And in an era where chastity was
vogue, I was liberal with my favors. I was very popular with
any number of young men attending NYU and Columbia,

and even as far away as Princeton. It wasn't that I liked sex so much. Because I didn't. Then. I don't know. I was too giggly to really dictate what I wanted. And besides, that was unheard of then.

(With authority) Women today are very lucky that it's become fashionable to actually indicate to their bed partners the location of their clitoris—excuse me, EXCUSE ME, but it's true.

But I was never stupid. And I saw my peccadilloes as escape routes. Remember, I was still propping her up and picking her clothes and cooking for her, unless I was willing to dine on Ajax, which she took to incorporating into her recipes the way homemakers on a budget work with tuna.

The point is, I quickly became pregnant. I never took precautions, knowing little about them, and wouldn't if I'd known more. I didn't see a doctor. I didn't have to. I knew it. I could feel it. So, I spent the next week dating the seven candidates who might be my baby's father. A couple, I was sure, would softly hold my hand all the way to their Park Avenue doctors to have my ticket to freedom scraped from inside me. But Philip was, then, a gentle man. And I could tell when he looked at me that he adored me. Even if I couldn't tell when we made love. So the following week, I informed him that I was carrying his child, and true to form, he asked me to marry him.

Three months later, my mother, who'd really deserted me ten years earlier, deserted me finally. She died of a stroke in mid-afternoon. She should have been dressed. She could have been up and doing things. But, I assume . . . she did not care to. I thought of leaving Philip, since I'd married him to escape my life, which now escaped me. But I was pregnant and he was wealthy and solicitous. In time, I had Philip, whom I loved. And Amy, whom I did not. I don't know why. Perhaps it's because she's such a graceful and delicate flower—I use sarcasm to illustrate myself.

Children are an odd phenomenon, don't you find? I

have to say, I've never really understood them. It seems so irrational to me. You create something. You carry something around, inside of you, for what seems an eternity, and then you are delivered a person. A stranger. And you can tell me otherwise, but from the minute we're born, we are people. My children had likes and dislikes from day one. Philip adored music and art and emulated me. While Amy, on the other hand, turned her nose up at my breast and never really came around!

(Lecturing) I see young mothers in the park walking their children, like poodles on leashes. I am aghast! They treat their children as if they were objects. I claim no expertise *BUT* it has been my experience that children are not dogs. Were they dogs, I'm afraid, I'd've been tempted to put Amy to sleep several times by now. I don't mean to be hard about Amy. I'm sure she has many fine qualities—which are not apparent to me. All people have goodness inside of them! Only some people have very little, and it's *very, very, very* deep down. And she is a stranger! That's what it comes down to. I know she came from me, but she's not part of— oh, God. I must sound awful. But it's true. My feet are part of me. My hands are part of me. My children are people I know. I do love them. Don't mistake my objectivity for indifference. I love my children very much. I just see that they are *other* people. And, if you ask me, we'd have a great deal less crime and drug addiction if mothers and fathers realized their children are not their pets. And this understanding would lead to happier children, healthier adults, less crime, lower taxes, a thriving economy, prettier architecture, less television, more theatre, less litigation, more understanding, less alienation, more love, less hate and a calmer humanity who felt less of a need to spit all the time in public!! Because that's what it is, really. All this spitting in public, is just a thinly veiled hostility for ME, MY TASTE, MY AESTHETIC AND THE COMMON CONSENSUS OF WHAT IS GENERALLY CONSIDERED

SOCIALLY ACCEPTABLE!!—AND ISN'T IT WONDER-
FUL HOW I HAVE COME FULL CIRCLE, AND CAN
NOW CONTINUE WITH MY STORY IN A NATURAL,
LOGICAL FASHION!!

Everything goes in circles really. Except things that go
in straight lines. Hmmm. I was counting spitters, vile,
angry, lost souls who felt impotent to change their lives in
view of what they think is fate. Well, after about a hundred
of these spitting villains, I could take no more. I was in a
rage! What has happened to my lovely city! What has happened to it? The buildings are suddenly eyesores. There are
placards everywhere, for so-called bands I've never heard
of with fascist-sounding names and illustrations of women
so wanton as to degrade women everywhere.

Finally, I could take no more. So I started following this
one young woman, who looked reasonably sane—except
for the fact that she was wearing a tweed skirt with sneak-
ers, but I allowed for a foot condition. She had on a blazer.
Her light brown hair was piled high on her head with a tor-
toise clip. She looked fine. She looked normal. I thought to
myself, "I will just stare at this young woman. I will not
look to her right. I will not look to her left. I will see only
her. And I will convince myself that I am surrounded by
similarly sane young women. I won't look, so I'll assume
everyone around me is just as polite and normal as she. . . ."
And it was working. I had myself believing it. Everything
was lovely . . . and then she *veered* over to the curb. *(A real
panic builds inside of her)* I said a silent prayer. This woman
had become, to me, a symbol: the last great kindness in a
once kind world. My breathing changed. I felt my hands
grow tense and saw my knuckles whiten in my clenched
fists. She walked along the curb for a few feet. I thought,
"Thank you, God, thank you. She's just walking along the
curb. She's a little erratic, but she's not one of them, she's
one of us!" And then slowly, it seemed as if everything was
in slow motion . . . she *leaned* over. I hoped, I prayed she

was going to faint! I hoped she was ill and going to die! "Let her die a martyr to beauty, but please God, *please*, don't let her spit! Let her fall over, into the street, into the traffic, let her be canonized the patron saint of civilization, but PLEASE GOD, don't let her spit!" And she made a small coughing noise. "She's coughing—you're coughing—she's coughing—aren't you?—please don't be clearing your throat—just be coughing!" If I shut my eyes, I'll miss whatever happens and I can pretend that nothing happened and I can go on, continue to live and hope! But they would not close! I couldn't shut them! I wanted to! I tried to! But I couldn't! I was hypnotized! I just stared and stared and the seconds became hours and the hours weeks and the weeks millennia! And then it happened!!!

SHE SPIT!!!

And the world went black and the sun fell out of the sky, burning the earth and sending the buildings tumbling, bricks flying, people crushed in the rain of debris and humanity, which had only recently learned to walk, was SMASHED into oblivion for all time!! "WHAT'S WRONG WITH YOU!?" I found my hand on her sleeve. "Don't you understand what you've done?!" She spun around with such a look of utter horror and disgust on her face that I was only spurred to continue—"The world is decomposing! Humanity is rotting away! We're reverting to the behavior of apes and YOU'RE TO BLAME!" "Let go of me!!" She shouted, very loudly, much more loudly than was called for. "I had to spit. What's it to you?!" And with that she shoved me, hard, and I fell onto the pavement.

All I could think about was how sad, how sorry, I was, that I'd chosen badly, chosen someone who didn't care, couldn't be convinced, didn't see that we are all just withering, dying, crumbling in on ourselves. . . . I looked around from my *position* on the sidewalk and I was the center of quite a crowd. And I thought, "Oh no. I'm sitting in it. She's gone, and I am sitting in her *expectoration*!"

(Sad and shaken) And. Then. I shut my eyes and I hurried to the dressmaker. I was late of course and she was already on her next client, my old friend, Phoebe Potter. We were girls in school together. She looked so old, and I was so distraught from my experience that I mistook her for a mirror. It broke me completely, to see myself in her eyes and the folds of her flesh. "I'll come back tomorrow." "No, no. Mrs. Potter's almost finished." And so I waited. . . . And, soon, it was my turn.

I looked into the mirror as I was pinned. And, I was me again. I was shaken, but I was myself. I heard music in my head while she worked. And. As soon as I could, I rushed home. To Tony.

(Quite still, forgetting herself) I did not speak. I unbuttoned his shirt and he wrapped his arms around my waist, mumbling something into my ear, which I couldn't or didn't understand. Didn't care. And I filled up the palms of my hands with his shoulders. He pulled my blouse from my skirt in the back and I pressed my hips against his genitals and felt his erection, under his jeans. I kicked off my shoes and unbuttoned his pants, holding him, hardened, in my right hand and pulling his hair with my left, while he penetrated my mouth with his tongue. He unbuttoned my blouse down the back and pulled it off, lowering himself to take my nipples in his mouth, while I stroked his eyelids with my fingertips. How late in life I came to understand sex, how much time I wasted. He unfastened my skirt and it fell to the ground. I bent over and licked his ears and the back of his neck. He licked my thighs and in between. And I led him to my bed. My baby. My baby boy. And he stood over me, making me want him, and understanding that I wanted to be made to want. And we made love with the violent passion of children and animals ripping at each other, biting and hurting beautifully. . . . And from my bed, the window views the river and the city beyond, and as he held me, as I had him, I became a child again, the years drip-

ping away and falling off of me, until I was a girl. And the river flowed and the city on the other side changed from what it is to what it was: the sharp angry teeth of the buildings, the glass angles and steel knives became rounded. Until he finished. And I finished. And I threw my head back and the sun was setting on a city of the past, where everything was beautiful, and we were children, and more . . . easily pleased.

(She looks around and realizes that she has exposed more than she intended)

So you see, sex, it seems, is very important, when it comes to seeing the beauty of things.

(She crosses to her dressing table, and slowly lets her hair down. Amy closes the chiffon drape quickly. Suddenly light comes up behind the drape and Tony and Vivian are there, as if by magic. Claire is seated, oblivious to their presence, looking into her mirror. Tony and Vivian are dressed in full evening clothes. We hear "The Physician," recorded by Gertrude Lawrence. As the song plays, Tony and Vivian do a dance that begins in traditional ballroom style, but changes rather quickly. The dance becomes a series of movements, rife with double entendres. As the song ends, Amy pulls around a burlap curtain. The new curtain is dirty, distressed, covered with blood and grime. There are words on the curtain: "Sex, Work, Girls, Men, God." The words appear to have been written in blood.)

SCENE 2

Philip emerges abruptly from a tear in the burlap curtain. He walks to a pool of light and addresses the audience.

PHILIP: Sex. Philip and Sex:

What a preponderance of time I spend, we spend, everyone spends, dwelling on, pursuing, planning, regretting, thinking about, and avoiding the subject of Sex. I don't know if preponderance was the right word, but you know what I mean, I hope.

I have a sick feeling in my stomach. I don't remember *when* I ate last, so naturally, I don't remember *what* I ate last, but it has upset my stomach—I think. I'm sure it was spoiled. It was probably some bad fish. I hate fish. I would never've eaten fish. You know what I mean. Pressed fish. Processed fish. And now I have botulism! I don't think that's the right word. You get that from canned goods. No one cans fish. Hell, you know what I mean. Trichinosis! No, God, that's something you get from undercooked pork. I may have eaten pork last, but if I did I didn't get trichinosis, I got—food poisoning! That's it, food poisoning! Oh the hell with it!

Philip and Sex:

Although I have tried to make sex less and less important in my life, which implies that it was at some point *im*portant, which really isn't accurate—but you know, the pursuit of it was important. That was my point. I have systematically tried to make the pursuit of sex, the planning and flirting, the buying of equipment, etc. etc., less important in my life.

I don't find my sex organs particularly attractive. I don't mean that. I mean, I don't find my sex organs particularly attractive. That's the same thing, isn't it? Let me clarify—oh hell! I don't think mine are any less attractive than anybody else's. I don't think my penis is any uglier than yours, say, or yours. But then, I'm assuming a lot, because I haven't seen your penis. But then you haven't seen mine. And let me tell you right now, you're not going to! And not because I think it's any uglier than anybody else's, but just because I *don't want to*! So, my point is: sex parts are ugly. Which, of course raises the invariable question, what is ugly and what is beautiful? We are all trained to see certain things as beautiful and other things as ugly, or less so. I haven't decided whether this is entirely environmental or whether genetics has a hand in it. But the pictures in *National Geographic* of women with long, pendulous breasts and disks, like garbage can lids, implanted into their lips, leads me to the conclusion that it is largely environmental conditioning. (I don't know if conditioning was the right way to end that sentence, but it was long and I lost the thread—DON'T JUDGE ME!)

Anyway, we are all trained that certain lines are attractive, angles, pleasing to the eye, cleanness of line and so forth. Anyone who's studied design or the Munsell color wheel knows what I'm talking about. And let's face it. *The scrotum* really falls through the cracks of what is generally considered attractive. Is it me, or does the scrotum look like you've been in the bathtub a long time before you even get in? Wrinkled and soggy. I know it's not me, so don't try to make me feel bad, I feel bad enough already. I have a terrible stomachache from fish or pork or something.

And I don't think women have it any better! What? Is the vagina such an oil painting? Apologies to Georgia O'Keeffe, but it's no Mona Lisa, which I realize is a mixed metaphor, I think. But they're not pretty. Although my penis has, from time to time, been my friend. It has, more often, not. It has been my enemy. Oh hell! That may be too strong. . . . I used to love to sit on the edge of my bed, naked, holding the head of my penis between my thumb and index finger, squeezing the hole on the end so it opened and closed, while I threw my voice and carried on a conversation. . . . YOU HAVE NO BUSINESS JUDGING ME! Everyone has done that! Haven't they? . . . Well, everyone with an imagination.

(He has a twinge of pain in his stomach) I have a sharp, twisting pain in my stomach, like I've eaten a lizard, or something alive, hot and thrashing around.

I thought, for a brief time—well, what's a brief time?

Everything is relative. More than an afternoon and less than a decade. Once! I thought once, that I was a homosexual, but I'll get into the specifics of that later. Oh, don't worry, there'll be nothing graphic. No slides or anything. Although some of you would like that, wouldn't you? I know what kind of people you are! You get pleasure from the pain and suffering of others! But then who doesn't really? Isn't it more or less human nature—or is it nurture!? I tell myself continue. I thought I was a homosexual. I was not comfortable with the image of myself as a homosexual. I was not comfortable with myself as a man. Or a woman. Or a human being. Or a plant or a tree or a doorstop or a lump of disemboweled protoplasm! Oh hell, you get my point!! I was tortured! Nature? Nurture? Or just a bad case of botulism, or trichinosis, or that parasite you get from undercooked pork—that microbe. What's it called?

(A second pool of light comes up. He moves into it.)

Philip and Girls:
    When I was thirteen years old—WHICH WAS SEVEN YEARS AGO, FOR THOSE OF YOU WHO'VE NAPPED AND LOST THE THREAD! You know who you are!— When I was thirteen, I had my first sexual experience. I don't mean I had sex. I had my first sexual experience. I KNOW! That's the same thing. I mean, I had an experience of a sexual nature with another person, which is more than a lot of people ever have. I didn't penetrate or anything. I didn't actually ejaculate at the time. Don't get me wrong, I'd been ejaculating for some time. I mean, from time to time over a period of time, I don't mean like one long stream of semen all afternoon. I mean—Oh you see what I mean!! I was thirteen and I was invited to a friend's house. A girl. I'll call this girl Cathy. I remember her last name, but I'm not going to use it. I don't want to. Not that I think she's

here or anything, she's probably dead by now. What a terrible thing to say. I must have a wealth of repressed hostility for this Cathy character. Anyway, I'm still not going to tell you her last name, because one of you might know her and you might tell her about this, that she's being discussed. And then, she might come here and try to shoot me. Who knows what kind of depravity she's lapsed into in the last seven years. I have to protect myself!! I think I'll call her Mona. Oh, I already said her name was Cathy—HELL! She invited me to a party. There were lots of little boys and girls at this party. And Mona had, I assume, a crush on me. Or else, she was insane with a persecution complex and she was punishing herself by leading me to the bathroom, where she turned off the lights and "did things" to me.

And she was not a pretty girl. I realize that's sexist, but fuck it. Mona had these big, buck teeth. Now everything is relative, but these teeth were big and buck compared to just about everything else on the planet today—or then. Big teeth! Like Mr. Ed, whom at thirteen, I found amusing, but not attractive, and certainly not the object of any sexual desire. NO ALAN STRANG AM I! And she had hair the color of Chinese noodles: no color. And she wore this transparent hair pulled back into a transparent ponytail. And you just knew she was five years away from a transparent bun. Am I being cruel? I think I'm being accurate. Were you there? I was! This is how it happened. She turned off the lights. I was unbelievably grateful. Once I could no longer see her, I responded to the *actual, literal, physical* stimulation, instead of the specific person in front of me. She kissed me. . . . I kissed her back. We didn't actually kiss each other. It was like tennis. That's odd. But you know what I mean, don't you? I hope so. And then it happened.

I got this big hard-on. And Cathy—I mean Mona!—felt it against her leg, reached down to touch it and let out a yelp like I had a hermit crab down there that'd just ripped off her fingers! She burst out of the room, ran into the party, screaming and carrying on and telling everyone about my *"boner"* and I just wanted to die right then and there. So. I shut the door and sealed myself up in the bathroom, in the darkness, wishing that there was a window for escape, or that everyone at the party would just die spontaneously!

So I masturbated. Then I dried myself of with toilet paper. When I turned on the light, I noticed I had this big *wet spot* on my pants and I knew I couldn't go out there until it dried. That's happened to everyone, hasn't it? . . . Well? So, I sat on the toilet. Waiting. Feeling very ashamed and embarrassed. I don't know why. Nature or nurture? Tidy huh?

(He has a sharp twinge in his stomach) The pain in my stomach has evolved from a piercing to a throbbing, like there's an orchestra, tuning up.

(A third pool of light comes up. He moves, reluctantly, into it.)

Philip and Men:

Last year, I was living in London, in Camden, where the *young people* live. Very *now*. You know. I was supposedly there studying music composition at the Royal Academy, where everyone has "hairdos." But I'd been there about six months and I'd stopped going to my classes completely— DON'T JUDGE ME!! I have terrible insomnia a lot of the time. I was working at the Mrs. Field's Cookie Store on Leicester Square. I figured, if I wasn't sleeping, I might as well be working. And although I am obviously much too intelligent to be shoveling cookies—WELL I AM!—it's hard for Americans to get work over there. So I was working late nights at the cookie store and sleeping during the day, or going to the movies. And mostly the people I was waiting on were creepy tourists: a lot of Germans, or Americans who just embarrassed me when I opened my mouth. So I didn't. I kept my eyes on my cookies.

And then, one night, at about eleven, I made the goddamn, awful mistake of looking up. And just about everything changed from then on. I saw, on the other side of the glass cookie counter, a person, a man, a boy. A human being.

(He fights emotion) He was obviously insane. He was very beautiful. But not in any stupid magazine kind of way, not that anyone else would think so. Not like that. He was tall and he had big hands and sandy brown hair, like everyone over there. And I didn't really notice his body, or what he was wearing. It was his face. It was round—I don't mean it was fat!—It was gentle. There was a gentleness to it. I'd never seen anyone like him. It was the angle of his chin and the fullness of his lips. And his eyes. I can't describe them, except that he was wearing eyeliner—although he wasn't effeminate! He wasn't a faggot! He was just wearing eyeliner! And I knew when I looked into them, that this person, this obviously insane person, this man, boy, lunatic, gentle thing, lost soul was half of me. And I knew it at once.

And we spoke! And I could tell I was right, he was insane and completely lost. When I say we spoke, I don't mean we had any goddamn long personal conversation. I mean we spoke. I asked him what he wanted and he told me and I didn't hear him and I gave it to him and he left. I watched him leave. I watched him disappear into the crowd of normal heads. I watched him disappear. And I went home that night and thought about this nameless, gentle lunatic . . . and . . . I . . . masturbated.

I DID TRY NOT TO THINK OF HIM!!! I TRIED NOT TO!! But it was out of my hands, beyond my control. I don't mean that night, or any night. I mean the days that followed. I tried to think of other things! I tried to do things! But everywhere I went, I looked for HIM! Around every corner and in every crowd! Every night at the store, I waited! I waited and waited and waited! And every time someone approached my heart jumped into my throat! Every customer was a possibility, every passerby a could-be! And they'd walk through the door and be some vulgar

American, or bloated Swede, AND IT WAS NEVER HIM! And the days became weeks and it was never him! And I tried with all my might to think other thoughts BUT I COULD NOT! I tried counting and reciting and thinking music and color and art, BUT I COULD NOT! DO YOU UNDERSTAND!? DO YOU? And when, for a moment, I'd accomplish it, my mind would lapse into some other thought, some more pressing need, I'd relax my efforts for a minute—AND THAT WAS IT!

Then. One night, a cold night, three weeks after the first night, he came in! *(He is quite out of control now)* He walked through the door! I couldn't breathe. I couldn't think. I studied him. I stared at him. I memorized him. I had to ALWAYS remember what he looked like, what he was! And he was just the same! He was me! He was a part of me! And I know it sounds nuts—I KNOW IT, ALL RIGHT?— But this is how it was! And while he was there it seemed like hours and after he left it was just a few seconds. But I managed to make friendly little conversation. Just friendly! Nothing more. Couldn't let him know, couldn't let him see, how important he'd become to me! He hadn't been in for weeks. I was nothing to him! Couldn't let him guess! He'd think I was insane, which I knew he was, and I was at this point, completely! I KNOW IT! BUT I WAS BEYOND MYSELF! I WAS OUT OF CONTROL! COULDN'T TELL MY MIND WHAT TO THINK! WHAT TO FEEL! IT HAD A MIND OF ITS OWN AND I WAS ITS VICTIM COMPLETELY! I KNOW IT!

—But I controlled myself, I did. I did. I did. . . . "How are you? How've you been? Where do you work?" . . . And his deep voice stoked mine, not with words, which I'd worry about later, but with sound and breath and music. . . . And he was gone. He worked in one of those Angus Steak Houses that are everywhere in London.

The next day, the next night—mind you I knew this was bad, I knew I was in the throes of something—the next night I didn't go to work. Didn't care. I was obviously better than selling cookies anyway. I went there! I went to his restaurant. I didn't go in! I couldn't! People kept passing me, looking at me. This was a busy street and people kept bumping into me and the fat morons eating dinner could see me! They could see me looking at them! FUCK THEM!! I was waiting for a friend! And I waited! And I waited! And I still couldn't find him! And I was freezing cold, but I simply could not leave—DO YOU UNDERSTAND? WHERE WAS HE! Was he lying to me? Maybe he could tell I was insane and he lied to me to get away—just said the first thing that came into his head and he didn't work in a restaurant and he could tell I was insane all along!

Then I saw him! He was there! He didn't lie! HE WAS THERE! Same person, boy, child, man, woman, smudged eyes. Same person. He came out the front door. I wanted to run up to him! I wanted to. I couldn't. I followed him. I walked behind, about fifteen feet. I didn't know where I was going. The streets are old and curve in on themselves and I was lost. And it was cold and snowing now, and I was sneezing and shivering and suddenly *very* tired, BUT I KEPT GOING!! We were headed downtown, down to Fleet Street, the financial district. Very deserted. Very quiet. No cars. I thought I would faint, or die. I didn't know what time it was. The street lights are far apart and even though the snow reflected in them, it was very dark. And I was sure I would die, lost in the financial district, alone in the snow. And so I ran ahead!! I ran ahead! I ran forward and called out "HEY!! HEY!!"

(Pause)

And he turned around. . . . He turned around and looked at me. And I knew, he knew who I was.

(Pause)

It was very quiet, and very still. There was nothing. The snow made our breath echo. There were no cars. We were in the snow, by a building they were building.

He asked what I was doing down there. I was out for a walk, enjoying the snow—can't let him know. He said he lived nearby. . . . "Oh." Hours passed between our words.

"I was wondering, I was curious, I was thinking. I was wondering would you like, would you care to, maybe sometime, some night after work, sometime when you're free, would you like to have a drink, have a drink, join me for a drink?"

"What?"

And I explained that I didn't mean anything, that I wasn't gay, but I wasn't bothered if he was, because, I said, hearing myself not hearing myself, I found him very attractive, which was absurd and really not the point.

(Remorseful, still) And he explained, that he lived with a man. And a woman. That they had an understanding. And that. He didn't think it was a good idea. And that. Etc. Etc. . . . etc. His words just filled up the space and I said I had to go . . . because I couldn't think of anything else to say. And he turned around . . . *AND I DID NOT PLAN IT!! THERE WAS NO PLAN!!*—He turned around, and I picked up a brick, from the building they were building, and as he stepped away from me, I threw it. I threw it with all my might. I threw it at him. I think it hit his head, although he didn't make a sound, when it hit him. Or when he fell, into the snow, which was quiet and white and very pretty. And I ran in the other direction and continued running, until I came to a tube station . . . where I stayed until morning.

(After a moment, more composed) I'm sure he was fine. I'm sure he didn't die or anything. And no one ever came around to ask me about it: the police or anything. And I never saw anything about it. On the news or anything. So I'm sure he was fine.

(After a moment, completely composed) I met Vivian about two weeks later. When I had long forgotten about that night. And the person whose name I never did learn.

(He has a severe twinge in his stomach) I CAN WILL

THIS PAIN IN MY STOMACH TO LEAVE ME! I CAN
DO THIS! AND I CHOOSE TO!!

*(He spins around abruptly and rips the burlap curtain
down, revealing Claire's bedroom. Claire is seated at her
vanity. Amy is seated in the shadows, with a liquor bottle.)*

SCENE 3

*Immediately following Scene 2. The scene is as described.
Claire is gaily finishing her makeup. Amy lurks in the shadows. Philip is where he was. As the scene begins, Claire
maintains her Act I "style." Philip is agitated, progressing
naturally from the last scene.*

PHILIP: Mother.

CLAIRE: Oh, Philip, I didn't see you come in. I can't talk right
now. I have to fix myself. By the way, is that what you're
wearing? Not that I don't like it. I do. It's cunning. But,
don't you think, a little dreary? Black, black, black?

PHILIP: What difference does it make?

CLAIRE: It makes *all* the difference. We must always look our
best. We are what we wear. Besides, we're going to dinner,
not a state funeral.

PHILIP: I'm not going.

CLAIRE *(Modeling)*: Do you like these earrings? Or something
simpler?

PHILIP: Listen to me!

CLAIRE: Oh, I'm sorry. What is it?

PHILIP: Vivian's gone!

CLAIRE: Gone? Gone where? Where does she live? Is she missing? Should we search? Have a hunt?

PHILIP: I mean she's gone!

CLAIRE: That's the same thing. Don't be cryptic.

AMY *(Stepping forward)*: He means for good.

CLAIRE: Amy, what are you doing?

AMY: Helping.

PHILIP: I threw her out!

CLAIRE: Oh no.

AMY: They've broken up.

CLAIRE *(To Amy)*: I understand.

PHILIP: I want to die!

CLAIRE: Don't even say that.

PHILIP: I loved her!

CLAIRE: I know you think so.

AMY: She was awful.

PHILIP *(To Amy)*: You didn't know her!

AMY: Well, she was.

CLAIRE *(To Amy)*: Go to your room.

AMY: No.

PHILIP: I loved her!

CLAIRE: We think so. We always do. We think we're Edison dis-
covering love. But we learn too soon.

AMY: It's for the best.

CLAIRE: I never liked her.

AMY: She was wretched.

CLAIRE: She had dubious posture.

PHILIP: She was beautiful!

CLAIRE: She wasn't right for you.

PHILIP: Can't you see? I was in love!

AMY *(To herself)*: So was I.

CLAIRE: She's better forgotten. Now, you must come out with
Tony and me tonight. I insist on it. You can't mope about
the house, wallowing in pity. It won't do. Now go change.
Go, go, go, go. We'll all have a marvelous time!

PHILIP: I'm not going out with you—

CLAIRE: Trust me.

PHILIP: You're to blame! It's your fault it happened!

CLAIRE: What are you talking about?

PHILIP: You brought him here!

AMY: He didn't belong.

PHILIP: He ruined everything!

AMY: We're a family.

CLAIRE: What happened?

AMY: Tony was here.

PHILIP: And I walked in!

CLAIRE *(To Amy)*: Send him up.

AMY: I can't.

PHILIP: I threw him out.

CLAIRE: What!?

AMY: Thank God.

CLAIRE: Why!?

PHILIP: I saw them together!

CLAIRE: Who?!

AMY: Tony and Vivian.

PHILIP *(To Amy)*: Don't interrupt—

CLAIRE: This doesn't concern you!

PHILIP: It's none of your business!

CLAIRE: Go to your room!

AMY: Leave me alone!

PHILIP: I caught them together and it was disgusting! He was on top of her! He was inside of her!

CLAIRE: STOP IT! I don't know what you're talking about—you must be—

PHILIP: I saw them!

AMY: So did I!

PHILIP: And I threw them out!

AMY: He did.

CLAIRE *(To Amy)*: I SENT YOU TO YOUR ROOM, GO TO YOUR ROOM!

AMY: NO!

PHILIP: My fiancée and your lover! Rolling around on the floor, filthy and fucking like dogs! I got rid of them!

CLAIRE *(Deadly)*: You had no right.

PHILIP: You're my mother!

CLAIRE *(Composure snapping)*: AND YOU SHOULD MIND YOUR OWN GODDAMN BUSINESS! HOW DARE YOU INTERFERE!—WHEN DID HE LEAVE?

PHILIP: He didn't love you.

CLAIRE: What would you know about it? There are different kinds of relationships! How could you do this to me?

PHILIP: What's wrong with you?

CLAIRE: Who are you to judge me? WHAT DO YOU KNOW ABOUT ME? I need him. Is that simple enough? BASIC enough? I need him holding me and listening to me and looking at me—GOD! Don't let me cry. I don't want to cry.

PHILIP: Oh my God.

CLAIRE: I'll call him. And he'll come back, and we'll make love like we did this morning and last night and the night before and the night before, beautifully and ruthlessly, like nothing ever happened. And we'll go on, because nothing ever happened. DO YOU HEAR ME?!

PHILIP *(Overlapping)*: Oh my God. Oh God. You don't care. You just don't care . . . at all.

AMY *(Overlapping Claire)*: You see?

PHILIP: BUT IT DID! You can pretend all you want! Pretend Tony loves you!!

CLAIRE: He does!

PHILIP: NEVER!

CLAIRE: THEN SO WHAT!? SO WHAT IF HE DOESN'T OR NEVER REALLY DID OR NEVER REALLY WILL? SO WHAT?! WHAT DIFFERENCE COULD THAT POSSIBLY MAKE!?

PHILIP: Pretend you love me! BUT THAT DOESN'T MAKE IT SO!! IT! DOES! NOT!

CLAIRE: You're insane!

PHILIP *(Wildly, happily)*: How else could I live? You mean you couldn't tell? My LOVING mother? My DEVOTED mother?! My doting, CHARMING mother!? Couldn't you tell that I'm sick? Couldn't you tell that I'm crazy? THAT I CAN'T FEEL A SINGLE FUCKING THING? DIDN'T YOU NOTICE? COULDN'T YOU TELL? MY PERFECT, MY FUCKING, MY BEAUTIFUL MOTHER! NOW YOU

CAN HATE ME FOR THIS! *(Spent, he falls onto the bed and withdraws from the scene, into himself)*

CLAIRE: Oh my God.

PHILIP *(Random, overlapping)*: You can hate me. You can hate me for this.

CLAIRE: It's all right, Philip. I'll go to him. I'll fix everything.

AMY: I did it.

CLAIRE *(After a moment)*: I cannot say that I'm surprised.

AMY: I told him the truth.

PHILIP *(Continuing, random)*: I'm sorry, I'm sorry, I'm sorry for whatever I did.

AMY: I told him about the boys before him.

CLAIRE: I see.

PHILIP: I'm sorry I remind you you're not eighteen.

AMY: And the boys after him.

PHILIP: I'm not what you want me to be.

AMY: I made him see he wasn't using you, you were using him. I made him hate you.

CLAIRE: Why?

AMY: I had to save Philip.

CLAIRE: At my expense?

AMY: I wanted to.

(Amy and Claire look at each other for a moment. Then Claire can take it no longer.)

CLAIRE: I've got to go. I've got to find him.

AMY: I know.

(Claire exits.)

PHILIP *(After a moment)*: Mother?

(Amy sits at Claire's vanity. There is a pause. Before she speaks, Amy dusts herself with Claire's powder and straightens her posture.)

AMY: Yes?
PHILIP: I didn't mean to do anything wrong.
AMY: I know.
PHILIP: Are you mad at me?
AMY: No. I love you.
PHILIP: I hate her.
AMY: Who?
PHILIP: Vivian.
AMY: Don't. It's not her fault. I learned, just recently, there is no happiness to be had.
PHILIP: I hate her.
AMY: We're alone. All alone. All of the time. It's our nature.
PHILIP: No.
AMY: We're alone and frightened and there's nothing we can do about it but cease existing and forget. We can take someone to our beds and pretend we love them. Or not bother. We can hold them against ourselves, feel their skin against ours, smell them and taste them, and for a minute or two, we can forget, that we are, afterwards and always, alone.
PHILIP *(Simply)*: I can't.
AMY *(Going to him)*: Try.

(She turns his head toward hers. He sees her for the first time.)

PHILIP: Amy?
AMY: Try.

(She holds him. They embrace. At first it is tentative. Then it becomes mutual and passionate. After a moment, he takes command: they lunge abruptly into a romantic embrace identical to that of Tony and Claire in Act I. As they kiss, we hear "Love Is Good for Anything That Ails You." The lights fade out.)

END OF PLAY

FAT MEN IN SKIRTS

Fat Men in Skirts was first presented by the Vortex Theater Company (Robert Coles, Artistic Director) in New York City under the author's direction in 1988. The lighting design was by Mark Andrew; the costume design was by Susan B., the production was stage managed by Lizze Fitzgerald. The cast was as follows:

PHYLLIS HOGAN	Stephanie Correa
BISHOP HOGAN	Chuck Coggins
HOWARD HOGAN/DR.NESTOR	Bill Christ
PAM/POPO	Debra Riessen

In 1991, the play was produced at the Woolly Mammoth Theatre in Washington D.C. (Howard Shalwitz, Artistic Director; Nancy Turner Hensley, Producing Associate). It was directed by Howard Shalwitz and Lee Mikeska Gardner; the set design was by Keith Belli; the costume design was by Helen Qizhi Huang; the lighting design was by Christopher Townsend; the sound design was by Daniel Schrader; the production stage manager was Scott Hammar. The cast was as follows:

PHYLLIS HOGAN	Nancy Robinette
BISHOP HOGAN	Rob Leo Roy
HOWARD HOGAN/DR.NESTOR	Grover Gardner
PAM/POPO	Desiree Marie

CHARACTERS

PHYLLIS HOGAN, An attractive,
sophisticated woman in her 40s at the play's opening.

BISHOP HOGAN, Her son.

HOWARD HOGAN, Her husband.

PAM, A young woman.

DR. NESTOR, A psychiatrist,
played by the same actor as Howard.

POPO MARTIN, A very cheery mental patient.
Played by the same actor as Pam.

TIME AND PLACE

ACT I
Five years on a desert island and various locations.

ACT II
The Hogan apartment, New York City.

ACT III
A hospital for the criminally insane. One year later.

ACT I

*In the darkness we hear Bobby Darrin's recording of
"Beyond the Sea." The lights come up on a beach. There is
no foliage, perhaps a lone palm tree. Phyllis Hogan is standing center, with her back to us. She is emptying her shoes of
sand. She is clearly overdressed for a day at the beach. She
turns and addresses the audience.*

PHYLLIS: I loathe the beach. I am Phyllis Hogan and I do so
loathe the beach. To me, it is the very definition of monot-
ony. Just sand and water and sand and water. And more
sand and more water. Ick. And look, a perfectly good pair
of shoes, Susan Bennis/Warren Edwards, crocodile, and
completely ruined! I have never understood the appeal of
the seashore: sand in your stockings and young girls with
better bodies in skimpy swimsuits. When I was a girl I used
to bury myself in the sand. Head first.

I've no idea where I am. I was supposed to be in Italy by
now, but I've been to Italy, and I always gain weight in Italy,
so here I am at the beach. My husband is in Italy, gaining
weight no doubt, gorging himself on the local delicacies and
the local girls—and perhaps, thinking, only fleetingly, "What
could have become of Phyllis?" He's scouting locations for a
new film. Something heartwarming about extraterrestrials.

I assume. My husband is a filmmaker. He was a director in the seventies, now he's a filmmaker. He makes heartwarming films about lovable extraterrestrials, mostly.

My plane crashed. It's a miracle that I'm alive. I suppose. There were eight of us on the plane, including the pilot. Only Bishop and I survived. Of course one died of a heart attack during the in-flight movie. It featured Tatum O'Neal. I can't say I was frightened when the plane went down—the film was beastly. I just watched the ground getting closer and closer, spinning around outside my window like a top. I just shut my eyes and waited for it to happen: the bang, the crash, the end. And knowing my life was over was kind of a relief in a funny way. The chore of my life was over and I could just relax and wait and see. . . . But then I opened my eyes and now a perfectly good pair of shoes is down the drain. Damn. You should meet Bishop. Bishop! He's my son. I sent him to go through the pockets of the others. I only have two packs of cigarettes with me and there's no telling how long it'll be before they find us. That was an hour ago.

BISHOP! I'll go mad if I don't have some cigarettes.

(Bishop enters from over a dune. He is 11. He's wearing a prep-school uniform. His posture is terrible, hunched over and pigeon-toed. He speaks with a stutter.)

BISHOP: Yes, M-m-other?
PHYLLIS: What've you been doing?
BISHOP: What did you t-t-tell me t-to do?
PHYLLIS: I told you to go through their pockets for cigarettes.
BISHOP: Well, that's what I've been d-d-doing.
PHYLLIS: And?
BISHOP: Two cigars.

(He offers her two cigars which she takes and puts in her flight bag.)

PHYLLIS: Thank you. *(Out)* You never know.

BISHOP: M-m-mother?

PHYLLIS: You needn't address me as "Mother," Bishop. There's no one else alive.

BISHOP: Oh.

PHYLLIS: Well, what is it?

BISHOP: M-m-mother?

PHYLLIS *(Irritated)*: Yes?

BISHOP: I'm f-f-fr—scared.

PHYLLIS: Of what? We've already crashed.

BISHOP: What will happen t-t-to us?

PHYLLIS: Someone will find us.

BISHOP: B-b-but—

PHYLLIS: Don't be gloomy. It isn't becoming on little boys.

BISHOP: B-b-but—

PHYLLIS: If we'd made it to Italy, you'd be fat by now.

BISHOP *(Out)*: Katharine Hepburn made a movie in Italy. *S-s-summertime.* With Rossano B-b-brazzi. It was ad-d-dapted from *The Time of the Cuckoo,* by Arthur Laurents, and later turned into the m-m-musical, *Do I Hear a Waltz?* While f-f-filming on the canals of Venice, which are sewers, she fell in and got an eye in-f-fection which caused her to tear all the t-t-time after that.

PHYLLIS: Very good, Bishop. Bishop is obsessed with Katharine Hepburn. Stand up straight.

BISHOP *(Out)*: K-k-katharine Hepburn was born November eight, n-n-nineteen-oh-nine. As a young girl, she wore her hair v-v-very short in the summer and was often m-m-mistaken for a boy. She was married to Ludlow Ogden Smith. But only for th-th-th—a little while.

PHYLLIS: Thank you, Bishop. That will be all about Miss Hepburn.

BISHOP: Her f-f-first play was *The Art and Mrs. B-b-bottle.*

PHYLLIS: That will do.

BISHOP *(Out)*: Her first film—

PHYLLIS: That's enough.

BISHOP *(Out)*: A *B-b-bill of Divorcement.*

PHYLLIS: Stop it now.

BISHOP *(Out)*: Her f-f-first Oscar was for—

PHYLLIS: Bishop—

BISHOP *(Out)*: M-m-m, was for—

PHYLLIS: Stop it, Bishop! *(Out)* Bishop can be quite the little show-off. *(To Bishop)* No one is interested. No one cares. And if they do, they can buy one of three thousand books currently in print about her.

BISHOP: Yes, Mother.

PHYLLIS: Thank you.

BISHOP *(Out)*: *Morning Glory*!!

PHYLLIS: There's no telling how long we're going to be here, so *please* try to behave.

BISHOP: I'm hungry.

PHYLLIS: Don't think about it.

BISHOP: What should I th-th-think about?

PHYLLIS: Don't you realize how lucky you are to be alive?

BISHOP: No.

PHYLLIS: Well, you are very lucky.

BISHOP: Oh.

PHYLLIS: Everyone else was killed.

BISHOP: I know.

PHYLLIS: They weren't so lucky.

BISHOP: Lucky me.

PHYLLIS: That's right.

BISHOP: I'm l-l-lucky. And I'm hungry.

PHYLLIS: Oh, dig for clams.

BISHOP: I d-d-don't like clams.

PHYLLIS: Have you ever had clams?

BISHOP: No.

PHYLLIS: Then, how do you know you don't like them?

BISHOP: They look like snot.

PHYLLIS: Not clams casino.

BISHOP: I'm sorry.

PHYLLIS: You're giving me a headache, Bishop.

BISHOP: I'm sorry.

PHYLLIS: Can't you go play with the dead bodies or something? You're eleven, you should like that sort of thing.

BISHOP *(Out)*: There were magazines in the cockpit, with p-p-pictures of naked boys doing things to each other.

PHYLLIS *(Out)*: Probably why we crashed.

BISHOP: I'm hungry.

PHYLLIS: You said that.

BISHOP: I'm s-s-sorry.

PHYLLIS: Try to say new things.

BISHOP: I'm st-t-tarving.

PHYLLIS: Interesting things.

BISHOP: I'm famished.

PHYLLIS: I should be dead now. I tell myself I should be dead or in Italy.

BISHOP: I'm h-h-h—

PHYLLIS: Bishop!

BISHOP: Thirsty.

PHYLLIS: Oh, I'll go look for food. Hold my shoes. They're ruined at this point, but the last thing I need is to lose a heel.

(Phyllis hands Bishop her shoes and exits over the dune. Bishop addresses the audience.)

BISHOP: I d-d-didn't mind crashing. Really. It was ek-ek-ek—cool. I'm lucky. We were s-s-spinning and spinning and it was just like being in a movie. K-k-katharine Hepburn played an avi-av-av—lady pilot in the movie *Christopher Strong*. It was never turned into a musical. I am Bishop Hogan. Th-that is my name, I am not a deacon of the church. I'm eleven. My father is famous. He hates Mother. He sleeps with the young girls in his m-m-movies.

(Howard enters from the wings.)

HOWARD *(Out)*: That's not true.

BISHOP *(Out)*: He doesn't love my mother and he doesn't love m-m-me.

HOWARD *(Out)*: She tells him these things—

BISHOP *(Out)*: He's ob-bsessed with his work.

HOWARD *(Out)*: To assuage her guilt over a failing marriage and to alienate my son from me.

BISHOP *(Out)*: He's self-absorbed.

HOWARD *(Out)*: Her words.

BISHOP *(Out)*: The only reason I have any friends at all, is b-b-because I give them *Arcky* dolls.

HOWARD *(Out)*: She fills his head with lies.

BISHOP *(Out)*: Arcky was the extrat-t-terrestrial in my father's movie.

HOWARD *(Out)*: They know Arcky. Everybody knows Arcky. Everybody loves him. *(Out)* They used him in the Pepsi-Cola commercials.

BISHOP: Why don't you love Mommy?

HOWARD *(Out)*: Who said I didn't?

BISHOP: She did.

HOWARD: Oh.

BISHOP: Wh-wh-why?

HOWARD: She's overbearing.

BISHOP: What's that?

HOWARD: It's complicated.

PAM *(Offstage)*: Hoowwaardd?

BISHOP: Do you think we're d-d-dead?

HOWARD: I haven't thought about it yet.

PAM *(Offstage)*: Hoowwwaarrddd!

HOWARD: Excuse me.

(Howard exits. Phyllis enters.)

PHYLLIS: There is nothing.

BISHOP: Oh?

PHYLLIS: Not so much as a coconut. Oh, give me those, I feel frumpish. This island is a parking lot. *(She takes the shoes)*

BISHOP: I'm hungry.

PHYLLIS: I know.

BISHOP: Do you think Daddy thinks we're dead?

PHYLLIS *(Bright)*: Let's talk about sleeping arrangements. Shall we?

BISHOP: I bet he's c-c—worried.

PHYLLIS: It'll be night soon.

BISHOP: He's crying. I bet.

PHYLLIS: Can you build a lean-to?

BISHOP: I miss Daddy.

PHYLLIS: Can you build a lean-to, or a hut, or something?

BISHOP: Do you miss D-d-daddy?

PHYLLIS: Can you, Bishop, build a lean-to?

BISHOP: Of course not.

PHYLLIS: What do you mean, of course not?

BISHOP: I mean I can't.

PHYLLIS: Don't be negative. Why can't you?

BISHOP: Because I can't.

PHYLLIS: That's no attitude. How do you know you can't? You have to try and find out that you can't.

BISHOP: Daddy c-c-could build a lean-to. He could build a split-level twin dwelling.

PHYLLIS: Do not mention your father again tonight.

BISHOP: I'm s-s-sorry. *(Out)* Katharine Hepburn made *Philadelphia Story* in n-n-n-nineteen-forty-one. After being labeled box-office poison.

PHYLLIS: I'm ignoring that. Now. What will you need to build a lean-to?

BISHOP: I can't build a lean-to!

PHYLLIS: Why not?!

BISHOP: Because I'm hungry!!

PHYLLIS: Don't raise your voice to me!

BISHOP: I'm s-s-sorry.

PHYLLIS: I realize you're frightened—

BISHOP: I'm hungry—

PHYLLIS: And hungry.

BISHOP: You hate me and you wish I was dead.

PHYLLIS: What a terrible thing to say.

BISHOP: Why won't you feed me?

PHYLLIS: Eat seaweed.

BISHOP: I'm not Chinese.

PHYLLIS: I thought you were hungry?

BISHOP: It's poison.

PHYLLIS: It's sushi.

BISHOP: It's creepy.

PHYLLIS: Eat rocks, eat sand—oh, hand me my purse.

(He does so.)

Here. Eat lipstick. It's not poison.

BISHOP: Thank you. *(He eats it)*

PHYLLIS *(Out)*: He was always a picky eater. As a baby, Bishop threw up everything five minutes after he ate it. Tell you the truth, I thought he was bulimic.

BISHOP: Done!

PHYLLIS: You didn't save me any?

BISHOP: I didn't think you l-l-liked lipstick.

PHYLLIS: That's not the point.

BISHOP: I'm sorry.

PHYLLIS *(Bright)*: Now. What will you need to build a lean-to?

BISHOP: M-m-mother?

PHYLLIS: You can get supplies from the wreckage—

BISHOP: M-m-mother?

PHYLLIS: You can build here, with a southern exposure and a view of the sea—

BISHOP: M-m-mother!

PHYLLIS: That'll be lovely—

BISHOP: Mommy!

PHYLLIS: What is it?

BISHOP: I'm still hungry.

PHYLLIS: You just ate a whole lipstick.

BISHOP: We're going to starve to death, aren't we?

PHYLLIS: Don't be ridiculous. I have lots of lipsticks. *(Out)* Different colors for different outfits.

BISHOP: You can't live on lipstick.

PHYLLIS: I don't see why not.

BISHOP: It has no v-v-vitamins.

PHYLLIS: We'll fish.

BISHOP: We have no t-t-tackle.

PHYLLIS: We'll hunt.

BISHOP: We're going to starve to death!!

PHYLLIS: We'll trim down!

BISHOP: I'm thin now!

PHYLLIS: Five pounds, and you'll be amazed at how clothing hangs off of you!

BISHOP: You don't care.

PHYLLIS: Please, I'm tired, I'm irritated and I have sand in my stockings! Try to cooperate. Now, if the lean-to faces this way, the morning sun will get in my eyes—

BISHOP: WE'RE GOING TO DIE! I DON'T WANT TO DIE! WE'RE GOING TO STARVE TO DEATH!! WE'LL DIE!!

PHYLLIS: ALL RIGHT!! All right. Hand me my purse.

(He does so. She pulls out a huge butcher's knife.)

Here's a knife. Now. Go back to the plane and cut the arm off that nun. Bring it back here and I'll cook it and we'll eat it.

BISHOP: What?

PHYLLIS: Go cut off the nun's arm and I'll cook it. All right?

BISHOP: I c-c-can't!

PHYLLIS: Pardon me?

BISHOP: I c-c-can't do that.

PHYLLIS: I thought you were hungry. I'm sorry.

BISHOP: I am.

PHYLLIS: Do you think it's going to start raining cheeseburgers?

BISHOP: N-n-no.

PHYLLIS: Can you eat the air? Can you eat the water?

BISHOP: N-n-no.

PHYLLIS: So what are you going to eat?

BISHOP: I don't know!

PHYLLIS: Do you want to starve to death?

BISHOP: I can't d-d-do it!!

PHYLLIS: Look! I'm frightened too! Don't you think I'm scared? I am. I'm scared. So what? What do we do? Do we sit here and watch each other decay? Quizzing each other on Katharine Hepburn trivia while we wither to skeletons? Is that it? Or do we take matters into our own hands? She's already dead. You're not doing anything wrong.

BISHOP *(Out)*: She was a nun!

PHYLLIS: That's why I picked her!

BISHOP: Don't m-m-make me.

PHYLLIS: It's time to grow up.

BISHOP: Why don't you love me?

PHYLLIS: Who said I don't?

BISHOP: If you loved me you w-wouldn't make me d-d-do this.

PHYLLIS: No. I'd let you starve to death. In front of me. I'd let you die. That, I take it, would be proof of my maternal instincts.

BISHOP: You do it.

PHYLLIS: Let's be realistic. You are wearing Dalton blues. I have on my Michael Kors.

BISHOP: What's that?

PHYLLIS: My dress, which I'd just as soon not splatter with blood.

BISHOP: I c-c-can't.

PHYLLIS: It's easy.

BISHOP: I'm not hungry anymore.

PHYLLIS: Just do it!

BISHOP: Lipstick filled me up. That was one big lipstick.

PHYLLIS: Make me proud? Please, Bishop.

BISHOP: But—

PHYLLIS *(Gentle)*: When you get back, we'll build a fire.

BISHOP: Yes, M-m-mother.

PHYLLIS: That's a good boy.

(Bishop exits over a dune. Phyllis addresses the audience.)
I had a child whom I loved and whom I taught to sever the arms of nuns.

(There is a light change, indicating a flashback. Howard enters, perhaps wearing tails. Phyllis may drop some piece of her costume. She joins him. It is their wedding night. She is giddy and young.)

HOWARD: Are you happy?

PHYLLIS: It was a beautiful wedding.

HOWARD: It was.

PHYLLIS: Canary and avocado.

HOWARD: You were a beautiful bride.

PHYLLIS: Do you love me, Howard?

HOWARD: I do, dumpling.

PHYLLIS: My name is Phyllis.

HOWARD: I know that.

PHYLLIS: Why did you call me dumpling?

HOWARD: It was a euphemism.

PHYLLIS *(As if he'd sneezed)*: God bless you. *(Out)* I was young and used to coasting on my looks.

HOWARD: You look very beautiful, there by the window.

PHYLLIS: Me? You mean me?

HOWARD *(Out)*: She was silly. She was a breath of fresh air. *(To Phyllis)* Let's go to bed.

PHYLLIS: Are you sleepy?

HOWARD: That's not what I meant, sweetpea.

PHYLLIS: Sweetpea? Who's sweetpea?

HOWARD: That's not what I meant.

PHYLLIS: What did you mean? By what? When? Where were we?

HOWARD: Let's make love.

PHYLLIS: Couldn't we get to know each other first?

HOWARD: It's our wedding night.

PHYLLIS: It's never too late.

HOWARD: Come to bed.

PHYLLIS: My sister Marie, who was always the smart one, says that sex is a beautiful, special event, and a woman's only real power over a man.

HOWARD: You have a beautiful neck.

PHYLLIS: My mother says, "What will you have and how would you like that cooked?" She's a waitress.

HOWARD: Beautiful ears.

PHYLLIS: My father just grunts if you block the TV.

HOWARD: Beautiful lips.

PHYLLIS *(Out)*: He has remote control. He likes wrestling.

HOWARD: Beautiful shoulders.

PHYLLIS: I want a baby.

HOWARD: Why?

PHYLLIS: You would like me better if I had a baby.

HOWARD: I don't know if that's true, cookiepuss.

PHYLLIS *(Frustrated)*: I keep telling you—

HOWARD: I know, I know. Your name is Phyllis.

PHYLLIS: I think if we had a child we would be bonded. And you would feel, even if only unconsciously, a debt of gratitude towards me for supplying you with a miniature version of yourself, who would in turn reproduce and continue the cycle, ensuring, in an abstract way, your immortality, thus easing your fear of death.

HOWARD: Phyllis?

PHYLLIS: I read it.

HOWARD: Let's go to bed.

PHYLLIS: I want to make a baby!

HOWARD: I want to hold you. I want to protect you. I want to keep you with me forever and shield you from the world. I want to take care of you.

PHYLLIS: I think I'd like that.

HOWARD: You would, cupcake.

PHYLLIS: My name is—

HOWARD: Stop talking.

(Howard embraces her and kisses her. Bishop appears, standing atop the dune. He holds high the nun's arm, dripping with blood, still clutching a rosary.)

BISHOP: I DID IT!!!

(Phyllis and Howard break their embrace and look up at Bishop. There is a blackout. Phyllis walks into a pool of light and addresses the audience.)

PHYLLIS: Lately, I have been having a recurring dream. When I was a little girl, we lived in a part of Philadelphia called Society Hill. In an apartment. Down the hall from us lived a Mr. Antonelli. Mr. Antonelli worked at the Museum of Natural History. And he was big. He was a big man. Must've weighed three hundred pounds. He was the fattest human being I'd ever seen, close up. But he was well-groomed. And on certain nights of the week, Saturdays, I think, Saturdays mostly and Thursdays, Mr. Antonelli would dress as a woman and go wherever three-hundred-pound men who dress as women go, to seek whatever they can mistake for love. He'd put on a skirt and a blouse, sometimes a mumu-Bloody-Mary-type thing. And a lot of makeup. He wore a wig, a reddish kind of Ethel Merman affair. And always lovely matching jewelry sets: green rhinestone earrings, green rhinestone bracelets, brooches. He got all dolled up and went off to seek others like himself (although I can't imagine there were many others like Mr. Antonelli; three-hundred-pound transvestites are pretty much on their own in the world, I should think). When I was six, I was going to a friend's birthday party one Saturday, and I was wearing the sweetest little powder-blue jumper, and Mr. Antonelli got into the elevator with my mother and me. He looked down at me—this great mountain of gelatinous white flesh, and said, "My goodness, what a sweet little blue dress you have on." And I said, "You could borrow it sometime, if you want, Mr. Antonelli." I was six, and the concept of Junior and Misses sizing had not yet been made clear to me. Well, my mother squeezed my hand so tightly I thought my fingers would snap off. Once on the street, she explained to me that I must never, ever speak to Mr. Antonelli again. If he spoke to me, I was to nod politely. But

I was never—under any circumstances—to speak to him again. And I was certainly not to get into the elevator with him. My mother explained to me that Mr. Antonelli was a freak. That he should be locked up. Forgotten about. That Mr. Antonelli, although not to blame him for his condition, was nevertheless, the lowest form of the species, a creature to fear, and his parents, poor souls, must have a terrible burden to bear. Now. In my dream, I'm a little girl again. And I'm wearing my little powder-blue jumper. The one I wore that day. Only, I'm not on my way to any birthday party. I'm on a field trip with my class from school. We're at the zoo. Riding the monorail and laughing. The sun is shining, balloons fill the sky and we have cotton candy for lunch. We go to the reptile house and the polar-bear cage and the tigers are sunning themselves. Then we go to the monkey house. But there aren't any monkeys. There are, climbing the jungle gym, picking salt from their hair, dozens and dozens of fat men in skirts. Huge fat men, with matching jewelry sets, swinging from limb to limb, laughing in no language. And everyone laughs and points. And then they turn around. All the monkeys. All the men turn around at once. They turn around and look at me, right at me. And they all have the same face. And it's Bishop's face. They all have my son's face.

(Bishop steps into the light, holding a trousered leg.)

Who's for dinner?
BISHOP: Leg of pilot.

(Phyllis takes the leg. Exits.)

My father has a mistress. I think he always has.

(The lights come up on Howard and Pam.)

HOWARD: I think I could love you.

PAM: Well, thanks.

HOWARD: What did you say your name was again?

PAM: I didn't.

HOWARD: You have beautiful legs.

PAM: It's Pam. Pamela. Pam.

HOWARD: It's a beautiful name. Would you like something to eat?

PAM: No thank you.

HOWARD: Are you sure?

PAM: I don't eat.

HOWARD: I don't understand.

PAM: I take liquid protein.

HOWARD: Oh?

PAM: And amphetamines.

HOWARD: Don't you get hungry?

PAM: I fill up on pills.

HOWARD: You look thin to me.

PAM *(Out)*: The camera adds ten pounds.

HOWARD: You're an actress?

PAM: Yes. Maybe you've seen some of my films? *Hannah Does Her Sisters, Lubricating Rita, Fatal Erection, True Clit, Star Whores, Anal Weapon, A Room with a View?*

HOWARD: You were in *A Room with a View?*

PAM: No. I just said that. I don't know why.

HOWARD: Oh. I direct films.

PAM: I know that. I've seen every one of your movies.

HOWARD: Really?

PAM: No.

HOWARD: Oh. Would you like a drink?

PAM: No. I don't drink.

HOWARD: Why not?

PAM: I gave it up.

HOWARD: When?

PAM: I drink. I don't know why I said that.

HOWARD: Well, would you like one?

PAM: Yes. No.

HOWARD: Are you nervous?

PAM: Yes. Not really. I took a Dietack at three o'clock.

HOWARD: You look thin to me—

PAM *(Out)*: The camera adds ten pounds—

HOWARD: Should we go to bed?

PAM: That's very direct.

HOWARD: I'm sorry.

PAM *(Out)*: I like that in a man.

HOWARD: Do you?

PAM *(Out)*: No. Of course not. All day on the set, that's what I get. Nice to meet you. Roll tape and penetration.

HOWARD: Would you like to go?

PAM: I think so.

HOWARD: I'll get your coat.

PAM: I mean I want to stay. I find you incredibly attractive. I think you might be the handsomest man I've ever seen.

HOWARD: Really?

PAM: Of course not. I mean you're nice-looking, but I just said that. I thought you'd like to hear it. I guess. I mean I do think you're fine. Is your penis big?

HOWARD: Yes.

PAM: Really?

HOWARD: No. I mean I guess it's average.

PAM: It doesn't matter.

HOWARD: Really?

PAM *(Out)*: To some people.

HOWARD: It matters to you?

PAM: No.

HOWARD: Good.

PAM *(Out)*: It matters.

HOWARD: Yes?

PAM: No.

HOWARD: Good.

PAM: You direct movies?

HOWARD: Yes.

PAM: You could put me in one.

HOWARD: I could.

PAM: Would you?

HOWARD: Yes.

PAM: Really?

HOWARD: No. I just said that hoping it would make you more eager to have sex with me and less concerned about my genital size.

PAM: I see. Your bluntness verges on insulting.

HOWARD: That's the way I am. Abrupt and self-absorbed.

PAM: I find it repulsive.

HOWARD: We're attracted to that which repels us.

PAM: Oh?

HOWARD: I hope so. My marriage is based on it.

PAM: I think I should go.

HOWARD: That might be best.

PAM: It was nice meeting you.

HOWARD: I'll get you a cab.

(They embrace and sink to the ground. Bishop enters a pool of light and addresses the audience.)

BISHOP: Katharine Hepburn made *Suddenly Last Summer* in n-n-nineteen-fifty-nine. It was based on a one-act play by Tennessee Williams. B-b-both she and Elizabeth Taylor were n-n-nominated for Oscars for the film. It is the story of Violet Venable, Katharine Hepburn's efforts to have her n-n-niece, Elizabeth Taylor, lobotomized by Doctor Montgomery Clift. She wants to stop Liz from telling the world about her son, Sebastian—named for St. Sebastian, who was pecked to death by crows, like Tippi Hedren in the movie, *The Birds*. *(His stutter is gone)* It seems, Sebastian was this homo who used to use Katharine to lure young men on tropical islands, until she got too old and he had to use Liz. (And Katharine had the hots for junior herself, sorta.) But last summer he was eaten to death by homo-cannibals, which according to the movie had something to do with sea turtles and Elizabeth Taylor's bathing suit becoming transparent when it got wet. *(He looks at his feet, which straighten themselves from their pigeon-toed stance)* According to legend, and her biography, by Charles Higham, Katharine Hepburn had to have homosexuality explained to her by Joseph Mankiewicz. Now, I don't think it's possible to have worked in Hollywood for twenty-five years and not to have figured it out. I think anyone who claims not to know that kind of thing is hiding something because they're nervous. I think this probably relates to why Katharine Hepburn only lived with her husband, Ludlow Ogden Smith for a few months, but had the same secretary, Laura Harding, for over twenty years. *(He takes a moment and stands up perfectly straight, for the first time)* Anyway, in the end of the movie, Monty saves Liz and Katharine loses her marbles. It was in black and white. *(His voice drops to a deeper register. He now speaks strongly, coldly)* I do not mind it on the island. The sky is almost always blue. I can do what I want. I can be by myself. It was not like that at home.

(Lights come up on Phyllis, young and silly, holding a baby, and Howard, reading. Bishop watches.)

PHYLLIS: He's a beautiful baby. Marie says he's beautiful. My mother says we're out of mashed potatoes and did you want dessert?

HOWARD: Uh-huh.

BISHOP *(Out)*: I can't remember this.

PHYLLIS: I think he looks like you.

BISHOP: But I do.

PHYLLIS: Except he doesn't have any hair. If we shaved your head he'd look more like you. Or we could get him a little wig. Do you think we could get him a little wig, Howard? Would you like a little Zsa Zsa Gabor synthetic wig, Baby?

HOWARD: I'm reading.

BISHOP: Look at me.

PHYLLIS: Look at him Howard.

HOWARD: I'm reading.

BISHOP: Look at me.

PHYLLIS: We should name him Howard—I don't mean we should name him Howard—although we could—I mean, Howard, we should name him.

BISHOP *(To Phyllis)*: Don't name me Howard.

HOWARD: Not now, I'm reading.

PHYLLIS: But it's been two months!

BISHOP *(To Howard)*: I need a name.

HOWARD: Darling—

PHYLLIS: Who?

HOWARD: Phyllis—

PHYLLIS: What?

HOWARD: You're in my light.

PHYLLIS: We can't keep calling him Baby. It's embarrassing—

HOWARD: Can't you see that I'm reading?

BISHOP *(To Howard)*: So what?

PHYLLIS: I'm sorry.

HOWARD: I have to read now.

PHYLLIS: What are you reading?

HOWARD: A book.

PHYLLIS: But Howard—

HOWARD: You're in my light.

PHYLLIS: I'm sorry.

HOWARD: Thank you.

PHYLLIS: I suppose we could call him Baby.

HOWARD: Uh-huh.

PHYLLIS: Baby Hogan. It has a ring. No, no. I don't like it. The other children will make fun of him.

HOWARD: He doesn't know any other children.

PHYLLIS: But he will.

BISHOP *(Out)*: Not really.

PHYLLIS: And I don't think Baby is an appropriate name. What if he's tall? People will say, "Here comes that big Baby."

HOWARD *(Out)*: This went on for months.

PHYLLIS: I'll name you baby. I don't mean I'll name you Baby, I mean, baby, I'll name you.

HOWARD *(Out)*: What was sweet became cloying.

PHYLLIS: That's kind of jazzy.

HOWARD *(Out)*: What was charming became grating.

PHYLLIS: You're pink. We'll call you Pink Hogan—no, no, that's faggy.

HOWARD *(Out)*: What was endearing became insufferable.

PHYLLIS: Blue. Blue is for boys—no, no. People will think you were a blue baby.

HOWARD *(Out)*: I worked more and more.

PHYLLIS: What do you think Howard, do you like pink or blue?

HOWARD: I like brown.

PHYLLIS: For a name?

HOWARD: As a color.

PHYLLIS: We can't call him brown, Howard. People will think we're Negroes.

HOWARD: Please stop talking.

BISHOP: Name me!

PHYLLIS: We have to name the baby, Howard.

BISHOP: Name me!

PHYLLIS: We have to! It's humiliating! The other mothers come up to me in the supermarket and they say, "Oooo what an adorable baby, what's his name?"

HOWARD *(Out)*: It's like living with a metronome!

PHYLLIS: And I just say the first thing that comes into my head! The other day he was Cap'n Crunch—I was in cereal.

HOWARD *(Snapping)*: WHAT AM I DOING!?

PHYLLIS: What?

HOWARD: WHAT AM I DOING?

PHYLLIS: Reading?

HOWARD: THAT'S RIGHT! THAT'S RIGHT!

PHYLLIS: Don't yell at me! *(To Bishop)* Hold this. *(She hands Bishop the baby)* Don't yell at me!

HOWARD: YOU CAN SEE THAT I'M READING!

PHYLLIS: You don't love me anymore!

HOWARD: What are you talking about?

PHYLLIS: You never used to yell at me!

HOWARD: You never used to get on my nerves—

PHYLLIS: I get on your nerves?!!!

HOWARD: Just a little—*(Out)* All the time. *(To Phyllis)* Now and then.

PHYLLIS: You used to think I was funny! Now you think I'm stupid!

HOWARD: No I don't. *(Out)* Like a post. *(To Phyllis)* Not at all.

PHYLLIS: I know you do! I see you roll your eyes when I ask you questions—you used to be flattered, now you're annoyed!

HOWARD: Calm down.

PHYLLIS: But how will I learn if I don't ask questions?! A person has to ask questions! I can change! You'll see! I can get smarter! I can get more sophisticated! GIMMEE THAT BOOK! What's it about?

(Phyllis grabs the book and exits. Pam enters and addresses the audience.)

PAM: Howard loves me. I am a hundred percent secure in that. We make love every day and it's beautiful and he holds me next to himself and he whispers my name over and over again and I hear music and I make him do things he doesn't know he wants to. Well maybe not every day. But Howard is a wonderful lover, and I'm in a position to know. I started when I was twelve, with a cousin-by-marriage. And I have had hundreds of lovers since—both in front of the camera and behind, if you know what I mean. But the fact of the matter is, I never felt anything before Howard. Oh sure, I felt things, other things, but not the thing I thought I was supposed to feel. And yes! I know he's married, and he can't let go. But listen. This is my life and my future and my old age around the bend and I can't worry about who I'm hurting, because everybody has to take responsibility for their own actions.

(Pam exits. Lights comes up on Bishop eating the baby which had been him in the last scene.)

BISHOP *(Out)*: There was a baby on the plane.

(Phyllis enters, weak, weary and disheveled. She drags a bloody, trousered leg.)

PHYLLIS: Bishop?
BISHOP: What?
PHYLLIS: You're eating the baby.
BISHOP: So?
PHYLLIS: I thought we were saving the baby.
BISHOP: For what?
PHYLLIS: Dessert.
BISHOP: Well, I'm eating it.
PHYLLIS: I wish we had more lipsticks.
BISHOP: For snacks?
PHYLLIS: For my lips. I feel frumpish.
BISHOP: You look fine. You look the same.
PHYLLIS: I can't go on.
BISHOP: Don't be negative.
PHYLLIS *(Mary Richards)*: The lean-to is a pigsty.
BISHOP: Don't whine.
PHYLLIS: Was it a boy or a girl?
BISHOP: Boy.
PHYLLIS: Was he cute?
BISHOP: I didn't notice.
PHYLLIS: He cried on the plane.
BISHOP: You can't remember that.
PHYLLIS: I do.
BISHOP: It was months ago.
PHYLLIS: Was it?

BISHOP: Or years.

PHYLLIS: But I remember. He cried on the plane. I guess the air pressure bothered him, made his ears pop.

BISHOP: Don't think about it.

PHYLLIS: He cried and cried and his mother tried to get him to stop but she couldn't. And I kept thinking they should just put him in the overhead baggage compartment.

BISHOP: You don't remember it. You think you do.

PHYLLIS: And now you're eating him. It.

BISHOP: It's good.

PHYLLIS: Is it?

BISHOP: Tender. You want some?

PHYLLIS: No thanks. I have a leg.

BISHOP: Baby's better.

PHYLLIS: Would you know it if I lost my mind?

BISHOP: I'd know it.

PHYLLIS: I think I've lost my mind.

BISHOP: You haven't. You were always queer.

PHYLLIS: But my hands look unfamiliar to me.

BISHOP: You need a manicure.

PHYLLIS: True. But it's more than that.

BISHOP: Let me see.

(She shows him her hands.)

They're your hands. That's them.

PHYLLIS: What if you lost your mind, too? What if we're two loons, nutty as fruitcakes and there's no one else around as a sanity barometer.

BISHOP: I haven't.

PHYLLIS: I can't hear you stutter anymore.

BISHOP: I don't stutter anymore.

PHYLLIS: You don't?

BISHOP: No.

PHYLLIS: When did that happen?

BISHOP: Months ago.

PHYLLIS: I didn't hear it go away.

BISHOP: It was gradual.

PHYLLIS *(After a long pause)*: I see things. I look up at the sky and the clouds arrange themselves into hot-air balloons. Beautiful balloons, all different colors, like a box of crayons. And they block the sun. And I'm in one, and I fly away.

BISHOP *(Sadistic)*: Katharine Hepburn played—

PHYLLIS *(Terrified)*: No.

BISHOP: A hot-air balloonist—

PHYLLIS: No, no. Please—

BISHOP: In *Olly Olly Oxenfree*!

PHYLLIS: No!

BISHOP: She did her own stunts!

PHYLLIS: I don't want to hear it! I don't want to hear about it!

BISHOP: She flew the balloon herself!

PHYLLIS: NO! NO! NO MORE ABOUT HER!

BISHOP: It was directed by Richard Colla!!

PHYLLIS: PLEASE, BISHOP, PLEASE!

BISHOP: IT WAS NEVER RELEASED!!

PHYLLIS: STOP IT STOP IT!!

BISHOP: IT WAS SOLD DIRECTLY TO HBO!!

PHYLLIS: I AM YOUR MOTHER!!

BISHOP: SO WHAT?

PHYLLIS: I FORBID IT!

BISHOP: Forbid what?

PHYLLIS: PLEASE!!

BISHOP: What do you forbid? WHAT?

PHYLLIS: LEAVE ME ALONE!

BISHOP: SAY IT!

PHYLLIS: No, don't make me!

BISHOP: SAY! IT!!

PHYLLIS: YOU MAY NOT—

BISHOP: I MAY NOT?!

PHYLLIS: MAY NOT MENTION—

BISHOP: WHO?!

PHYLLIS: HER!!

BISHOP: WHO!!?

PHYLLIS: YOU KNOW WHO!

BISHOP: Who do you mean? I'm not sure I understand.

PHYLLIS: YOU KNOW WHO I MEAN!!

BISHOP: SAY IT!! SAY IT!! GODDAMN YOU!!

PHYLLIS *(In a wild frenzy, she tries to begin the play again)*: Iloathethebeach.IamPhyllisHoganandIdosoloathethebeach. Itistheverydefinitionofmonotony.Justsandandwaterandsand andwaterandmoresandandmorewater.Andlookaperfectly goodpairofshoes.SusanBennis/WarrenEdwardscrocodile andcompletelyruinedI'veneverunder—

BISHOP: SAY IT!

PHYLLIS: Iloathethe beach/Iloathethe beach/Iloathethe beach—

BISHOP: WHO CAN'T I MENTION!! WHO! SAY IT!!

PHYLLIS: KATHARINE HEPBURN!!!!

BISHOP: WHO!!!??

PHYLLIS: KATHARINE HEPBURN! KATHARINE HEP-BURN!! KA-THA-RINE-HEP-BURN!! THERE! I FORBID YOU!! I FORBID IT! YOU WILL NOT SAY HER NAME AGAIN!!!

BISHOP: Who, Mother?

PHYLLIS: KA! THA! RINE! HEP! BURN! KATHARINEHEP-BURN!!

BISHOP: HA HA HA HAAAA!

PHYLLIS: I hate you, I hate you, I hate you, I— I *(She rushes off stage)*

BISHOP: It's so easy to get under her skin.

(Bishop sits and eats "the baby." Pam enters, followed by Howard. She takes a pill.)

HOWARD: I wish you'd stop.

PAM: I wish I was the Queen of France.

HOWARD: I thought, if you were happy, you would stop.

PAM: If I were to stop, I wouldn't be happy.

HOWARD: Aren't you happy?

PAM: Yes. No.

HOWARD: Don't I make you happy?

PAM: It's not that simple.

HOWARD: Of course it is.

PAM: Leave me alone.

HOWARD: I want you to stop taking pills.

PAM: You're not my father.

HOWARD: Please.

PAM: What do you care?

HOWARD: I don't know, maybe it's me. But I'd just as soon not have you shriek in the night that your feet are gone and the walls are laughing at you.

PAM: My feet were laughing at me and the walls flew away. You are so self-absorbed.

HOWARD: I'd rather not have to worry, when we go through customs, that they'll find LSD in your *Harper's Bazaar*.

PAM: Well they didn't, did they?

HOWARD: That isn't the point.

PAM: No. The point is, it was *House and Garden*.

HOWARD: How can that be the point?

PAM: It is. It is exactly the point. Because you're so wrapped up in yourself you don't even know if I'm smuggling stuff in *Harper's Bazaar* or *House and Garden* when the two magazines are completely different. They have absolutely nothing in common.

HOWARD *(Out)*: They're both magazines.

PAM: Have you ever read *Harper's Bazaar*? I don't think so. I don't think you could have or you couldn't confuse it with *House and Garden*. *House and Garden* is just pictures of rich people's homes and decorating ideas. *Harper's Bazaar* is fashion and gossip and much trendier. But it doesn't relate to you, so you wouldn't know that.

HOWARD: What's that got to do with your drug problem?

PAM: I don't have a drug problem.

HOWARD: I think you do.

PAM: It's strictly recreational.

HOWARD: You are continually stoned.

PAM: I have a lot of free time.

HOWARD: What do you want?

PAM: Marry me.

HOWARD: Stop and I'll marry you.

PAM: Marry me and I'll stop.

HOWARD: You go first.

PAM: You go first.

HOWARD: You go first.

PAM: You go first.

HOWARD: You go first.

PAM: They're not coming back.

HOWARD: I don't want to talk about it.

PAM: It's been three years.

HOWARD: Let's go to bed.

PAM: They're dead, Howard. They are.

HOWARD: You don't understand.

PAM: Marry me, Howard.

HOWARD: No.

PAM: I think we should separate.

HOWARD: Maybe you're right.

PAM: I think maybe it's time.

HOWARD: I think maybe we should.

PAM: I think you should move out.

HOWARD: I think maybe I ought to.

PAM: I think that would be best.

HOWARD: I think maybe you're right.

(They embrace. Bishop walks down center. He addresses the audience. He is now a frightening, feral beast, rhythmic, ruthless and savage in his manner.)

BISHOP: My body is like this building, that I'm building one brick at a time. One brick at a fucking time. There is life on the island. The monkeys have come outta the trees. There are maggots on the rotting branches and a fistful makes lunch. There are birds in the sky and I can hit them with rocks and we eat them. I'm not afraid of the animals. They're afraid of me, brilliant motherfuckers. My body is a weapon. And my stomach feels good against my hands. And my face and my legs and my dick are made of concrete. And I can run faster than the monkeys and I can catch the fish with my metal hands. And there are wild dogs with open sores and monkeys fucking all around us in the night. I watch 'em. And they hump each other like crazy wild animals, screaming, crying, making fucking monkey sounds and twisting like epileptics tied up with rope. And I watch 'em. And they pound each other, hard, like parents. And I watch 'em. And they foam at the mouth and their eyes roll back in their heads. And I watch 'em and I pull my stone dick with my metal hands. And their ape arms flail away like insects in water. And I hold my breath so they don't hear me. And I stay in the dark so they don't see me. And they cry like fucking monkey bastards, shrill shrieking "fire" and "help" in monkey tongues. And I pull harder my concrete joint with my man-made hands and they don't even know I'm there! AND I SHOOT MY SHIT INTO THE AIR AND I SCREAM, "YAAHHHHH!! YAHHHHH! YAHHHH!" AND THE DUMB FUCKING MONKEY BASTARDS DON'T KNOW WHAT THE FUCK'S GOING ON! AND THEY DON'T KNOW WHAT THE FUCK I AM! AND THEY SCREAM BACK STUPID FUCKING MONKEY SOUNDS AND RUN AND I LAY BACK AND LAUGH. THE STUPID FUCKING MONKEY BASTARDS!!

(Phyllis and Howard enter. Bishop's rage is echoed by Phyllis.)

PHYLLIS: HOWARD!

HOWARD: Phyllis?

BISHOP *(Now referring to Phyllis and Howard)*: Stupid fucking bastards!

PHYLLIS: There's someone else, isn't there?

HOWARD: No.

BISHOP: Liars!

PHYLLIS: Don't lie to me!

HOWARD: All right.

PHYLLIS: There is, isn't there?

HOWARD *(Out)*: I don't want to hurt her.

PHYLLIS: I hate dishonesty.

HOWARD *(Out)*: I hate scenes.

PHYLLIS: I hate lies!

HOWARD: I hate confrontations.

PHYLLIS: I hate my life.

HOWARD: I love you.

PHYLLIS: Do you? Do you really?

HOWARD: You mean right now? Right at this moment in time?

PHYLLIS: Yes!

HOWARD *(Going to her)*: Phyllis—

PHYLLIS *(Breaking away)*: Don't touch me!

HOWARD: We have to talk.

PHYLLIS: I DON'T WANT TO TALK! What do you want Howard? Do you have the vaguest idea!? You didn't want me stupid, and you don't want me smart! Well tell me what you do want! Tell me what new permutation you want this year! I can do it Howard! I can make myself again and again and again! Only be careful, because I will!

HOWARD: What are you talking about?

PHYLLIS: Do you even remember what I was? Do you? When you thought you wanted someone nice? When I was nice! Because I was!

HOWARD: No. I don't remember that at all.

PHYLLIS: Do you want me to be hurt? Do you want me to retaliate?

HOWARD: I want you to be happy!

PHYLLIS: WHO IS IT!!

HOWARD: It's no one.

PHYLLIS: No one in particular? You mean it's many?

HOWARD: Let's go away.

PHYLLIS: For what?

HOWARD: Try again.

PHYLLIS *(Arch)*: The irony is, I think I stopped loving you a long time ago. But I didn't notice. And I was faithful because I was busy. And I never noticed how little I cared.

HOWARD: People make mistakes.

PHYLLIS: They certainly do.

HOWARD: I'm sorry.

PHYLLIS: Contrition becomes you.

HOWARD: I have to go to Italy.

PHYLLIS: Enjoy the pasta.

HOWARD: Join me?

PHYLLIS: I gain weight in Italy.

HOWARD: Come with me.

PHYLLIS: Why?

HOWARD: We could be happy.

PHYLLIS: What about Bishop?

HOWARD: Leave him.

(Bishop's head turns at this.)

It'll just be us.

PHYLLIS: No.

HOWARD: Think about it. I have to go. Join me next week, please.

PHYLLIS: I've been very stupid Howard.

HOWARD: Think about it.

(Phyllis crosses and sits by Bishop. Howard addresses the audience.)

They called me in Italy to tell me the plane went down. I was relieved. And sorry. And sad and happy and guilty. I can't remember Bishop's voice anymore. When I close my eyes, I can see his face. But I can't make his voice in my head.

(Pam crosses the stage.)

PAM: It's five years, Howard.
HOWARD: What?
PAM: They're dead.
HOWARD: I suppose.
PAM: Howard?
HOWARD: Yes?
PAM: I'm pregnant.

(Pam is gone. Howard exits. Lights come up on Bishop and Phyllis. She reaches spastically for the sky. She seems shell-shocked; he in control.)

PHYLLIS: The sky.
BISHOP: What?
PHYLLIS: The sky. The sky—is—very blue.
BISHOP: Yeah so and.
PHYLLIS: Blue and bottomless.
BISHOP: It's up.
PHYLLIS: What?
BISHOP: It's up, asshole.
PHYLLIS: What is?
BISHOP: The sky is up, fucking dusthead.
PHYLLIS: Oh.
BISHOP: So, of course it's bottomless.
PHYLLIS: Oh?
BISHOP: If it had an end, it would be a top.
PHYLLIS: Oh.
BISHOP: Not a bottom.
PHYLLIS: Of course.
BISHOP *(He starts doing push-ups)*: Fucking dusthead.
PHYLLIS: Of course. What are you doing?
BISHOP: Push-ups, crudbrain.
PHYLLIS: Oh.
BISHOP: What's it look like?

PHYLLIS: It looks like push-ups. Days. Years. Push-ups. You do push-ups. A sit-up would kill you. A squat-thrust would be too much—

BISHOP: Look at my body! My body is a fucking building! A cocksucking tower. My body is the fucking fabulous French Eiffel Tower!

PHYLLIS: It's very nice.

BISHOP: It's the ass-kicking pyramids.

PHYLLIS: What day is it?

BISHOP: Monday.

PHYLLIS: It was Monday yesterday.

BISHOP: It was fucking Sunday yesterday. Fucking dusthead.

PHYLLIS: No, no—I asked you what day it was yesterday and you said it was Monday.

BISHOP: Fuck you.

PHYLLIS: Didn't you?

BISHOP: It was Sunday so I said it was Sunday.

PHYLLIS: You always say it's Monday.

BISHOP: Crumbhead.

PHYLLIS: Maybe I only ask once a week.

BISHOP: Lintbrain.

PHYLLIS: Time flies.

BISHOP: Crudhead.

PHYLLIS: See that cloud?

BISHOP: Sandhead.

PHYLLIS: It looks like her.

BISHOP: Like who, trashhead?

PHYLLIS: Like her. Like Katharine Hepburn.

BISHOP: Garbagenoodle.

PHYLLIS: She looks beautiful. She looks young. I feel frumpish.

BISHOP: Christ.

PHYLLIS: I'm tired.

BISHOP: I'm hungry.

PHYLLIS: I want to sleep.

BISHOP: Cook something.

PHYLLIS: I'm sleepy.
BISHOP: Cook, slophead!
PHYLLIS: No.
BISHOP: Don't "no" me!!
PHYLLIS: Bishop!
BISHOP: Don't answer me!!
PHYLLIS: I'm sorry.
BISHOP: Muckbrain.
PHYLLIS: Bishop?
BISHOP: What is it?
PHYLLIS: No one is coming.
BISHOP: Shut up.
PHYLLIS *(After a moment)*: Could you kill me?
BISHOP: I could.
PHYLLIS: Then do.
BISHOP: Shut up.
PHYLLIS: I do not want to go on. I just don't think I want to.
BISHOP: Turdhead.
PHYLLIS: Monday after Monday. After Monday.
BISHOP: Then it's Tuesday. If you want a Tuesday, it's fucking
  Tuesday. Are you happy? I make it Tuesday.
PHYLLIS: I want someone else.
BISHOP: If I say it's fucking Tuesday. It is.
PHYLLIS: My voice sounds very strange to me. It's been too
  long. It's been forever. Just air and space and Katharine
  Hepburn looking down at us. I want someone to take care
  of me.
BISHOP: I take care of you.
PHYLLIS: Thank you.
BISHOP: I catch things!
PHYLLIS: I know.
BISHOP: We eat!
PHYLLIS: We do.
BISHOP: So shut up.
PHYLLIS: I want someone to protect me.
BISHOP: I protect you.

PHYLLIS: I don't want to wait anymore. I've waited long enough. I'm all dressed up, on the stoop, waiting and waiting and no one is coming. I want to go inside. I want to give up. I want to lie down. No one is coming for us, Bishop.

BISHOP: They are too.

PHYLLIS: THEY ARE NOT!!! —And you can kill me. You can kill things. You can. I've seen you.

BISHOP: Shut up!!

PHYLLIS: I'VE SEEN YOU KILL THINGS! YOU KILL THEM WITH THE ROCKS AND THE BRANCHES AND YOUR HANDS, AND YOU CAN, AND YOU CAN KILL ME!! PLEASE!

BISHOP: SHUT UP!!

(He knocks her down, she may be crying.)

PHYLLIS: I wish—

BISHOP: Always thinking of your fucking self.

PHYLLIS: I wish someone—

BISHOP: Who would I talk to?

PHYLLIS: I wish someone would—

BISHOP: Fucking monkeys?

PHYLLIS: I wish someone would hold me. I wish I had, I wish I was, I wish, I wish. I wish.

BISHOP: Be quiet. *(He approaches her. He puts his hand on her hair)*

PHYLLIS: Bishop?

BISHOP: Be quiet.

PHYLLIS: Bishop.

(He places his hand on her breast and kisses her mouth.)

No.

BISHOP: Shut up.

PHYLLIS: No, no, no! Stop it!! Stop it!

BISHOP: SHUT UP!

(He yanks her head back and kisses her again. She struggles.)

PHYLLIS: PLEASE!! GOD!! HELP!! THIS ISN'T WHAT I MEANT!!
BISHOP: SHUT UP!! SHUT UP!!! SHUT UP!!!
PHYLLIS: GOD HELP ME!!!!

(He forces her to the ground and tears at her clothes in a frenzy.)

GOD!! GOD!! HELP ME!! PLEASE!!!

(Pam rises and walks down center, blocking our view of Phyllis and Bishop.)

PAM *(Out)*: There will now be a brief intermission.

(Blackout. We hear "Bali Ha'i.")

ACT II

SCENE 1

The living room. Actually, the furniture is on the beach, arranged as if it were in a living room. There are two chairs, a sofa, a bar, and a television with its back to the audience. Pam is watching television.

PAM: Howard! Howard! They're on again! They're showing it again! *(Out)* I love CNN. *(To Howard)* Howard! They're showing Phyllis and Bishop getting off the plane again!— *(Out)* the same footage over and over. That Ted Turner—a genius. *(To Howard)* Howard!

HOWARD *(Enters, tucking in his shirt)*: What?

PAM: They were showing that clip again. Phyllis and Bishop getting off the plane.

HOWARD: Oh, what time is it?

PAM: Almost three.

HOWARD: They should be here.

PAM: Are you nervous?

HOWARD: No. Yes. What time is it?

PAM: It's almost three.

HOWARD: They should be here.

PAM: You said that.

HOWARD: Did I?

PAM: Do you want me to leave?

HOWARD: Yes.

PAM: Where would I go?

HOWARD: No. Stay.

PAM: You love me, Howard.

HOWARD: What?

PAM: Remember that. And our baby inside of me. We're going to have a whole new life together.

HOWARD: Maybe you should go.

PAM: I live here.

HOWARD: But I don't think she should walk in and find you.

PAM: We could say I'm the maid.

HOWARD: Yes.

PAM: And you could explain things to her gradually.

HOWARD: Do you have a uniform?

PAM: No.

HOWARD: Can you cook an egg?

PAM: No.

HOWARD: What if someone wants eggs?

PAM: Why would they want eggs?

HOWARD: What if they're hungry and they want some eggs?

PAM: You don't eat eggs. We don't have eggs.

HOWARD: You can't be the maid.

PAM: Maybe I should go.

HOWARD: Where will you go? Will you be all right? I'll take care of you. I'll support the baby. You won't have to worry.

PAM: I meant to the movies.

HOWARD: Oh.

PAM: Or for a walk. I meant for a little while.

HOWARD: Of course.

PAM: So that you could have some time alone with them. To talk with them. To explain what we've discussed. What we decided.

HOWARD: What we decided?

PAM: They can't stay here, Howard. I mean, they can stay here overnight, or through the weekend. But we agreed, they can't stay here. You have a new life now.

HOWARD: But I can't just throw them out. He's my wife and she's my son.

PAM: But we agreed.

HOWARD: What are you saying Pam?

PAM: I'll go out. You talk to them.

HOWARD: I think you should stay.

PAM: You do?

HOWARD: You're right. We have a life together and a baby coming and I think we should face this together. It was over a long time ago with Phyllis and I'm sure if we present ourselves—I'm sure she's fine, I'm sure she's mature, I'm sure she's rational, I'm sure she's calm, I'm sure she's—

(Doorbell.)

Hide!!

PAM: What?!

HOWARD: It's them! Hide!

PAM: What? Where?

HOWARD: Get in the closet! Just get in the closet!

PAM: Howard!

(Howard shoves Pam into the closet. Phyllis and Bishop appear at the door.)

HOWARD: Phyllis! Son!

BISHOP *(To Phyllis)*: Go IN.

PHYLLIS: I don't want to.

BISHOP: GET IN THERE!

PHYLLIS: No.

HOWARD: Come in?

PHYLLIS: No thank you.

HOWARD: Pardon?

PHYLLIS: No thank you.

BISHOP: MOVE!

HOWARD: Won't you come in?

PHYLLIS: I don't think so. I like the hallway.

BISHOP: Shit.

HOWARD: I don't understand.

PHYLLIS: It's nice. The wallpaper is pretty. It's mint. I think I would describe this color as mint. I never noticed it before. It has a very delicate stripe.

HOWARD: You're not coming in?

PHYLLIS: Could you bring me some shoes? They gave me flats. I feel short.

HOWARD: Shoes?

PHYLLIS: Yes please.

BISHOP: We're late because the shithead kept making the taxi drive around the block.

HOWARD: I don't think you should call your mother shithead. I think it's disrespectful.

PHYLLIS: Shoes please?

HOWARD: Just a minute. *(He runs off)*

BISHOP: Get in there!

PHYLLIS: I don't want to. Please don't make me. Please. I'll do anything. I don't want to go in.

BISHOP: It's our home, dirthead!

PHYLLIS: Can't we move? Get something smaller across town? A studio maybe? Something with a tub in the kitchen.

BISHOP: NO! Now go in.

PHYLLIS: You go in. I'll stay here.

BISHOP: You have to go in eventually.

PHYLLIS: No I don't. You can go in and slide food through the mail slot.

HOWARD *(Reenters carrying a pair of shoes)*: Here we go! Shoes!

PHYLLIS: Take them.

(Bishop takes the shoes from Howard and passes them to Phyllis, who puts them on her hands.)

BISHOP: Here.

PHYLLIS: These shoes are beautiful.

HOWARD: Thank you.

PHYLLIS: They're too small. Do you have something in an eight?

HOWARD: An eight?

PHYLLIS: These aren't my shoes. These are a six. I'm an eight. These are sixes. Bishop, are these your shoes?

BISHOP: God!

PHYLLIS: Bishop, have you been wearing ladies' shoes? I should never have sent you to a private school. I don't mean to be judgmental—

BISHOP: THEY ARE NOT MY SHOES!

PHYLLIS: Oh.

HOWARD: Don't you like them?

PHYLLIS: Are you a transvestite now, Howard?

HOWARD: They're my mother's shoes.

PHYLLIS: Your mother died when you were five.

HOWARD: They're an heirloom.

PHYLLIS: That's touching.

HOWARD: Won't you come in now?

PHYLLIS: And they look right up-to-the-minute. Funny how fashion repeats itself.

HOWARD: Someone will get off the elevator. Someone will see you.

BISHOP: I'm going in.

PHYLLIS: Bishop!!!

BISHOP *(He rushes into the room and stands center)*: Look. Look, airbrain—

HOWARD: I don't think you should call your mother an airbrain.

BISHOP: Shut up.—Look. I'm in. I'm inside and nothing happened. It's fine. It's fucking fine. There's nothing to be afraid of.—What the fuck you staring at?

HOWARD: I don't understand.

BISHOP: The crudhead's afraid to come in—

HOWARD: I don't think you should call your mother a crudhead.

PHYLLIS: I'll never get out.

HOWARD: What?

PHYLLIS: If I come in. I'll never get out again. And the room doesn't look very big. And I don't recognize the furniture.

HOWARD: It's new.

PHYLLIS: Oh.

HOWARD: Don't you like it?

PHYLLIS *(Waving at furniture)*: I don't even know it. How could I like it?

HOWARD: Bishop likes it. Don't you, Bishop?

BISHOP: I HATE IT!!!!

PHYLLIS: He forms opinions quickly.

BISHOP: IT'S UGLY!!!

PHYLLIS: Someone's getting off the elevator! Someone's coming! *(She runs into the room)*

HOWARD: There.

PHYLLIS: I don't like it here! I don't like it. I want to go. This isn't my home. This isn't my furniture!

BISHOP: Get a hold of yourself, vomithead.

HOWARD: I don't think you should call your mother vomithead.

PHYLLIS: This isn't my living room. Everything's different! This isn't my chair!

HOWARD: It's new.

PHYLLIS: I want my chair! Where's my chair!

HOWARD: It's gone. You like this one.

PHYLLIS: I don't! It's strange. Ooh, ick, I hate this chair.

BISHOP: The chair is fine, bilebrain.

HOWARD: I don't think you should—

PHYLLIS: I WANT MY OLD CHAIR!

HOWARD: But.

BISHOP: Get her old chair, for Christ's sake.

PHYLLIS: I WANT IT. I WANT IT.

HOWARD: I threw it out.

PHYLLIS: WHY!!

BISHOP *(Threatens)*: That was stupid.

HOWARD: I redecorated. I just got some new furniture. That's all.

PHYLLIS: This isn't my home. Where am I? My home has a wingback chair. Where am I?

HOWARD: You are home.

PHYLLIS: I don't think so.

BISHOP: You shouldn'ta thrown it out, craphead.

HOWARD: I don't think you should call me craphead—

BISHOP: Shut up.

PHYLLIS: Wherever I am. I want to leave. Can I leave here? Do you think we could go, Bishop?

BISHOP: We just got here—

PHYLLIS: But I don't like it.

HOWARD: What's wrong with her?

BISHOP: She's nuts, splitbrain—

HOWARD: I don't think—

PHYLLIS (Hiding her eyes with the shoes, she sinks to the ground): This is not my home.

BISHOP: She's a dusthead.

PHYLLIS: Is not. Is not. Is not.

BISHOP: Ignore her.

PHYLLIS: Is not. Is not. Is not.

BISHOP: Yeah. She'll shut up.

HOWARD: Maybe she should lie down.

BISHOP: Do you want to lie down?

PHYLLIS: My feet hurt.

HOWARD: What does that mean?

BISHOP: It means her feet hurt, phlegmhead.

HOWARD: I don't think you should call me—

BISHOP: Yeah, yeah, yeah.

PHYLLIS: My feet hurt.

HOWARD: Would you like to lie down?

PHYLLIS: These shoes are pretty, but they're too small.

BISHOP: She doesn't want to lie down.

PHYLLIS: I think they're a six.

BISHOP: Ignore her.

PHYLLIS: I'm an eight.

HOWARD: Ignore her?

PHYLLIS: Do you have anything in an eight? A pump?

BISHOP: She'll shut up. You'll shut up, won't you dusthead?

PHYLLIS: Black crocodile, maybe?

HOWARD: Well, sit down, son.

BISHOP: You sit down.

HOWARD *(Sitting)*: All right.

PHYLLIS: Do you have anything in patent leather?

HOWARD: How are you son?

BISHOP: Gee, I'm fine, thanks. And you?

HOWARD: Good, good. I'm good.

BISHOP: That's good.

HOWARD: I'm fine.

PHYLLIS: I'd like to see this in an eight.

HOWARD: It's good to have you home.

BISHOP: Mmmmmmm.

HOWARD: It's good to have you home.

BISHOP: You said that.

HOWARD: Oh. *(Reaching out to Bishop)* Tell me. Was it terrible. Do you want to talk about it?

BISHOP: Want to make a movie of it?

HOWARD: Well, maybe.

BISHOP: Fuck you.

HOWARD: I don't think—

PHYLLIS *(Out)*: Excuse me, could someone help me?

HOWARD: What?

PHYLLIS *(Out)*: Could someone—I'd like to try something on.

BISHOP: Ignore her!!

PHYLLIS *(Out)*: Could someone help me?

HOWARD: Well. I guess you're anxious to get back to school, back to your friends?

BISHOP: What friends?

HOWARD: Your little friends—

BISHOP: I'm not going back.

HOWARD: You have to go to school.

PHYLLIS *(To Howard)*: Could someone help me please?

HOWARD: Everybody goes to school.

BISHOP: Do you?

PHYLLIS *(Out)*: This is a terrible store.

HOWARD: You used to like school.

PHYLLIS *(Out)*: The salespeople hate me.

HOWARD: You used to enjoy it.

BISHOP: That was then.

HOWARD: Well, once you go back—

BISHOP: I'M NOT GOING BACK!

PHYLLIS *(To Howard)*: Could someone please, please help me?

HOWARD: You try it. You go back and give it a try.

PHYLLIS *(More desperate)*: Please, please, please!

BISHOP *(To Howard)*: Fuck you.

HOWARD: Maybe not this week. You rest this week.

PHYLLIS: Please, please, please!

HOWARD: Maybe next week. You'll go back next week and you'll see you like it.

BISHOP: It's summer! You asshole! It's fucking summer! What will I do at the fucking school when I get there! It's fucking summer!

HOWARD: Well there is summer school!!! Maybe you've heard of summer school!!! It's school! And they have it in the summer!!

BISHOP: Shut up!

HOWARD: I don't mean to shout.

BISHOP: Fuck you!

HOWARD: I don't mean to lose my temper.

BISHOP: Drop dead!

HOWARD: I mean to be a good father!

PHYLLIS *(Out; breaking down)*: All I want—all I want to do, all I want to do is, I want to try, I want to try on some shoes! Shoes! Shoes. And no one will pay any, no one will wait, wait on me! I need some, some, no one will, will, will someone help me, help me, help me, help me—

HOWARD *(Going to her)*: Calm down Phyllis, calm down. It's all right. I'm here. I'm here.

BISHOP *(Almost chanting)*: DO NOT TOUCH HER! DO NOT TOUCH HER! DO NOT! DO YOU UNDERSTAND ME!!!? DO NOT!

PHYLLIS: I—

BISHOP: DO NOT! DO NOT! DO NOT! DO NOT! DO NOT! DO NOT!

(There is a blackout and Howard steps into a pool of light. As he speaks, the lights come up dimly behind him. We see Bishop dragging on a huge bag of shoes, mostly tattered-looking. Bishop and Phyllis arrange the shoes around her on the floor.)

HOWARD *(Out)*: I don't know if Bishop went to school. About three days after he came back, he started leaving. Going out in the morning and coming back at night. I thought, if he went to school, if he saw people his own age, he would calm down. Are you going to school, Bishop?

BISHOP *(From his place by Phyllis)*: NO!

HOWARD: Where are you going?

BISHOP: NONE OF YOUR FUCKING BUSINESS!

HOWARD: We had what you might call a negative rapport. And Phyllis sat in the living room. Arranging her shoes. Breaking my heart. Occasionally, she made sense, but mostly, Bishop was right. It was best to ignore her. She slept on the floor of the living room and Pam came to me. Creeping past her.

(Pam enters and joins Howard in his pool of light. While they talk, we see, dimly, Bishop caressing, fondling and making love to Phyllis.)

PAM: It's long enough Howard.

HOWARD: What?

PAM: I can't go on like this.

HOWARD: Like what?

PAM: Living in the closet.

HOWARD: Oh.

PAM: With them here.

HOWARD: Be patient.

PAM: I need you Howard.

HOWARD *(Out)*: I felt so guilty.

PAM: Send them away.

HOWARD: I feel so guilty.

PAM: You didn't do anything.

HOWARD: They need me.

PAM: She's insane.

HOWARD: She's confused.

PAM: He's dangerous.

HOWARD: He's high-strung.

PAM: They need help.

HOWARD: I'm his father.

PAM: Put them away.

HOWARD: You look very beautiful.

PAM: Howard.

(Pam leaves the light. The light behind Howard goes out so he is alone onstage.)

HOWARD: And Pam pushed me. And we made love. And in her breasts I forgot my savage son and my addled wife. Her skin is as white as beach sand, and I made circles around her nipples with my tongue. And in the darkness as I fucked her, as she panted, not to wake them, Bishop saw us. He watched from the hallway. He stared at the door. He stood in the dark. And I knew he was watching, and I pounded harder and she said I was a god. And I was trapped, unable to move in any direction.

(Howard exits. The lights come up on Phyllis playing with her shoes. Pam enters, now visibly pregnant. Some time has passed. She is dressed in a maid's uniform. She dusts.)

PAM: 'Scuse me.

PHYLLIS: I was arranging my shoes.

PAM: I was going to dust in here.

PHYLLIS: You can.

PAM *(Sarcastic)*: I won't disturb you?

PHYLLIS: I am so disturbed already.

PAM: It's a lot of shoes.

PHYLLIS: None of them fit.

PAM: Where do they come from?

PHYLLIS: Shoe stores, I think.

PAM: Oh.

PHYLLIS: Or the garbage.

PAM: Oh.

PHYLLIS: Bishop brings them.

PAM: Oh. That one's nice.

PHYLLIS: You can have it.

PAM: Well, thank you.

PHYLLIS: I don't like it.

PAM: Oh.

PHYLLIS: And it has no mate.

PAM *(Dropping it)*: Well thank you anyway.

PHYLLIS: I'm hungry.

PAM *(Miserable)*: Would you like me to get you something?

PHYLLIS: You're a bad cook.

PAM: I know.

PHYLLIS: I feel like . . . eggs!

PAM: What?

PHYLLIS: I think I'd like some scrambled eggs.

PAM: How about a sandwich?

PHYLLIS: No. Eggs.

PAM: Ice cream? We have ice cream.

PHYLLIS: Why can't I have eggs?

PAM: We don't have any eggs.

PHYLLIS *(Sinister)*: What kind of a maid are you?

PAM: Howard doesn't eat eggs.

PHYLLIS: I eat eggs.

PAM: He doesn't like them.

PHYLLIS: You are a terrible maid.

PAM: I'm not the maid, Phyllis.

PHYLLIS *(Frightened)*: Are you her evil twin sister?

PAM: No.

PHYLLIS: Then you're the maid.

PAM: No, no. I'm not.

PHYLLIS: You look like the maid.

PAM: I'm me. That's not what I mean.

PHYLLIS: You're trying to drive me insane.

PAM: I'm not.

PHYLLIS: I think that's cruel.

PAM: Listen to me.

PHYLLIS *(Out)*: And redundant.

PAM: I'm not really a maid.

PHYLLIS: Is this an argument for existentialism?

PAM: No.

PHYLLIS: If you're not the maid, then why are you dressed like that? Not that I don't like it. I do. It reminds me of my mother.

PAM: Is she a maid?

PHYLLIS: She's a waitress.

PAM: I'm an actress.

PHYLLIS: And you're preparing for a part?

PAM: Not exactly.

PHYLLIS *(Giving up)*: Can't you just dust?

PAM: I want to prepare you. I want you to understand.

PHYLLIS: I don't think I want to.

PAM: You know I'm going to have a baby.

PHYLLIS: I just thought you had bad posture.

PAM: And Howard is the baby's father.

PHYLLIS: Howard? Howard, who?

PAM: Your husband.

PHYLLIS: He's sleeping with the maid?

PAM *(Losing her patience)*: Pay attention.

PHYLLIS: How cliché.

PAM: I wasn't a maid when I conceived!

PHYLLIS: And he gave you a job. I think that's big-hearted.

PAM: No Phyllis! Listen to me. Concentrate. Howard and I are in love. I'm not a maid. I've been pretending. He doesn't want to hurt you. He feels responsible for you. But time is passing and I think you're strong enough to see. To understand.

PHYLLIS: Understand what?

PAM: I plan to marry Howard. As soon as possible. I plan to marry him.

PHYLLIS: I see.

PAM: You do?

PHYLLIS: Yes. That's why you never go home and you're here when I wake up and here when I fall asleep and why you creep past me at night and why you pretend there's a room where I know there's a closet.

PAM: I hate that closet.

PHYLLIS: It's a nice closet.

PAM: Are you upset?

PHYLLIS: No. What do I care if you like the closet?

PAM: About Howard? About me?

PHYLLIS: Oh. No.

PAM: Really?

PHYLLIS: Now I feel we can talk like friends. I felt class distinction prevented that when you were the maid.

PAM *(Out)*: There is dignity in any job well done.

PHYLLIS: Howard plans to send me away then?

PAM: He's afraid to.

PHYLLIS: I know I should leave this room.

PAM: He's not very strong.

PHYLLIS: But I don't want to. I thought, when I was on the island, I thought all I wanted was walls. I thought I wanted a television. I thought I wanted cars and people. But when I try to get up, when I try to leave the room, I feel sick.

Sometimes when no one's around, I try and I get really sick. It's not in my mind. I know you hate me.

PAM: What?

PHYLLIS: I know you hate that we're here. Please don't. I'm sorry. I'm sorry we came back. No one asked us.

PAM: I'm sorry.

PHYLLIS: No one ever asked me.

PAM: Was it terrible?

PHYLLIS: It wasn't that the sky went on forever, it was seeing the nature of things. The way things really are. It was being watched at night and seeing how the world really is.

PAM: You don't have to talk about it.

(Bishop enters behind them, unnoticed.)

PHYLLIS: I was always the pretty one and my sister Marie was the smart one. And I was nice. Before I met Howard, I was. I was a nice person. I was pretty then. I thought that mattered.

PAM: You're still pretty.

PHYLLIS: No, my feet are too big. I'm an eight.

PAM: I don't think so.

PHYLLIS: No, I know I am. I've had my feet measured. I'm an eight.

PAM: That's not what I meant.

PHYLLIS: What did you mean? By what? When?

PAM: Forget it.

PHYLLIS: I'm confused. I want to leave the room. I do. I want to leave for Howard. Because he wants me to. And even though he wants me to for his own reasons, like he wants to sleep with the domestic help, I want to for him, because I don't hate him. Really. And I want to do it for me. Because I know people do. And I know that's what I should want. I should want to leave here and go shopping and have a life, and change my clothes—I think I've been wearing this dress forever—do I smell funny?—I know I should want these things, but I don't seem to be able to make myself. When I close my eyes all I see is the high high sky and the birds flying stupidly around Katharine Hepburn's face the way she looked in *Summertime* or *The Rainmaker* or *Sea of Grass*. And what scares me most of all—and this is really embarrassing—is I think I miss it.

PAM: What?

PHYLLIS: And that makes me want to just stop. And I cry. And Bishop comforts me. He protects me. And he holds me. When no one is looking. Late at night, when you're in your closet and Howard's in bed. Bishop comes to me and makes me feel all right for a minute. And I hold him against myself and pretend that she's watching and we're on the sand by the sea . . . and it's really very beautiful—when we can pretend.

PAM: Oh my God!

PHYLLIS: What?

PAM: I can't believe it! The two of you—that's terrible—

PHYLLIS: You shouldn't judge.

PAM: You poor—

PHYLLIS: No, no, it's not his fault.

PAM: We'll send him away.

PHYLLIS: No.

PAM: Howard doesn't know this, does he?

PHYLLIS: Please—

PAM: We'll send him away! He will.

PHYLLIS: Don't tell him—

PAM: Don't worry, Phyllis. He'll take care of it.

PHYLLIS: He won't understand.

PAM: I've got to go.

BISHOP (*Lunging at Pam with a knife*): NO!

(*Pam screams. Blackout.*)

SCENE 2

The lights come up on Phyllis frantically packing shoes, trying to get all her shoes into a suitcase.

PHYLLIS: Bishop! Bishop!

(Bishop enters, eating a sandwich and dragging what must obviously be Pam's leg.)

BISHOP: What?
PHYLLIS: What are you doing?
BISHOP: Eating. I'm hungry.
PHYLLIS: Please. Don't get blood on the chair.
BISHOP: Yeah yeah yeah.
PHYLLIS: Help me.
BISHOP: T'sorta dry. It could use some barbecue sauce. D'ya think we have any?
PHYLLIS: I don't know. Help me. We've got to pack.
BISHOP: Or soy sauce. Soy sauce would be good.
PHYLLIS: What are you talking about?
BISHOP: I'm talking about condiments!
PHYLLIS: We've got to pack. We've got to get out of here.
BISHOP: Why?
PHYLLIS: You killed someone, Bishop.
BISHOP: Yeah so and.
PHYLLIS: Don't you understand?
BISHOP: You want some?
PHYLLIS: God no.
BISHOP *(Out)*: It's good but it's dry.
PHYLLIS: Not "It's good," Bishop. "She's good."
BISHOP: Maybe ketchup.
PHYLLIS: You've committed murder!
BISHOP: Or mayo.
PHYLLIS: We have to get out of here.

BISHOP: You overreact.

PHYLLIS: Someone will find out! They'll find out and put you away! We need disguises. Can you grow a mustache? Do I have a wig? They'll catch you!

BISHOP: Who?

PHYLLIS: The police!

BISHOP: Morons.

PHYLLIS: You can't just murder people willy-nilly—

BISHOP: I can.

PHYLLIS: Where can we go? Have you ever been to Detroit?

BISHOP: We don't have to.

PHYLLIS: I'll dye my hair. Can you grow a beard?

BISHOP *(Threatening)*: Do you like your shoes?

PHYLLIS: Help me think. Where can we hide?

BISHOP: Do you?

PHYLLIS: What's that got to do with anything?

BISHOP: Just answer the fucking question!

PHYLLIS: Yes.

BISHOP: Where do you get them?

PHYLLIS: You bring them to me.

BISHOP: And where do you think I get 'em?

PHYLLIS: I don't know.

BISHOP: Where!

PHYLLIS: Shoe stores?

BISHOP: Wrong, crapnoodle.

PHYLLIS: The garbage?

BISHOP: Wrong, pissnoggin.

PHYLLIS: You steal them?

BISHOP: WRONG, sewageconk.

PHYLLIS: I don't want to know.

BISHOP: Why not?

PHYLLIS: I'd rather not—

BISHOP: People don't just give up their shoes!

PHYLLIS *(Realizing)*: Oh my. Oh my God.

BISHOP: There are barefoot bodies all over town.

PHYLLIS *(Frightened)*: Bishop, all these shoes?

BISHOP: I take care of you.

PHYLLIS: You did this?

BISHOP: For you.

PHYLLIS: You had no right.

BISHOP: Why not?

PHYLLIS: I don't know. It's not right. It's not moral.

BISHOP *(Indicating the leg)*: With her it's moral *(Indicating the shoes)*, with them, it's not?

PHYLLIS *(A confidence)*: Well, I never really cared for her.

BISHOP: Some morals.

PHYLLIS: I feel sick.

BISHOP: Have a bromo.

PHYLLIS: We have to go. Now. Before your father comes home.

BISHOP: He can be dessert.

PHYLLIS: You shouldn't have killed her. I think he liked her. He's bound to notice.

BISHOP: Leave it to me, assholehead.

PHYLLIS: Don't call me that!

BISHOP: What?

PHYLLIS: What do you want to take?

BISHOP: You hate me. You wish I'd died in the plane crash.

PHYLLIS: Don't be absurd.

BISHOP: You hate me. I can tell!

PHYLLIS: You should not have murdered her. It showed poor judgment. You act in haste.

BISHOP: I had to!

PHYLLIS: Why?

BISHOP: You told her. She knew about us—she'd get them to put me away—you told her! It's your fault!

PHYLLIS: Don't blame me!

BISHOP: Why not? It's your fault!

PHYLLIS: You just wait until your father gets home—

BISHOP: You want them to catch me, admit it. You want to be alone with *him* again. You prefer him to me, don't you? It's obvious!

PHYLLIS: I didn't kill his little concubine, you did! It's fine as long as you do away with random strangers—you were fine when you couldn't be traced—but now you'll get caught. You never think ahead, that's your problem! There are repercussions.

BISHOP: I'M SORRY! ALL RIGHT! I'M SORRY! BUT IT'S DONE! WHAT DO YOU WANT ME TO DO ABOUT IT NOW!!

PHYLLIS *(Deadpan)*: Well, stop eating her for one thing.

BISHOP: I hate you.

PHYLLIS: Help me shut this—

HOWARD *(Offstage)*: I'm home!

PHYLLIS: Don't speak.

BISHOP: I'm not afraid of him.

PHYLLIS: Let me handle this. *(Hiding "the leg" in the sofa)* I'll stall him. We'll leave tonight.

BISHOP: Yeah yeah yeah.

PHYLLIS: Please.

(She sits on her suitcase. Howard enters.)

HOWARD: How is everyone?

PHYLLIS: Oh fine. Fine, fine, thank you.

HOWARD: And the shoes?

PHYLLIS: Oh, they're happy shoes.

HOWARD: Why the suitcase.

PHYLLIS: What suitcase?

HOWARD: That one.

PHYLLIS: Oh, this?

HOWARD: Planning a trip?

PHYLLIS: Redecorating. Like it?

HOWARD: Did you learn anything in school today, son?

BISHOP: I don't go to school, you moron.

HOWARD: I don't think you should call me a moron, Bishop. I think it's disrespectful. How can we be a family—

BISHOP: I don't go to school, you dipshit.

HOWARD: What's wrong with him?

PHYLLIS *(Shrugging)*: Kids today?

BISHOP: Christ.

PHYLLIS: I feel all in. Time for bed!

HOWARD: Where's Pam?

PHYLLIS: I'm pooped. Did we spring forward or fall back or something?

HOWARD: Where is Pam?

PHYLLIS: Who?

HOWARD: Pam.

PHYLLIS *(Relocating onto the sofa in order to hide "the leg")*: I don't know anyone named Pam. Do you know a Pam, Bishop?

BISHOP: You bet.

PHYLLIS: I don't know who you mean.

HOWARD: Pam. Pamela. The maid.

PHYLLIS: Oh. Pam.

HOWARD: Where is she?

PHYLLIS: Out. Pam went out.

HOWARD: Out where?

PHYLLIS: Howard, I know I've been nutty and you've been unfaithful, but I feel all better now and I'd like to start over. Could we renew our vows?

HOWARD: Out where? Where'd she go?

PHYLLIS: Nevada. She went to Nevada.

HOWARD: What?

PHYLLIS: Yes. She wanted to play blackjack.

HOWARD: Pam!

PHYLLIS: She's gone. She wanted to play Big Six.

HOWARD: God.

PHYLLIS: She wanted to see Siegfried and Roy.

HOWARD: Bishop!

BISHOP: What?

HOWARD: Where's Pam?

(Bishop belches.)

PHYLLIS: She wanted to see Elvis impersonators.

BISHOP: How the fuck should I know?

PHYLLIS: She left you to become Barry Manilow's maid.

HOWARD *(Losing his patience)*: What are you talking about!

PHYLLIS: Barry Manilow. I love him. He writes the songs.

BISHOP: Ignore her.

PHYLLIS: It's hard to find loyal help.

(Bishop reaches into the sofa and pulls out a handful of "Pam.")

HOWARD *(Disgusted)*: What is that?

PHYLLIS *(Rising)*: Let's remember happier times.

BISHOP: Dinner. You want?

PHYLLIS: Fresh air and sunshine. When Betty, and Bud and Kitten were kids. Why, I remember once—oh, no, that's not us. That's *Father Knows Best*. Damn.

HOWARD *(Looks closer)*: What is that?!

BISHOP *(Revealing the leg)*: What's it look like?

HOWARD: MY GOD!

PHYLLIS: Anyone for Yahtzee?

BISHOP: She's good but she's dry.

HOWARD: What happened here?!

PHYLLIS: Not to change the subject. But.

HOWARD *(Revolted)*: What the hell is that?

BISHOP *(Mock gee-whiz)*: Well, gosh Dad. I know it's the first time I brought a girl home, but I think it's love—I'd like ya ta meet Pam.

HOWARD *(Reaching out)*: Pam.

BISHOP: I knew ya'd like her.

HOWARD: Oh my God. Pam. *(Running off)* Pam! Pam!

BISHOP: If you want a leg there's more in the fridge.

HOWARD *(Returning)*: What are you?

BISHOP *(Yanking the leg)*: Starved!

HOWARD: You did this!

BISHOP: That's right.

HOWARD: I'll kill you!

PHYLLIS: Bishop, go to your room.

BISHOP: Drop dead.

HOWARD *(Lunging at Bishop)*: I'LL KILL YOU!

BISHOP *(Pulling a knife)*: I don't think so.

HOWARD: Try it! Try it, you little bastard!

PHYLLIS: I wouldn't taunt him dear. He's high-strung.

HOWARD: You're sick! You're insane!

PHYLLIS: Don't do it Bishop! I don't even like his shoes.

HOWARD: You're evil.

PHYLLIS: They're too clunky. I'd feel all masculine.

BISHOP: Shut up!

PHYLLIS: Howard, talk to your son. He shouldn't tell me to shut up.

HOWARD: Kill me! Kill me now, or I'll kill you!

PHYLLIS: I just said you should "talk" to him.

BISHOP: You never cared about me!

PHYLLIS: He has a point.

HOWARD: You killed someone—someone I cared about, cared for, someone I loved!!

BISHOP: I could never please you!

PHYLLIS *(Momentarily affected by what she's heard)*: You loved her Howard?

HOWARD: Yes!

BISHOP: You see!

PHYLLIS: I knew, but I hoped—

HOWARD: I loved her!

PHYLLIS: Oh kill him, Bishop.

HOWARD: Phyllis!

PHYLLIS: Go ahead. You have Mother's permission.

HOWARD: What are you talking about?

PHYLLIS *(Going to Bishop, cheerily)*: We're freaks and we belong together.

HOWARD: I'm calling the police.

PHYLLIS *(To Bishop)*: Get him.

(Bishop lunges at Howard. There is a struggle.)

Men being men.

HOWARD *(Straddled by Bishop)*: Get off me! WHAT ARE YOU?

BISHOP: I could kill you like *that* and eat you for breakfast!

HOWARD: Please. You're sick. You should be in a hospital—

BISHOP: You just want to send me away! You're sorry I came back!

HOWARD: That's not true—I want to help you, I'll help you!

BISHOP: Lying mother motherfucker!

PHYLLIS: Name-calling is a dirty business.

HOWARD: You're my son. You need help!

PHYLLIS: Someone's changed his tune.

BISHOP: You don't get rid of me! I get rid of you! WATCH!

HOWARD: Phyllis!

PHYLLIS: Yes dear?

HOWARD: Help me! Stop him—call the police!

BISHOP: YOU CAN'T GET RID OF ME! I'M YOUR CHILD!

HOWARD: CALL THEM!!

PHYLLIS *(After a moment of internal debate)*: No.

BISHOP: YOU NEVER LIKED ME! YOU NEVER WANTED ME!

HOWARD: CALL THEM!

PHYLLIS: I feel . . . inert.

HOWARD: Please Phyllis! I love you!

PHYLLIS: Oh Howard. You love her, you love him, you love me. You just love everyone when there's a knife at your throat.

HOWARD: HELP ME!!!

PHYLLIS *(Bored)*: Would you like a glass of water?

HOWARD: Dear God oh God oh God—

BISHOP: You should have killed me, you asshole! You should have killed me years ago! When you had the chance, when I was little—you didn't want me then—you don't want me now—and it's not MY FAULT! IT'S YOURS! BUT YOU COULDN'T! YOU'RE TOO SCREWED UP! YOU'RE TOO FUCKED UP—WHAT'S RIGHT AND WHAT'S MORAL AND YOU DIDN'T HAVE THE GUTS! BUT I'M NOT YOU! I CAN DO IT! I CAN KILL THINGS! I

CAN KILL YOU!! AND IT FEELS TERRIFIC! IT FEELS
LIKE RUNNING AND RUNNING AND GUNSHOTS IN
MY HEAD! AND THERE ARE BIRDS IN THE SKY,
JUST LIKE YOU AND I CAN CATCH THEM AND PULL
THEM DOWN! AND IT'S BETTER THAN FUCKING!
WATCH! JUST WATCH! JUST WATCH!!!

*(He cuts Howard's throat. There is a long pause. Bishop
collapses. Phyllis looks at him. Then at us. Then at
Howard. Then at us again.)*

PHYLLIS: Well . . . that was cleansing.

BISHOP: Uh-huh.

PHYLLIS: I feel good.

BISHOP *(At Howard)*: What a drip.

PHYLLIS: You know, dear, I don't mean to criticize, but it
would've been tidier to stab him in the chest.

BISHOP: EVERYONE'S A MONDAY-MORNING QUARTER-
BACK!!!

PHYLLIS: Sorry. *(There is a pause)* Bishop?

BISHOP: What.

PHYLLIS: What now?

BISHOP: C'mere, slophead. *(She joins him)* We'll go back.

PHYLLIS: Back?

BISHOP: Home.

PHYLLIS: Tonight?

BISHOP: Tomorrow.

*(They look at each other and fall into a kiss, mutually. It is
passionate.)*

I'm starved.

(They look at Howard, then at each other and start to giggle.)

Don't eat the toes!

PHYLLIS: I won't!

BISHOP *(Out)*: Toes are my favorite.

PHYLLIS *(Out)*: I like privates.

BISHOP: That's my slophead.—We'll go back and start over and always be together.

PHYLLIS: I love you Bishop.

BISHOP: Get the salt.

(Phyllis cheerily exits, and Bishop rises and addresses the audience.)

And the next thing I remember, I was someplace else completely.

(Blackout. We hear "Save the Bones for Henry Jones.")

ACT III

A year later. A hospital. There are two areas set up on the sand. One is a consulting room: a desk with chair, and a chair for the patient. The other is Bishop's room: a cot and a small chest of drawers. Dr. Nestor is seated at the desk.

NESTOR: Send in Bishop Hogan.

(After a moment, Bishop enters.)

Hello.

BISHOP: Hello.

NESTOR: You are Bishop Hogan. Do you know who I am?

BISHOP: Do you know who *I* am?

NESTOR: I just said, you're Bishop Hogan. I am Dr. Nestor. *(Pause)* Do you know why you're here?

BISHOP: Do you know why *you're* here?

NESTOR: I work here. I'm the new doctor.

BISHOP: *I'm* the new doctor.

NESTOR: Do you think you're a doctor?

BISHOP: Do you think *you're* a doctor?

NESTOR: I know I am.

BISHOP: I know *I* am.

NESTOR: I see.

BISHOP: I see.

NESTOR: I am Bishop Hogan. I am here because I murdered my parents. I killed my father and his mistress, and the next day, my mother. I am here because it was the judgment of the court that I was mentally ill at the time of these acts.

BISHOP: *I* am Bishop Hogan. *I* am here because I murdered my parents. *I* killed my father and his mistress, and the next day, my mother. *I* am here because it was the judgment of the court that I was mentally ill at the time of these acts.

NESTOR: I LIKE IT HERE.

BISHOP: I LIKE IT HERE.

NESTOR: I am all better and the psychological demons which tormented me have receded into the dark recesses of my unconscious.

BISHOP: Yeah yeah yeah, recesses, unconscious.

NESTOR: I thought you wanted to play a game.

BISHOP: Fuck you.

NESTOR: Fuck you.

BISHOP: What?

NESTOR: What?

BISHOP: Fuck off.

NESTOR: Fuck off.

BISHOP: You can't talk to me that way.

NESTOR: YOU CAN'T TALK TO ME THAT WAY!

BISHOP: I'm the patient. You're the doctor!

NESTOR: You're the doctor.

BISHOP: Fuck you!

NESTOR: FUCK YOU! *(Laughing)* You see how irritating that can be.

BISHOP *(Out)*: Dr. Nestor is eerily like my father.

NESTOR: Now. Shall we start over? *(Pause)* Hello.

BISHOP: Hello.

NESTOR: Now, you're Bishop Hogan. Do you know who I am?

BISHOP: Fuck you.

NESTOR: That's better.

BISHOP: You're the new doctor?

NESTOR: Yes.

BISHOP: You remind me of my father.

NESTOR: It says here, you killed your father.

BISHOP: Yeah so and.

NESTOR: Do you remember that?

BISHOP: Like it was ten minutes ago.*

NESTOR: Why did you kill your father?

BISHOP: I was hungry.

NESTOR: Pardon me?

BISHOP: I was hungry and there was no spareribs in the kitchen.

NESTOR: Do you like Chinese food?

BISHOP: Comme ci, comme ça.

NESTOR: You killed your father in a rage over an ill-stocked refrigerator?

BISHOP: No. You moron.

NESTOR: I don't think you should call me a moron, Bishop. I think that's disrespectful.

BISHOP: I killed my father, to eat him. Didn't you read that thing?

NESTOR: I meant to, but it got boring.

BISHOP: Well, that's why I did it.

NESTOR: All right. Why did you kill your mother?

BISHOP: I didn't.

NESTOR: I did read that far—

BISHOP: I didn't kill my mother, you cocksucking, needlenosed dick!

NESTOR: Do you feel hostile?

BISHOP: Can we look at ink blots?

NESTOR: You don't remember killing your mother?

BISHOP: Since I didn't do it, why would I remember it?

NESTOR: Maybe it slipped your mind?

BISHOP: I remember things. I'm not insane.

NESTOR: Then why are you here?

BISHOP: You mean in the metaphysical sense?

NESTOR: How did your mother die, if you didn't kill her?

*Substitute actual elapsed time since Act II killing of Howard.

BISHOP: She didn't.

NESTOR: It says here—

BISHOP: I don't give a shit what it says there! I didn't write that! It's not true.

NESTOR: So you think the other doctors are liars?

BISHOP: Yes.

NESTOR: And the judge?

BISHOP: Yes!

NESTOR: And the police?

BISHOP: Yes!!

NESTOR: And the courtroom stenographer?

BISHOP: Yes!!!

NESTOR: And the mortician?

BISHOP: YES!!!

NESTOR: And the undertaker?

BISHOP: YES!!

NESTOR: And me and Miss Fitch and the embalmer and the man who carved the headstone and the people from CNN and *Geraldo*?!

BISHOP: YES! YES! YES! A BUNCH OF FILTHY-FUCKING-FREAKASSED LIARS!

(Phyllis enters. She looks composed and well-kept, as she did at the start of the play.)

PHYLLIS: Bishop.

BISHOP *(Rushing to Phyllis)*: Mommy.

PHYLLIS: Calm down, Bishop.

BISHOP: They think you're dead.

PHYLLIS: Don't be absurd—stand up straight.

BISHOP: It's starting again. They're saying you're dead.

PHYLLIS: Do I look dead?

BISHOP: You're standing up.

PHYLLIS: Do I sound dead?

BISHOP: What do dead people sound like?

PHYLLIS: Not like this.

BISHOP: They say that I killed you.

PHYLLIS: That's not true.

BISHOP: I love you.

PHYLLIS: Why would you kill me?

BISHOP: I wouldn't.

PHYLLIS: I know that.

BISHOP: Why do they keep saying it then?

PHYLLIS: They're incredibly stupid.

BISHOP: All of them?

PHYLLIS: Yes. They want to make you feel bad so they feel better themselves. They're insecure. They know they're stupid and they want to bolster their egos. They're jealous of us.

BISHOP: What should I do?

PHYLLIS: What would Katharine Hepburn do?

BISHOP: Re-re-rely on her Yankee strength.

PHYLLIS: That's right.

BISHOP: Th-th-that's what I'll do then.

PHYLLIS: And don't tell them anything. Don't give away your secrets. They'll use them against you. They'll judge you like God. Which they have no business doing.

BISHOP: I love you Mommy.

PHYLLIS: Why would you kill me? Don't chew gum.

(Phyllis and Bishop embrace. Popo enters wearing a bathrobe and sits on the cot.)

NESTOR: Send in Popo Martin, please.

(Popo rises and addresses the audience. She is very cheerful.)

POPO: I am Popo Martin. My friends call me Popo Martin. Dr. Nestor says I'm a paranoid schizophrenic. I think I have Marnie's disease. You know, like Tippi Hedren in that movie. When I see red, I see red! I mean, I have an episode. Although sometimes it happens when I don't see red. And sometimes I see red and it doesn't happen. I am the most popular girl in the hospital. I gets lots of visitors! I was a cheerleader. I'd do a cheer for you now, but I don't have my pompoms. All my teachers love me. The girls on the squad come to visit me every Sunday. The principal sent me a get-well note and the boys autographed a football. You can ask anyone in school about me, and they'd all say the same thing. Popo Martin is always cheerful. Popo Martin is a natural leader. Popo Martin looks on the bright side. Popo Martin has a smile on her lips and a kind word for a sad-dened stranger. Which is probably why everyone was so surprised when it happened. I tried to kill myself! I took thirty-five sleeping pills out of my mother's purse. I didn't want to smile anymore. My jaw hurts. And whistling gives me a headache. I want, more than anything, to wallow in a hopeless depression—but it just goes against my grain. So I tried to kill myself. That's why I'm here.

(Bishop and Phyllis have been watching her. Popo turns to Bishop and addresses him. As they speak, Phyllis recedes, but does not exit.)

I'm Popo Martin. You can call me Popo Martin.

BISHOP: Yeah so and.

POPO *(Holding out a potholder)*: Look what I made!

BISHOP: It's a square of fabric.

POPO *(Proud)*: It's a potholder!

BISHOP: Mmmmmm.

POPO: Don't you think it's beautiful?

BISHOP: No.

POPO: I do! I think it's the most beautiful one I've made yet! I've made thirty-seven potholders. Thirty-seven potholders and twenty-two ashtrays—which is odd, because they won't let you cook here, or smoke cigarettes. Do I seem cheerful to you?

BISHOP: Grossly.

POPO: I hate you.

BISHOP: What are you doing here?

POPO: I wanted to show you my potholder. I noticed you. You go after me, to see Dr. Nestor. *(She holds a potholder over each eye)* Look, look! I'm Kitty Carlisle!

PHYLLIS: She's an idiot Bishop.

BISHOP: You're an idiot.

POPO: You said something negative. So I didn't hear it. I tried to kill myself.

BISHOP: Try, try again, I always say.

POPO: Why are you here?

BISHOP: This is my room.

POPO: You look familiar. I know! You're that person who was on that desert island! You killed your parents! I saw you on *Geraldo!* You look thinner in person.

BISHOP: That wasn't me.

POPO: Can I have your autograph? Can I have your child? You're like a movie star. You look so much thinner. Wait till everyone hears that I know you! Could I kiss you?

PHYLLIS: Bishop!

BISHOP: No.

POPO: Could I? You can put your hands on my breasts.

PHYLLIS: Bishop!

POPO: You can tie me up if you want. You can fuck me if you want!

PHYLLIS: Bishop!

POPO: Bishop?

NESTOR: Bishop!

BISHOP: What?!

(Bishop leaves Popo, who returns to the cot. He joins Nestor at the desk. Phyllis follows.)

NESTOR: How are you today?

BISHOP: You tell me.

NESTOR: You tell me.

BISHOP: Don't start.

NESTOR: Tell me about the island.

BISHOP: Well there was the Skipper and the Professor and Mary Ann and a millionaire and his wife—

NESTOR: You were alone with your mother.

BISHOP: Yes.

NESTOR: How did you feel about that?

PHYLLIS: Tell him nothing.

NESTOR: Did you care for your mother?

BISHOP: You tell me—

NESTOR: I can't.

BISHOP: Too bad.

NESTOR: What was she like?

PHYLLIS: Was?

BISHOP: You mean "is" she like.

NESTOR: All right.

BISHOP: She's beautiful.

PHYLLIS: Thank you.

NESTOR: All right.

BISHOP: She loves me.

PHYLLIS: That's enough.

NESTOR: Do you love her?

PHYLLIS *(Warning)*: Bishop.

BISHOP: Why?

NESTOR: Do you, believe, Bishop, that it's possible to love someone, to care for them and still hurt them?

BISHOP: I don't know.

NESTOR: You don't know?

BISHOP: It's too abstract.

POPO *(On the cot, doodling his name)*: Bishop Hogan.

NESTOR: Do you think I want to hurt you?

PHYLLIS: Yes.

NESTOR: Do you think I care about you?

BISHOP: No.

NESTOR: Why not?

PHYLLIS: He's insane. You're fine.

BISHOP: Why would you?

NESTOR: Why wouldn't I?

BISHOP: I asked you first.

NESTOR: I asked you last.

BISHOP: You're insane.

NESTOR: You're a dick.

BISHOP: Fuckhead!

NESTOR: Asshole!

BISHOP: Dipshit!

NESTOR: Moron!

BISHOP: Spitbrain!

NESTOR: Crapnoodle!

PHYLLIS: This is absurd!

BISHOP *(To Phyllis, who is stopping his fun)*: Leave me alone.

PHYLLIS: Bishop!

BISHOP: I'm sorry. *(To Nestor)* Fuck you!

PHYLLIS: Atta boy!

POPO *(Still on the cot, writing a letter)*: Dear Mom and Dad. Everything is great. I love it here. The food is really good and the weather is beautiful. The sun is always out and I can hear birds from the window of my room. The nurses are really nice and I am organizing a cheerleading squad of delusionary schizophrenics—but really they are just nice people who hear voices coming from inanimate objects. I think they do very well, considering the amount of Phenobarbital they get pumped into them. I make really pretty potholders and ashtrays in workshop. I will make someone a great wife one day, assuming I cook and he smokes. On that subject, I have met the coolest guy. His name is Bishop Hogan. Maybe you heard of him. He's famous. He killed his parents. And some other people, I think. He's been on TV. But he's thinner in person. You'd like him. I can't wait for you to meet him. If you overlook the fact that he's delusionary, and that he butchered his parents and ate them, he's a fine catch. Love, Popo Martin.

NESTOR: Bishop.

BISHOP: What?

NESTOR: You killed a young woman.

BISHOP: Did I?

NESTOR: Didn't you?

BISHOP: You tell me.

NESTOR: You did.

BISHOP: If you say so.

NESTOR: I do.

BISHOP: Fine.

NESTOR: How did it feel?

BISHOP: I don't remember.

NESTOR: How it felt?

BISHOP: Anything.

NESTOR: What?

BISHOP: I have amnesia.

NESTOR: I see. And how did this happen?

BISHOP: I guess I took a bump on the head.

NESTOR: You guess?

BISHOP: I can't remember.

NESTOR: I see.

BISHOP: Sorry.

NESTOR: You remember this morning?

BISHOP: Nope.

NESTOR: Your mother?

BISHOP: No.

NESTOR: Your father?

BISHOP: No!

NESTOR: The island?

BISHOP: NO!

NESTOR: Your name?

BISHOP: NO!

NESTOR: CUT THE CRAP!

BISHOP: What?

NESTOR: You remember everything! You insignificant little
slime! I know it! And you know it! You remember!

BISHOP: I don't!

NESTOR: Listen to me. You'll do as I say you little bastard. Or
else! You will stay here in this hospital with paper slippers,

FAT MEN IN SKIRTS

soiled sheets and jello three times a day! You will stay here forever. We will pump you full of drugs and sit you in a yellow room with yellow walls and give you clay for ashtrays and yarn for placemats. And there you'll sit, till the days become years and your teeth fall out. And your hair falls out. And your muscles grow limp and you drool on yourself. And no one will visit you and no one will talk to you and no one will remember you and no one will care! And you'll really hear voices and you'll become old and your fingers will twist like the roots of a tree. And your organs will fail, one by one! And breathing's a chore! And you're just a body! Shuffling along! To no place at all! Every day! After day! After day! Until DEATH, FINALLY, MERCIFULLY, PATHETICALLY, PICKS YOU UP IN HER ARMS AND CARRIES YOU OUT OF HERE! NOW CUT THE CRAP!!!!

BISHOP: Mommy!

PHYLLIS and POPO: Bishop.

(Bishop starts to go to Phyllis but is cut off by Popo.)

POPO: I made this for you. *(She offers him a potholder)*

BISHOP: Leave me alone.

POPO: I call it "Potholder Number 38."

BISHOP: Put it away.

POPO: It looks like Number 37, but it's not. It's better.

BISHOP: Go away.

POPO: You're welcome. *(She leaves him)*

NESTOR: Bishop!

BISHOP: Go away!

NESTOR: What happened to your mother?

BISHOP: Nothing.

NESTOR: She's alive?

BISHOP: Yes!

NESTOR: Where is she?

BISHOP: Here!

NESTOR: Right here?

BISHOP: Yes!

NESTOR: I don't see her!

BISHOP: That's your problem!

NESTOR: Look at me!

BISHOP: What!

NESTOR: You see her?!

BISHOP: Yes!

NESTOR: Where is she?!

BISHOP: HERE!

NESTOR: WHERE?

BISHOP: I DON'T KNOW!

NESTOR: Atta boy.

BISHOP *(To Phyllis)*: Help me.

PHYLLIS and POPO: I'm here.

(Bishop and Phyllis embrace.)

BISHOP: I couldn't find you.

PHYLLIS: Don't leave me.

POPO: I love you Bishop.

PHYLLIS: I need you.

BISHOP: I'm sorry.

POPO: I love you Bishop.

PHYLLIS: My feet hurt. I need new shoes.

POPO: I love you Bishop.

PHYLLIS: I need a place to sleep. I can't sleep on the beach with
the clouds watching me. I need someone to protect me.

BISHOP: I'll protect you.

PHYLLIS: Tuck your shirt in.

POPO: I love you Bishop!

(Bishop hears Popo for the first time and moves to her.)

BISHOP: What?

POPO: I think about you all the time. Dr. Nestor says I'm fixated.
Dr. Nestor says I'm obsessing. Dr. Nestor says I'm off my nut!

BISHOP: He's right.

POPO: I dreamed about you last night.

BISHOP: Go back to your room.

POPO: I dreamed we were on a desert island.

PHYLLIS: Imagine.

BISHOP: Take a sleeping pill.

POPO: And I looked like Brooke Shields and you looked like Christopher Atkins.

BISHOP: Take a dozen.

NESTOR: Do you remember killing your mother?

POPO: And everything was idyllic.

BISHOP: Take a long walk off a short pier.

POPO: And the sun was very bright and our hair was blond.

NESTOR: Bishop!

BISHOP: Take a hike.

POPO: And our bodies were perfect, and we went swimming.

BISHOP: Take a rest.

POPO: Naked.

NESTOR: Do you?

BISHOP: Take a leak.

POPO: And we climbed out of the ocean, like Adam and Eve.

PHYLLIS: What's the matter with her?

BISHOP: She's obsessing.

POPO: Like the birth of Venus.

PHYLLIS *(Out)*: God.

POPO: And the water stuck to our skin, in droplets.

PHYLLIS: Who cares?

POPO *(Calm)*: And the droplets reflected the sun and turned the rays of sunlight into prisms off our skin. And we stood on the beach, on the sand, nude with colors.

PHYLLIS: Get rid of her.

POPO: And we didn't speak.

PHYLLIS: Bishop.

POPO: Because we spoke with our arms and we spoke with our skin and we understood each other without any words. And you stood very close to me. And your breath was very

warm on my face and the wind blew my hair and the waves
filled my head.

PHYLLIS: Don't touch her.

NESTOR *(To Phyllis)*: Leave him alone!

PHYLLIS: SHUT UP!

POPO: And I touched you. I put my hand on your shoulder.

PHYLLIS: Don't let her.

POPO *(She does so)*: And your skin was soft and felt like singing
to my fingers.

PHYLLIS: Bishop.

BISHOP: Leave me alone.

POPO *(As she continues, she becomes more and more relaxed,
both in body and voice)*: And the wind held my breasts and
I kissed your neck. *(She does so)* And it was sweet and
smelled like flowers. *(Again)* And I stopped hurting because
I stopped smiling. *(Again)* And I looked into your eyes.
(Again) And I saw my reflection.

PHYLLIS: STOP THIS!

NESTOR: LEAVE HIM ALONE!

PHYLLIS *(To Nestor)*: HE CANNOT DO THIS!

NESTOR: YOU'RE DEAD!

POPO: And you kissed me.

PHYLLIS: NO!

POPO: And you put your tongue in my mouth, and held my
breasts, in the wind, your hands.

PHYLLIS: STOP IT!!

POPO: And you entered me, and the sun went behind a cloud
and the shadows made dances on your chest—

PHYLLIS: STOP!

POPO: And it rained, on us, in the sand, on the beach, at the tide,
in my arms, in your eyes, in my mouth, on my back, at your
feet, by the sea, in my dream—

(Bishop and Popo embrace. Phyllis crosses to them.)

PHYLLIS: Get rid of her Bishop!

NESTOR: Don't hear her Bishop.

PHYLLIS: Remember what it looks like!

NESTOR *(To Bishop)*: Let her go!

PHYLLIS: Remember what it feels like!

POPO: I love you Bishop!

NESTOR: LET HER GO!

PHYLLIS: It feels like running and running Bishop—the taste of flesh in your mouth! Remember the taste! Remember the sounds! You said it Bishop! You can do it! Like gunshots in your head, better than fucking! Get rid of her!

(Bishop is holding Popo as if he might kiss her or kill her. Nestor removes his coat and becomes Howard.)

POPO: I love you Bishop.

PHYLLIS: Kill her!

HOWARD *(To Phyllis)*: STOP IT!

PHYLLIS: What do you care?! You never wanted him to begin with!

HOWARD: HE DOESN'T BELONG TO YOU!

PHYLLIS: HE DOES!!

POPO: I LOVE YOU!

PHYLLIS: HE'S MINE!

HOWARD: LOOK WHAT YOU DID!

PHYLLIS: I DIDN'T DO ANYTHING—

POPO: I LOVE YOU—

PHYLLIS: YOU DID IT—

HOWARD: HE KILLED YOU TOO—

PHYLLIS: I LOVE HIM—

POPO: I LOVE YOU—

BISHOP: STOP IT!

(At this, Bishop pushes Popo off him. She removes her bathrobe, revealing Pam's costume. Nestor puts on his coat again and goes to his desk. Phyllis dishevels herself and sits where she sat before exiting at the end of Act II. Pam and Phyllis revert to their Act II personas.)

I killed her. I killed her. I did.

PAM *(After a long moment)*: I miss being alive.

PHYLLIS: Bishop?

PAM *(Out)*: Go date married men.

BISHOP: We ate my father through the night.

PHYLLIS: I'm full.

PAM *(Out)*: Ick. *(She exits)*

BISHOP: And the sun came up. And we sat on the floor, the crap-head and me.

PHYLLIS: That was good. Do you want to watch TV?

BISHOP: We have to go!

PHYLLIS: Maybe something good is on the morning movie.

BISHOP: We have to get out of here. You said it yourself.

PHYLLIS: Maybe *African Queen*—

BISHOP: Someone'll find us.

PHYLLIS: Or *Philadelphia Story* or *Adam's Rib*—

BISHOP: Someone will find them!

PHYLLIS *(Growing desperation)*: Or *Break of Hearts*! Or *Morning Glory*!

BISHOP: You know we can't stay here!

PHYLLIS: I could miss *The Lion in Winter*! Or *Christopher Strong!* Or *Woman of the Year!*

BISHOP: We have to go back!

NESTOR: She wouldn't cooperate?

BISHOP *(To Nestor)*: I didn't understand.

PHYLLIS: We could play with my shoes?

BISHOP: We can bring your shoes.

PHYLLIS: It's a lot. I can't carry them all.

BISHOP: I'll carry half.

PHYLLIS: I want to see *Bringing Up Baby!*

BISHOP: They'll find them. They'll catch us.

PHYLLIS: Who?

BISHOP: The police.

PHYLLIS: I thought they were morons?

BISHOP *(Forceful)*: People are up. We have to go.

PHYLLIS: I can't.

BISHOP: Why not?

PHYLLIS: I'm afraid.

BISHOP: Of what?

PHYLLIS *(After a moment)*: You of course.

BISHOP: I protect you.

PHYLLIS: And . . .

BISHOP: What?

PHYLLIS: You kill people.

BISHOP: But I love you.

PHYLLIS: So?

BISHOP *(To Nestor)*: She wouldn't come.

NESTOR: And then?

BISHOP: Do you want to go to prison?

PHYLLIS: No.

BISHOP: You will. They'll lock you away and never let you out.

PHYLLIS: But I didn't do anything wrong.

BISHOP: They don't care. Everyone is guilty and they'll put you
    away.

PHYLLIS: What's on TV?

BISHOP: You've got to come.

PHYLLIS: Don't make me.

BISHOP: I won't leave you.

NESTOR: Why not?

BISHOP: I love her!

PHYLLIS: You have to.

BISHOP: I do what I want!

PHYLLIS: You have to go.

BISHOP: I'll stay with you.

PHYLLIS: You'll get on my nerves.

BISHOP: I'll be quiet.

PHYLLIS: No. No. Bishop. You go. You go without me. You'll
    kill me someday, if I come.

BISHOP: Maybe not.

PHYLLIS: So kill me now. I'm tired.

BISHOP: What?

PHYLLIS: Kill me now.

NESTOR: She asked you?

BISHOP *(To Nestor)*: SHUT UP!

PHYLLIS *(Positive; with love)*: We've done such things.

BISHOP: I don't understand.

PHYLLIS: I can't go on with you and don't want to without you. Please.

BISHOP: You hate me. You wish I was dead.

PHYLLIS: No. I love you. But see what I made.

BISHOP: I can't.

PHYLLIS: You can. You said it. It feels wonderful. It feels like running and running.

BISHOP: Don't make me.

PHYLLIS: Make me proud. Please, Bishop.

(Bishop and Phyllis embrace.)

BISHOP: I love you, Phyllis.

PHYLLIS: I love you, Bishop.

(They kiss. It is long and romantic. As they kiss, he lowers her to the ground; there is no overt act of violence, but she is dead. Bishop rises and addresses the audience.)

BISHOP: I am Bishop Hogan, that is my name, I am not a deacon of the church. I killed my father and his mistress and the next day, my mother, whom I loved. . . . It was the judgment of the court that I was mentally ill at the time of these acts. . . . And it was my mother's fault. And my father's. And my own. Because I am what I create: And I understand that I must stay awake all the time, because when I sleep, when I shut my eyes, the monkeys come again. And it is no one's fault. It is the nature of the monkeys.

END OF PLAY